T0381006

NOW I ASK YOU...

Questions and Reflections on Everyday Life

Dr. Sherry L. Meinberg

authorHOUSE®

AuthorHouse™
1663 Liberty Drive
Bloomington, IN 47403
www.authorhouse.com
Phone: 833-262-8899

Published by AuthorHouse   02/13/2024

ISBN: 979-8-8230-2095-4 (sc)
ISBN: 979-8-8230-2094-7 (e)

Library of Congress Control Number: 2024901619

Many of these anecdotes were first included in previous volumes.

This book is dedicated to you, Dear Reader.
I happily invite you to walk with me,
as I share some of the incredible memories
that happened during my life.
I hope my stories
speak to you and your experiences.

PREFACE

I have tasted both the bitter and the sweet. My life has been filled with amazing pivotal moments, and splinters of experience, of which 120 stories I am sharing with you. In this once over lightly account, I show my struggles and survival, the lessons I've learned, and how I have changed over the years. I have earned every line on my face, and clearly there are a lot of hard miles on my body. But I'm here to tell you, that it was all worth it. Don't give up the ship! Hang in there. And like my experiences, sooner or later, out-of-the-blue, unusual, unexpected, mind-blowing, improbable situations will happen to you, that may startle you out of your everyday life. The split-second timing is amazingly unbelievable; the odds are incredible. You will acknowledge that something significant has occurred, although you might not know exactly what it is, at the time. The most important events of our lives are little understood at first. Such events are powerful, and can change the course of your life, and even transform it. They may increase your openness to new ideas, new possibilities, and new ways of understanding. Such experiences can be your own little miracles. Know that you don't have to expand or grow at any particular rate. Hold on to those memories that are meaningful, and give the others the old heave ho. Free yourself from yesterday's negatives.

Understand your life as
a kaleidoscope of experiences
that move and change.
—L.D. Thompson

We do not remember days,
we remember moments.
—Cesare Pavese

The little things and little moments,
aren't little.
—Jon Kabat-Zim

We should learn
from the mistakes of others.
We don't have time
to make them all ourselves.
—Groucho Marx

Contents

INTRODUCTION

As tempting as a white picket fence with flowers lifestyle might be, I wouldn't want it, and I didn't get it. But I didn't want the opposite either, but that's what I got. My life unraveled for a number of years, as I learned to live with disappointment. I longed for a no fuss, no drama existence, and I finally got it. But in both cases, it was hard to make the adjustment.

There are no chapters in this book. The stories are placed willy-nilly, somewhat loosely based on my age progression. So you can randomly dive in anywhere. They are just my musings—muse, muse—throughout the decades. These memorable moments represent good times, bad times, and weird times. I've been known to have the occasional disaster. Like daily. Hope you will snicker, or laugh out loud, at some of the ridiculous experiences that I have had throughout the decades of my life. My stories, be they short, long, or simple, were all totally unexpected. Perhaps you can identify.

Some of our most unique and memorable milestones happened when we were children. During my first year of being, experiences were told to me about that beginning year, so I only know them via family members. I am sure this is the same for you, too.

For instance, there was a major tornado in Oklahoma, and many people took shelter in my Grandparents' cellar. Twelve men were holding the door closed, while the women were wailing, and the children were crying. Everyone was freaked out, except for me. I was around six weeks old, and having a grand time, with all the attention I was receiving. I was smiling and cooing, which brought some laughter to the very scary event.

Another story was told when I was around six months old. My aunt and uncle came to visit. They couldn't have children, so when we all went to the store, my aunt asked to hold me. She pretended that she was my mother. When the store manager asked if he could put me in their front bay window, to attract customers, she said yes. So I was having a great time, crawling around, interacting with the people on the other side of the glass. A whole crowd of people was watching me. When my mother asked my aunt where I was, she was furious upon finding me, and hauled me up and away from the window. Both she and the manager were upset with my aunt. So I was the only one having a good time.

A third story told to me was that my father was concerned that I was starting to walk too soon, and he was afraid that I would get bow legs, as a result. As such, he hammered slats across the top of my baby bed, so I couldn't stand all the way up. So I was a prisoner in my own crib, but I never knew. I was as happy as a lark.

You may have some stories that were told to you about your first year. And you may have some of your own remembrances from two years through your fourth and fifth years. (I have only included one story I remember as a two-year old, although off the top of my head, I can count 14 major memories that are meaningful to me, that are not included here.) Once school started, you probably have many more memories for each grade level. So, I am sharing just a few of mine.

Life isn't a matter of milestones, but of moments.
—Rose Kennedy

Life is the autobiography we write as we live it.
—Jim Phillips

Some people think we're made of flesh and bone.
Scientists say we're made of atoms.
But I think we're made of STORIES!
When we die, that's what people remember,
the stories of our lives and the stories we told.
—Ruth Stotter

People are meaning-making creatures.
We understand ourselves and the world through stories.
—Dr. Richard A. Heckler

Stories can be the easiest and
most pleasant way to learn.
—Cathleen McCandless

God made man
because he loved stories.
—Isak Dinesen

NOW I ASK YOU . . .

Do you remember the first major event in your life? How old were you when it happened? My first big remembrance has to do with a snake. Do you like snakes? Do you know anything about them? Do you know that there are over 3,000 species worldwide? Australia has the most species. Texas has the highest number of species in the nation (68). Yikes!

SIGNIFICANT INFLUENCE

Now this event I vividly remember: I am not fond of snakes, in any way, shape, form, or fashion. The first time I dealt with a live snake, I was two years old, and didn't know anything about them. Mother was cooking, and my job was to go out into the garage, and get three potatoes, and bring them back. The potatoes were inside the garage wall, by the floor, in a long line. As I leaned down to pick one up, there was a very long snake, staring at me. What a shock! I naturally screamed to high heavens, and both my parents rushed out of the house, as did all our local neighbors, who stood at a respectful distance in a wide semi-circle behind us. The second shock was that my father had been shaving in the bathroom, and had charged out of the house in his undershorts. (I had never seen him in anything but a uniform, as both mom and dad taught aviation cadets in WWII.) The third shock was when he grabbed a huge stick, and immediately began to wildly fight the snake, bashing it to smithereens. He was a country boy, having grown up around snakes on his family farm, and therefore knew a poisonous snake when he saw

1

one. So nakedness, violence, death, and snakes, became all mixed up in my tiny mind.

Nor did movies help, as I got older. I vividly remember the scene in *True Grit*, starring John Wayne and Glen Campbell, where the young girl falls into a mineshaft, and is surrounded by snakes. And that of *Alexander* (the Great), wherein he (Colin Farrell) is talking to his mother (Angelina Jolie) in her room, with about a hundred snakes undulating around on the floor. Ugh! And tales of Medusa didn't help, either. So the less I hear of snakes, the better.

Not all snakes are poisonous, and
not all poisons are deadly!
Keep this in mind when bitten.
—Mehmet Murat Ildanb

NOW I ASK YOU . . .

Did you have a tricycle when you were a small child? Did you want one? I don't know if I had a tricycle, or if my parent's friends' owned the tricycle, but I got to ride it, and it was fun, fun, fun, until it wasn't.

TRICYCLE

When I was three years old, my parents took me to their friend's house. I was left alone in a big empty dining room, that was next to the living room, separated by a huge wall of glass panes. It was the division between the two rooms, with a glass door in the middle. I have never seen anything like it, before or since. There was a tiny tricycle sitting there, all by itself, and just my size. So I took it for a ride, circling around in a big circle, faster and faster. At length, I lost control, smashing into the glass wall, and breaking out several glass panes. Naturally, I was bleeding and crying, when all the adults came running into the room. Someone called for the doctor (in those days, doctors made house calls), and I distinctly remember him attending to me on a countertop. I remember nothing else, that night. But in the morning, it was quite obvious that something had happened, as I had a big bandage around my arm. At a later date, when the bandage came off, there was a set of stiches in a circle, where my cut had been. So he had put me asleep somehow, and took care of me right then and there. I don't recall riding on any tricycles thereafter. But my stiches were apparent until my late seventies, and then they slowly moved on elsewhere. So

I wonder if my leadfoot ways, when I was in my twenties, and thirties, was a throwback to my youthful accident.

Life is better on three wheels.
—Unknown

A unicycle met a bicycle and
made a tricycle. That's a life cycle.
—Mario Ortiz

People say "third wheel" like it's a bad thing.
But tricycles can be super fun and stable.
—Unknown

NOW I ASK YOU . . .

When growing up, did you always heed your parents' directives? Did you remember what they said, and you deliberately did the opposite? Were consequences involved?

LEARNED MY LESSON

When I was five years old, in the beginning of first grade, as I went out to play one day, my mother told me to keep my shoes on. This was odd, as she had *never* said that beforehand, and I wondered why. So my friend and I were playing Tarzan, and we were swinging back and forth on the T clothesline poles, in her backyard. *How could we play Tarzan*, I thought, *if my shoes and socks were on? Tarzan never wore shoes*. So off they came, no matter what my Mom had said. *How would she ever know?* So we decided that the patch of grass between the two clothes hanger T poles, was a giant lake. So we would swing on the two poles, and jump forward into the lake. Fun, fun, fun! Until, that is, when I landed on the grass, in a sitting position, and broke my right wrist. I didn't cry at all (I never let anyone see me cry!), I was just worried that I was in big, BIG trouble. My wrist held limply, and wouldn't move, while I tried to pull my socks on, with my left hand. It wasn't easy. When I finally got my shoes on, I realized that I was unable to make a bow in my laces with only one hand. I knew that Mom would be furious, but I had to face the music. As I walked across the street, Mom was standing on the front lawn, and saw the way I was holding my hand. She screamed bloody murder and started crying, as she rushed me to the hospital. I wore a cast for six weeks. It was a hard way to learn that I needed to always follow my parents' directions. (I never knew if Mom even noticed that my shoelaces weren't tied).

The only mistake in life is the lesson not learned.
—Albert Einstein

The difference between school and life?
School teaches you lessons, and then gives you a test.
Life gives you a test, and you learn the lessons.
—Unknown

To learn anything, you must put aside
the safety of your ignorance.
—Richard Bach

NOW I ASK YOU . . .

Do you know that as you increase your vocabulary, you expand your mind? Are you learning new words? If so, you are improving all areas of your communication—listening, speaking, reading, and writing.

WORDS

"You know more words than a dictionary!" a child once complained to me. Unfortunately, it wasn't always so.

When I was a five-year-old first grader, my father decided that it was high time for me to have a bank account. (I didn't know what a bank was, and I didn't know what a bank account was, and I didn't have a job, and I never had any money given to me for any reason, but that apparently was a minor point that didn't concern him, as his motivation was pure: financial responsibility, and all that.) We walked into the bank together (which was a first, going anywhere together alone, so I knew this was important). Father asked for the proper forms, which he filled out. Then he thrust a card at me, asking for my *signature*. I had no idea what he was talking about, never having heard the word before. I froze, thinking it was something that I ought to know. (I had always been told that I was soooo smart, and didn't want to show my ignorance by asking.) My mind was desperate for a clue, as his voice was getting louder and more demanding. He kept repeating the word signature, but never the words *name, print*, or *write*. As all eyes were on me, I left in disgrace. I was in high school before I heard the word signature again.

7

*The difference between the right word
and the almost right word
is the difference between
lightning and the lightning bug.*
—Mark Twain

*Words can inspire, and words can destroy,
Choose your words well.*
—Robin Shama

*Handle them carefully,
for words have more power
than atom bombs.*
—Pearl Strachan Hurd

NOW I ASK YOU . . .

Family relationships can have long-lasting effects. Disagreements, misunderstandings, and unsolved issues, are bound to happen. As a child, did anything happen in your family that you didn't understand? As an adult, did you privately question other family members, trying to trigger some honest and open discussions? Were you satisfied with their observations, or are you still in the dark? Know that, over time, peoples' behaviors, circumstances, views, beliefs, and understandings can change.

FAMILY MATTERS

When I was six years old, it was clear that Father had something bothersome on his mind. He wasn't speaking to me, as he walked me out to the car, and had me sit on the front passenger seat. As he walked around the back of the car to enter the driver's seat, I reached out to close the door, but the Buick door was way too heavy for me to shut, so the door didn't quite close properly. I could see that door wasn't tightly closed, but I didn't want to bother him. So I held onto the door handle with both hands, thinking I could keep it from opening. Father began driving, and all went well until he turned a corner, and the door flew open, and I went with it—hanging on for dear life (there were no child seatbelts in those days). My father was freaked out, needless to say.

He took me to a house that I had never been to before, but I recognized the boy who lived there. We were in the same 2nd grade class at school. I saw him playing with his toy cars, in a huge pile of sand, next to the garage.

Father told me to go play with him, while he went to talk with the boy's mother. So we started playing together, and the next thing I knew, my father had gone. He left me without even saying goodbye. I decided that he was upset with me for not fully closing the car door. But as the day turned into night, and I ate dinner there, and then slept there, I decided that my parents didn't like me anymore, and had given me to this family (the major clue being that my clothes were in a suitcase).

I don't know how long I stayed there, when one day, Father came walking up the driveway, and took me home. And I thought that my mother and father must like me again. But I really couldn't figure out what I had done, for them *both* to just give me away like that. When I went into the kitchen to find my beautiful mother, she looked terrible. Her face had a pinched look, and there were dark circles under her eyes. She had lost a lot of weight, and she walked in a bent over position, and she was wearing a robe in the middle of the day. She seemed to be tired and in pain. And what was that in the kitchen sink? Mother was washing a baby! Where did that baby come from? I instantly thought I might have been replaced by the baby, but that later my parents decided to keep me anyway. And I hoped that maybe they had actually *missed* me. I thought about this situation many times, over the following years, before I finally put it all together, and understood the situation.

Families are like branches of a tree.
We grow in different directions
yet our roots remain as one.
—Unknown

Home should be an anchor,
a port in a storm, a refuge,
a happy place in which to dwell,
a place where we are loved
and where we can love.
—Marvin J. Ashton

No matter what you've done for yourself or humanity,
if you can't look back on having given love
and attention to your own family,
what have you really accomplished?
—Lee Iacocca

Hold your family close
and show them they are important.
Family matters.
—John H. Osteen

There's no place like home.
—Judy Garland (as Dorothy, in the 1939 classic film
The Wizard of Oz)

NOW I ASK YOU . . .

Have you ever had intuitive hits that are so sudden, so immediate, and so unexpected, that it takes your breath away? Intuition is a natural state, like breathing. First and foremost, it is a survival tool.

DANGEROUS STRANGER

When I was six years old, an elderly man tried to kidnap me from a department store. He kept following me around, talking to me, and making me feel *uncomfortable*. He said that he wanted to buy a set of China for his sick wife, and didn't know what pattern to choose. He asked me to choose it for her. The housewares section was way in the back of the store, in an *unlighted* area where no one was, with a wide open door to the alley. Even though I was only in the second grade, I knew that a grown man—old enough to be my grandfather!—wouldn't need a child to help him in that regard. And I also thought that if it were only he and his wife, why would they need a whole set of dishes? And if she were so sick, why would she be cooking, anyway? At some subtle level, I felt threatened in a way I didn't understand, and I didn't know how to deal with him, without being disrespectful. But I knew in my bones that I would be in deep trouble, if I got anywhere near that back door. The situation didn't *feel* right—dark and unpleasant—and I felt small and vulnerable, which was a first for me. So I just pointed to the first pattern that I saw, saying, "I choose that one!" and turned around and fled into the sizable crowd up front. Everyone was choosing valentines, so no one paid any attention to me, as I ran inside the clerk's counter, and hid. He came looking for me, as I saw him talking with the clerks. I felt vaguely ashamed at being so frightened, and not knowing why. I wasn't sure what might have happened, or why it was danger I sensed. I had no words for my experience, nor did I know what to complain about, and therefore told no one. Ever. Even though I was raised to respect adults, and follow their directions, my intuition told me to get away from that man, as fast as possible.

This was the one and only time that my mother left me by myself in a store. She went across the street, to buy something there, and because I was so excited about choosing valentines, she left me, saying that she would be right back. At length, I was so scared hiding from that man, that I decided to go find my mother. I fairly flew out the front door and onto the sidewalk, and saw my mother at the stoplight across the street. The traffic light had just turned red, but I saw two adults still walking across against the light. I knew I shouldn't walk against a red light, but those two were still in the crosswalk, so I ran to catch up with them. I didn't want to be on the same side of the street with that man. My mother was understandably *furious* that I had run across the street against the red light, and she scolded me royally, up one side and down the other. But I never told her why I had disobeyed, as I clung to her hand. She represented safety. It was just too scary, and I had no words to explain the situation. Intuition is a valuable tool. Parents and teachers didn't talk about predators in those days. Remembering that situation always gives me the creeps.

Intuition is a perception,
of seeing, or hearing, or feeling,
rather than thinking.
—Mona Lisa Schulz

Trust your intuition to the end,
though you can render no reason.
—Ralph Waldo Emerson

The only real valuable thing
is intuition.
—Albert Einstein

Trusting your instinct and intuition
is a way of listening
to your highest wisdom.
—Dan Millman

The most reliable advice we can ever receive,
comes from our intuition and gut feelings.
—Doreen Virtue

NOW I ASK YOU . . .

Whatever your religion, as a child, were there religious stories that you just didn't understand? Ones that you couldn't wrap your mind around? Did you ask questions of adults, or try to figure them out for yourself? Did you ever follow up your questioning in later years? I knew not to ask my father about church matters, because he had a scientific mind, and never went to church. (My father received straight A's in college, except for a required course in religion, in which he deserved an A grade, but the professor said that "Nobody is perfect," and he *never* gave out an A to anyone, ever. So that was the last straw for my father.) When I asked my mother about the *Parable of the Lost Sheep*, she said, "Honey, I just don't know." Maybe she just didn't want to talk about the adult version, having to do with sin. In any case, I didn't bother her with questions anymore, and tried to figure out all the answers by myself.

UNDERSTANDING

When I was in the second grade, I had Mrs. Edwards for my teacher. Everyone loved her. She looked like a grandmother to me. (I had two grandmothers, one in Texas, and the other in Oklahoma, but we only got to see them every so many years, because we lived in California.) All the class loved Mrs. Edwards.

One day at recess, the merry-go-round was full of students, and it was really zooming. Those of us who were standing around the circle, held out our hands, to slap the hands of those on the ride, making lots of interesting sounds. When I stuck out my hand to be slapped, someone grabbed my hand instead, and didn't let go. I toppled over, hitting my head on the pavement. My head hurt so bad that I wanted to cry, but I wouldn't do so in front of all those kids. The recess bell rang, and I told my friends to tell Mrs. Edwards that I was going home, because I didn't feel good. As everyone else was running to stand in their lines, I walked off the playground, and across the large grassy area, out the front double doors, and sat down on one of the middle steps. With nobody around, I allowed myself to cry a little.

Then I checked out my bloody hurts, and took stock of my situation. It was clear that I was a long way from home (which is why I took a bus to school), and that it would take a long, long time to walk there. And the house would be locked up, because both my parents worked. So I sat there trying to make a choice. Should I go, or should I stay? Then a surprising thing happened. Mrs. Edwards walked through the doors, and sat down on the steps next to me. In a soft voice, she asked how I was feeling. And I showed her my bloody hurts, and she produced some Band-Aids, and helped me put them on. We chatted for a few minutes, and then she asked if I felt well enough to go back to class. And of course, I nodded my head, yes.

So, back in the classroom, pondering the situation, I suddenly understood the story in the bible, about the shepherd, who left his flock, to look for a lost lamb (Matthew 18:12 and Luke 15: 4-6). I never understood why the shepherd would leave all 99 sheep, and go to find the missing one. I thought it was a risky thing to do (because four or five sheep might wander away while he was gone, and he could lose more than just one), but it was certainly understandable. Nobody wants to get lost, and everyone would want to be found. It would be easy to search for one puppy or one hamster, because many others weren't involved. But, to me, Mrs. Edwards was the shepherd who left her *safe* group of students, to find one sick or hurt lost lamb (me). And I was so glad she did. This was my understanding, as a six year old, and it made sense to me. Granted, the whole adult version is a tad different.

How think ye? If a man have an hundred sheep,
and one of them be gone astray,
doth he not leave the ninety and nine,
and goeth into the mountains, and seeketh
that which has gone astray?
And if so be that he find it, verily I say unto you,
he rejoiceth more of that sheep,
than of the ninety and nine which went not astray.
(Matthew 18:12-13, p. 1000)

What man of you, having
an hundred sheep, if he lose one of them
doth not leave the ninety and nine in the
wilderness, and go after that which is lost,
until he find it? And when he has found it
he layeth it on his shoulders, rejoicing.
(Luke 15: 4-5, p. 1066)

(*Holy Bible*, The John A. Hertel Co.,
Chicago, IL,1948)

NOW I ASK YOU . . .

Have you ever had a goal in mind, that you thought about, over and over again? A goal that was yours *privately*, that you hadn't shared with anyone? How did it feel, to have waited and waited for it to happen? Well, I had such a goal, at a very early age.

PERSISTENCE PAYS OFF

Way, way back, when I was a seven-year-old third grader, I loved to play baseball. The big boys—4th, 5th, and a couple of 6th graders—always played 500 in the street in front of my house. (It was a noncontact game, in which the batter would hit the ball, and the players would get so many points for catching it: 100 points for a fly ball, 50 points for one bounce, 25 points for two bounces, and 10 points for grounders. I would sit on the curb, watching, aching to take part, periodically asking if I could play. They always refused, since I was just a little girl. Finally, the boys tired of running after some of the grounders that rolled into the next block, and let me chase after them. So I would stand behind six or seven guys, and chase after the rolling balls that nobody wanted to bother with. One day I actually made 500 points. Then all the boys ran towards me, begging to take my place at bat. I refused, walking through an angry gauntlet. As I picked up the bat, they all moved up as close as possible. I kept telling them to back up, because I was worried about hitting them, when I swung the bat around. They reluctantly took a couple of steps backward. Satisfied that I had a bigger space to swing, I threw the ball up, and when it came down I socked that sucker clear into the next block. The way their heads followed the arc of the ball, and their whistles, shouts, and wild responses as they chased after it, was very satisfying to me. And I got to play 500 with them forever after. It was the first major achievement of a goal that I was really proud of, but I never told anyone about it. It was personal.

> *Persistence is not a long race;*
> *it is many short races*
> *one after another.*
> —Walter Elliot

> *Persistence is the key to success.*
> —Unknown

NOW I ASK YOU . . .

Are you still living under the decisions you made when you were in elementary school? Do you think that you're not good enough for sports? Dancing? Art? Speaking? Writing? Math? Tests? You've got to examine your life. Make sure that you are not *limiting* yourself. Widen your horizons! Have you tried to change your mind? Your attitude? Your dreams? Or do you feel that it's just not worth your time and effort? I understand, totally.

EARLY WRITER

As a seven-year-old, in the third grade, I could read adult books, although I didn't always understand what I was reading. For instance, in one book, after a boy meets a girl, they lay down on a mat. And that's what I thought they did: sleep. A couple of chapters later, I'm saying to myself: *Hey, where did this baby come from?* So I was always book smart, but not street smart. I wanted to be a writer, and I wrote stories each night, about the twins, Tizzy and Izzy. My teacher let me read them to the class each morning, while she got her materials altogether. But my written stories were of the Dick and Jane variety. I was reading a war book, and thinking I could never know all about that stuff in the author's book. I thought his brain was much bigger than mine would ever be (I didn't know anything about research). So I compared my beginner writing efforts with that of professional writers with years of practice under their belts, and realized that I couldn't compete. *And quit!*

Later, as an adult, I never thought to reconsider the

decision I made as a young child. Oh, woe is me! Forty-plus years later, my first book, *Into the Hornet's Nest: An Incredible Look at Life in An Inner City School* (1993), was published. It was a wild success. *Can you imagine?* I could have been *practicing* all those years! What a waste! The book you are now reading is my 24th book.

> *Going the long way*
> *is not the same as*
> *going the wrong way.*
> —Neale Donald Walsch

> *Don't be afraid to write crap*
> *because crap makes good fertilizer.*
> —Jessica Brody

Are you anything like me? Do you recognize some of your short-comings, but continue on in the same manner? Learn from my mistakes, and stay open to what you *can* do, and could do. Erase the word *can't* from your vocabulary. Don't set limits on yourself. And don't allow other people's limited perceptions to define you. Break past your self-imposed boundaries. Value your efforts. Become your own cheering section.

NEVER SAY NEVER

Years later, after writing several books, I continued to tell myself that I could never be a short-story writer. When I finally took a good look at my books, I saw that many were actually a bunch of little stories all cobbled together. My *Imperfect Weddings Are Best*, features close to 150 short, wacky wedding stories, and this book, *Now I Ask You . . .* has 147 short stories. So, I *can* write short stories, after all.

Similarly, for decades, I loved reading mysteries, but thought that I could never write them. But when I looked at some of my nonfiction children's books (which I considered only as science books), I saw that they were also mysteries that the students solved. (The first book in that series is titled *The Cockroach Invasion*, the subject of which adults can't abide, but children love, because of the ick factor. I had soooo much fun with that book!) *A Squirm of Worms*, and *The Angry Ants* followed. So I *can* write mysteries, after all.

Never say never, because limits, like fears,
are often just illusions.
—Michael Jordan

Never say never. Never is a long undependable time,
and life is too full of rich possibilities
to have restrictions placed upon it.
—Gloria Swanson

There's gonna be times when people tell you
that you can't live your dreams.
This is what I tell them: Never say never.
—Justin Bieber

NOW I ASK YOU . . .

Have you ever made a wish? Surely, as a child, you've made a wish on the earliest star you've seen that night, or wished while blowing on a dandelion puff, or said your wish as you threw pennies in a wishing well or fountain. Surely you've said, "I wish I could do that," and then didn't give it another thought. But have you ever had a desire or specific intention, just hoping it would come true (without doing anything about it)? Take a tip from a kitchen sign: Wishes don't do dishes. Or from an old fisherman's saying: Forty thousand wishes won't fill your bucket with fishes. And any baker can tell you that recipes don't make cookies.

A POWERFUL WISH

While in the fifth grade, on a family road trip across the states, we were driving in the middle of nowhere, through a seemingly endless Arizona desert. Although the weather was clear, the car radio mentioned a chance of flash floods, and I excitedly said that I would *love* to see one, since I couldn't picture it in my mind. Mother became quite upset that I would say such a thing, and admonished me for doing so, ending with: "Be careful what you wish for!"

The sentence was barely out of her mouth, when, on cue, a powerful flash flood swept across the highway, washing the pickup truck in front of us off the road. It landed nose-down in a ditch. An enormous amount of water coursed around it, with such force that the doors couldn't be opened.

All traffic was stopped both ways, unable to cross the

dangerous fast-moving water. So we had a front row seat to the awesome destruction that a flash flood can wreak. I was further shocked to see that the driver of the truck was a young woman—gender issues were stuck in 1949—and that she had a small baby with her. Both were crying, so we didn't know if they were injured, or just freaking out about the unexpected situation. But we were unable to help, as our doors wouldn't open either.

Since cell phones were nonexistent at that time, someone had to turn around, and drive all the way back to the closest town, to get the sheriff. He and a helper finally arrived, with a heavier truck, ropes and chains. We watched the ropes being used, as the sheriff battled through the water to rescue the baby first, and then went back to pull the woman to safety. Both were hauled out through the cab window. It was a long and arduous process. At length, the heavier truck pulled the pickup back onto the highway, and shortly thereafter, the flash flood had lost its punch. At that point, traffic was able to continue on, as if nothing had happened. Mother acted as if the whole experience was *my* fault, and I realized just how powerful our spoken words are.

We all have our own life to pursue,
our own kind of dream to be weaving,
and we all have the power to make wishes come true,
as long as we keep believing.
—Louisa May Alcott

A goal without a plan
is just a wish.
—Unknown

Some people want it to happen,
some wish it would happen,
others make it happen.
—Michael Jordan

If a man could have half his wishes,
he would double his troubles.
—Mark Twain

Many of us spend half our time
wishing for things we could have
if we didn't spend half our time wishing.
—Alexander Woollcott

The most fantastic magical things can happen,
and it all starts with a wish.
—Pinocchio

NOW I ASK YOU . . .

Have you ever made a threat to someone, either spoken or written? Has anyone ever threatened you? How did it make you feel? As an adult, I have received face-to-face threats, phone threats, and lengthy letter threats. (According to the FBI, I have the dubious honor of being the longest-stalked person in the nation: **50** years!) So I have been threatened Big Time! But I have survived and outlived my stalker.

SPLASH!

Way back, when I was about 11 years old, and my brother was probably six, we were in the kitchen, doing our chores. I was washing the dishes, and he was drying them. He kept bugging me about something, and wasn't doing his job. I do not recall what he was doing, but I kept telling him to stop, and he wouldn't. We were making a lot of noise. I was so angry, that I started threatening him, saying that if he didn't stop, I was going to throw the pan of water on him. But he didn't stop. And I was so incensed that I *did* throw the pan of water on him! And he was *drenched,* and water was all over the floor. We were both shocked into silence, as we stared at each other in disbelief. Then we started whispering that we had to quickly clean up the floor, because Mom and Dad would get mad. (Of course, they were both In the living room, and had heard the whole shouting match, but let us take care of the problem ourselves, without interfering.)

I always thought of this experience as only a way we had dodged a bullet, by avoiding a tongue-lashing and possibly further repercussions (restriction, or a loss of weekly allowance). And I never gave it much thought, other than relief. Over 50 years later, however, I found that my little brother (who was brilliant even then!), had considered this well-remembered event as *life-changing*, as it was the first time we had collaborated to avoid conflict. It was pivotal in seeing that anger issues and emotional explosions often get in the way of sensible resolutions. Decades afterward, as a leader (he founded and ran a number of businesses and corporations within 37 countries), he realized that nothing is more stressful and emotionally draining, than a full-blown argument (whether with an angry family member—me!—or an acting out friend, or an aggressive subordinate, or an unruly customer). He had learned early on—from our little experience—that conflict management was a valuable tool. And I realized that if you threaten someone, you have to follow through (or no one will believe you thereafter!), so that was my first and last threat that I made.

> *Threats are the last resort*
> *of a man with no vocabulary.*
> —Tamora Pierce

> *The quality of our lives*
> *depends not on whether or not*
> *we have conflict,*
> *but how we respond to them.*
> —Thomas Crum

NOW I ASK YOU...

*Because people aren't perfect
and relationships are messy,
we all need to learn
how to resolve conflicts.*
—John Maxwell

*Empty threats are for dreamers.
And I am a realist.*
—Natalya Vorobyova

*Empty threats are often worse than saying
nothing at all. It's like leading from behind.
Eventually, no one thinks you're leading at all.
And, after a while, no one is even listening.*
—Kathleen Troia McFarland

Loud threats often indicate deep fears.
—Napoleon Hill

NOW I ASK YOU . . .

Did your early choices of a career pan out? (As two-year-olds, both Jason, my great-nephew, and Haydon, my great great-nephew, were obsessed with trash trucks, and both wanted to be trash truck drivers when they grew up. It didn't happen.) As a youngster, did you have a lot of jobs you would like to have had, or like Scarlett O'Hara, did you choose to worry about it tomorrow? Or even later, when you grew up?

BUBBLES

By the fifth grade, I thought that the search for my adult career was over. I knew I couldn't be a teacher, and I couldn't be a writer, and I couldn't be a runner (I was the fastest runner in the whole school, but girls and women weren't encouraged to be athletes in those days. They received no support whatsoever). So I decided to be an archeologist.

I thought archeology was fascinating! And, one day, I got to tell all my classmates all about it. Mr. Pike, our teacher, simply asked each student, one by one, to stand up, and tell the class what job we wanted to have when we grew up, and why. Everyone had the most common answers, until he got to me. The girls wanted to be a mother, a secretary, or a nurse. The boys wanted to be a fireman, a policeman, or a doctor. When I said that I had a burning desire to be an archeologist, no one knew what that was. So I got to tell everyone how exciting a job that would be. So many of the students after me, said that they, too, wanted to be an archeologist. And some of the students that had already told what they wanted to be, decided to change their minds. So, with that many interested kids, I founded an Archeology Club. And we met every few weeks, at a different kid's house, and the mother's provided cup cakes or ice cream, or something to eat. If anyone brought articles from magazines or newspapers, we would all discuss them. I kept a big scrapbook, with all the magazine and newspaper articles pasted inside. Also, we included book reports on the subject. We had lots of fun. This was all after school, with no adults guiding us.

*Oddly, my brother had the same interest, although we had never talked about it. Not even once, as we were living in two different worlds, then, with a six and a half year difference between us. When he was an adult, he made many trips into the jungles, and had discovered old pyramids that were covered over by all the trees and vegetation, but it would cost too much to excavate them. Once when he was telling me about one of the pyramids, I showed him my old archeology scrapbook, and he went absolutely nuts reading through it. He excitedly said that the articles were all the original information. He use to give speeches about his trips, to various groups, and so he took my scrapbook to show others. And I never got it back!

When I recently emailed him, asking how many times he went exploring over the years, he said that he actually ended up making well over 50 trips to Mesoamerican archeological sites, saying: "One trip took over a half-dozen different archeological sites over a six week period. However, I have actually been to Mexico, Belize, Guatemala, and Honduras, many times, to consider newly discovered ancient cities. How many times? I quit counting years ago, but places like Palenque, Chichen

Itza, Uxmal, Teotihuacan, Coba, etc., I have been to at least a dozen times each. Many of those locations are no longer in jungles, and have become major tourist destinations. However, 35 and 40 years prior, most were still very remote and unusual." He has had so many wild adventures, that I often thought that my brother had been a prototype for the *Indiana Jones* books and movies.

So, anyway, I was enamored with the idea of being an archeologist through the 5th, 6th, and part of the 7th grades. But then reality hit me like a Mack truck. I never factored in the working conditions. The digging part was not a problem. (When I was in the first grade, I tried to dig a hole to China, behind the garage. I spent days shoveling dirt. My hole was huge, and when my father saw the depth of it, he freaked out, and made me fill it back up.) I would have to deal with long hours, with no air conditioning. (Nor did I know of the prevailing bias that women archeologists were not being hired, because they *shouldn't* be out in the blazing sun where they would *sweat!* How unladylike!) And I wouldn't be able to go home at night, and stores wouldn't be close by. When I found out about what the camps looked like, and what the workers ate, and that they slept in tents, and that there was little privacy, that's when my love affair with archeology started to crumble. But what really burst my bubble was when I found out that there was often a water shortage, and there would absolutely be NO Bubble Baths at any excavation campsite, EVER! That was the end of the dream, for me.

I LOVE bubbles! I have always had a thing for bubbles. I love to hear the bubbles when I pop open a can of Pepsi. I love to see bubbles in the washing machines, or dishwashing, or instant foaming hand soap. I especially like to watch bubbles in a brook, or coming out of a fountain, a bubble gun, or a bubble machine. Soap bubbles don't fly, they float, and I love to see them levitate, waft, glide, hover, and drift. I love to see the two-foot mountains of bubbles in my jet bathtub. I love to follow these shiny, iridescent orbs, even though they don't last long. There is something magical about soap bubbles, as they seem to defy gravity. As such, I simply couldn't imagine giving up bubble baths forever.

Even still, I eagerly read recent books by archaeologists, and watch all the documentaries about recent finds. And I cried for their success (in private)! It is so exciting to get another peek at our world's history, which widens our understanding of ancient days gone by.

Oh well, so it was back to the drawing board. I was back to deciding on a career I would like to have as an adult. But I didn't need to explore career options, nor did I need to strain my brain about it. I simply took my fall back position, and said, "Okay, I'll be a professional dancer!" That was an easy choice, since I had been dancing on the stage for 15 of my 17 years. (At the age of two, I was offered three movie contracts, but my parents refused to sign on the dotted line, saying I needed to have a *normal* life. I was supposed to take Shirley Temple's place, since she was then in high school, and was considered too old). While in high school, I was offered a job as a ballet teacher, but I had already taken a job at the newly built Disneyland. My friend, who was a year older than me, had been begging me for some time, to follow in her footsteps. She had signed her dancing contract, to go on tour. She would be on the circuit for a year before I graduated. But by then, she would know the ropes, and we would do the circuit together, and be roomies. That was the plan, anyway.

> *Far and away the best prize that life offers*
> *is the chance to work hard at work worth doing.*
> —Theodore Roosevelt

> *Choose a job you love, and you will never have to*
> *work a day in your life.*
> —Confucius

> *Pleasure in the job puts perfection in the work.*
> —Aristotle

NOW I ASK YOU . . .

Have you ever had a situation is which you were not believed? When all were against you? If so, did you feel bad about it? Not being believed is a frustrating, disappointing, and challenging experience to endure. Did you try even more to convince others, or did you drop the subject entirely?

BROKEN FINGER

I loved to play softball. As such I was always picked first on a team. One Monday, when in the 7th grade, during gym class, we were playing in the heat of the day. A perfect, easy catch was headed right towards me. But the noon sun was shinning directly overhead, blurring my vision. And I misjudged the ball by about a half-inch, and it smashed down onto my extended middle finger, as I loudly yelled and dropped the ball. And it hurt, BIG TIME (but I'm not one to weep and fall apart)! The gym teacher grabbed my finger, and shook it back and forth, declaring that it was not broken, and the game played on. I complained to my next period teacher, who grabbed my finger, shook it back and forth, and said it was not broken. I then complained to my next teacher (because it was *still* hurting!), who shook it, and said that it was not broken, but he had the presence of mind to send me to the nurse. The nurse, however, grabbed my finger, shook it back and forth, and declared that it was not broken. When I went home, unfortunately, both parents did and said the same thing. Several days later, my finger was *still* hurting! A lot. And it was hard to hold a pencil. So, on Friday, as I walked home from school, I stopped at a doctor's office, and asked if he would check out my finger, as I told him my sob story. He did so, and said, "YES, indeed, you *do* have a broken finger!" as he placed a metal splint under the length of my finger, and bandaged it securely in place. "But your finger will never be straight again, because it took you so long to see a doctor." The doctor called my father that night, and read him the riot act. And the doctor was right, as my middle finger is still crooked. I have rarely played softball, since.

> *"Sorry" is like a bandaid.*
> *Just because you use it,*
> *doesn't mean its going*
> *to heal the wound.*
> —Daniel Brindusa

NOW I ASK YOU . . .

Do you know anyone with epilepsy? How would you know? Seriously, what is a person with epilepsy supposed to look like? Have you ever seen someone having an epileptic seizure? Statistics tell us that over one million people in the USA have uncontrolled epilepsy. Yikes! This "falling disease" condition has been known for 4,000 years: ancient tablets found in Mesopotamia, and later Babylonia, and then the Egyptians (1700 B.C.), then the Chinese (770-221 B.C.), and later in Greece (5th century). Hippocrates first suggested that the brain might be the cause of epilepsy (instead of a Sacred Disease).

EPILEPSY

Apparently, I had been having small seizures throughout my childhood, but I was unaware of it. When I would freeze and stare off towards the heavens, my best friend knew, but she just thought that I was just having great ideas (since everyone always thought that I was "so smart"). But it all came to a head, when I was in the 7th grade, in a history class. The teacher asked a question, and I excitedly waved my arm around (as did several other students), but he called on me. As I started to answer, I froze, and when I came out of the seizure, everyone was staring at me, while another student was in the middle of stating the answer. So I knew time had gone by, without me being conscious of it. I must have had a perplexed look on my face, and my teacher seemed concerned, but just then the bell rang to race to our next class, and we all moved out quickly. I thought about my loss of time all day, and realized that I had had similar experiences beforehand (the most recent when I was presenting a puppet show in my science class), and decided to tell my parents that night.

I couldn't explain it, other than to say, "I wasn't there," "I wasn't awake," "I wasn't aware of anything," or "It was like I was *dead* for awhile." I didn't have the proper words to explain it. But they figured that I was talking about a seizure. They were concerned enough, that my Dad called specialists in Los Angeles, and the next day I was suddenly having x-rays of my head. The doctor said that I had been having petite mal seizures for a long time, and if I had waited just two more weeks to tell my parents, then I would be having grand mal seizures (a loss of consciousness, with violent muscle contractions causing me to fall down, with confusion upon awakening, and severe headaches). Geez, I figured I was really lucky!

In those days, epilepsy still had a bad reputation: the social stigmas said that I was either an evil spirit (a demonic possession), holy, or mad as a hatter (depending on the culture), causing those with epilepsy to be feared and isolated. As a result, my parents cautioned that I must *never, ever,* tell anyone that I had epilepsy. So I didn't, for many decades, as discrimination still raged, from a lack of health or life insurance, few jobs being available, no driver's licenses were given, and in a few states epileptics couldn't get married. And a few state laws even forced sterilization. Nowadays, people with epilepsy are protected under the Equality Act, even if they don't consider themselves to be 'disabled.'

I began taking three pills three times a day: morning, noon, and night. By the time I was in college, I didn't have to take them anymore. Years later, I only had one episode, when I was pregnant, but I figured that my body had all changed because of the pregnancy, and didn't worry about it.

Later on, however, when I was in my late seventies, and was the only caregiver for my husband, Wayne (with lots of stress and strain involved), I had one seizure, which was very scary. I drove up to the outside window of Kentucky Fried Chicken, and ordered a meal for Wayne, and then had a seizure. I came aware when my head was leaning backward, and when I opened my eyes, I was looking at the headliner of my car, and I could *feel* the car moving backward. I freaked out, looking through the back window, and luckily, there were no cars behind me, as I stomped on the brakes. This was totally unlike any other day, as there was always a bunch of vehicles in line at KFC (a small miracle!). I was so happy that I hadn't plowed backward into a line of cars. Can you imagine the insurance problems that would have entailed? I was so scared that I was afraid to drive home, but I had to, in order to take care of my husband. So I drove as slowly as possible, taking side streets, just in case. Because I had that one seizure, my driver's license was revoked (understandably!), and I didn't get it back for two years or so (which required permission from doctors). It was a long and involved process.

I may have epilepsy, but epilepsy doesn't have me!
Never let epilepsy win . . .you've got this.
—Unknown

Epilepsy may be hard to live with,
but it's how you deal with it,
that can make all the difference.
—Unknown

NOW I ASK YOU . . .

Have you ever changed your mind about something important (a decision, an opinion, a choice, or a plan)? Your willingness to change your mind, in the light of new information or evidence, is a sign of rationality. It takes courage to change your mind (especially if others are involved), and it may be uncomfortable, but you have the *right* to change your mind.

PEERING THROUGH A WINDOW

Throughout my youth, I wanted to be a teacher when I grew up. So every morning, before I went to school in the 2nd grade, I would dress my dolls, and place them on my bed (which I pretended was their school). I surrounded them with little books that I had made for them. Then (as their mother), I pretended to go to work and teach (like my mother and my father).

From Jr. High on, I would critique my teachers during their daily lessons. I knew what they could have said, to interest the sports-minded, or the popular kids, or the nerds, or the "bad boys," or even those with no interest in school, whatsoever. I wished I could have explained it, so those students would interact in class discussions, and get excited about the subject, and get more out of the lessons. As such. I felt well-prepared to be a teacher.

Unfortunately, both my parents, and several aunts and uncles, as well as three neighbors on our block were teachers. They were all very strict, formal, permanently serious, and quiet. These role models rarely smiled, their mouths habitually pursed in thought or disapproval. They were not into frivolity. Whereas, I had an outgoing, loud and sunny disposition, always smiling, laughing, singing, or dancing, wearing bright colors, and being highly creative, which I felt didn't go hand-in-hand with the role of an educator—judging from my role models.

I felt that I was way "too different," and that I wouldn't be accepted as a teacher, since my attitude appeared to be unlike other teachers. Basically, I was a right-brained kid trying to fit into a left-brained world. So, because it was my groundless observation that *all* teachers acted in the same manner, I put my passion on hold.

As a senior in high school (1957), I had my life all planned out: I was to sign a dancing contract shortly after graduation, as I had been dancing on stage for 15 years, since I was two-years-old. An older girlfriend was already on the dancing circuit, and I was to join her on tour, and we would be roomies.

That Christmas, our parents threw a party, that neither my brother, nor I, knew anything about. As we were leaving the house for our separate dates that night, guests began arriving early. We were absolutely dumbfounded, as our parents had never hosted a party before (or since). They didn't even go to parties! They only rarely interacted with neighbors.

We watched in total amazement, as many bottles of liquor were being carried through the door.

Now we had been raised with a teetotal mindset (no drinking, no smoking, no gambling, no swearing, no carousing, no drugs, no nonsense, and such). Total abstinence. Our lives were reminiscent of the later 1982 "Goody Two Shoes" song by Adam Ant, with the lyric refrain: "Don't drink, don't smoke, what do you do?", to which I would always shout, "Not much!"

So my brother and I decided to stick around for a bit, and watch through the windows. We were absolutely fascinated to see the teachers—strangers from two different school districts, and grade levels —happily carrying on together: talking, laughing, singing, dancing, and obviously having a grand time. A smaller group was huddled around the piano in the dining room, singing Christmas carols at the top of their lungs, when for some reason, Mother wanted the piano moved to the living room. So the piano player kept banging away on the keys, as several burly men picked up the piano, and the crowd of carolers moved as one, into the next room. Neither the piano nor the singers skipped a beat. I was thunderstruck!

As we left our window-watching perches, I had reached my turning- point. My whole life changed in an instant. Teachers could have *fun!* They could act silly, shout, be creative—and even drink and smoke! What a shocker! Teachers could actually have FUN! (Not that I would ever act silly or drink or smoke, but it was the idea that I couldn't if I wanted to: it was a matter of freedom of choice, and too many implied rules.)

In one fell swoop, I followed my heart, and danced my last dance. I immediately scrapped my dancing career, and went on to the university, and earned several degrees. And then taught for *fifty* years as a teacher and a professor. I find it remarkable that, by observing one unexpected party, my life was profoundly altered. It staggers the imagination.

We're constantly affected by our experiences of life,
and our experiences change our
personality, our world-view,
and our behaviors.
—Thom Hartmann

NOW I ASK YOU . . .

Have you ever wondered what really lies below the surface of someone you just recently met? Whether what you see is actually what you get? Before becoming involved in a relationship, do you know what warning signs to look for in potential stalkers? Do you know that abusers often become stalkers? Stalkers know how to make a good impression. Psychopaths and sociopaths appear to be average, ordinary citizens, very good at camouflage (remember Ted Bundy? Jeffrey Dahmer, John Wayne Gacy, or Samuel Little? How about The Green River Killer?). Harvard psychologist Dr. Martha Stout says that one in every 25 people is a sociopath, and they exist in all walks of life. Never trust appearances. You need to pay less attention to what a person says, than to what a person does. *See without putting your own spin on it* (which has always been my problem). My idealized emotions were not even close; they were not even in the same ball park, zip code, or even in the same time zone. Be diligent about tiny clues. Is there something that doesn't seem quite right? Something that seems a little off kilter? Something that doesn't quite track? Stop, look, listen, and *feel*. Keep your eyes as wide open as your heart. Do your homework. Make informed decisions. Meet at a number of public sites, before handing out your address. While the dinosaurs never saw it coming, you can.

A SKEWED VIEW

Once upon a time, long before DNA testing, nanoseconds, cyberspace, cell phones, robots, and AI, in the olden days of rock 'n roll and Sputnik (the stone age when it comes to the Internet), I met Chuck at a Teen Dance in 1957, when I had just turned seventeen. And as is common in literature, it all began so innocently. I arrived with a date, as did he. Chuck and I wouldn't even have connected, if his date hadn't asked me for some mascara, as I was walking out of the Women's Room. Apparently, the two of them had been necking in the parking lot, and she needed to reapply her makeup. I loaned her my mascara (nobody thought of health implications in those days!), and waited outside, happily chatting with Chuck.

I'm sure the giddy flush on my face couldn't help but display my pleasure at being in a conversation with such a handsome *older* man (around 24 years old). When his date returned, we went our separate ways. Much later, Chuck found me again amid the mass of teens, and asked for my phone number. He smiled a lot and seemed so nice, I thought it terribly romantic. I was thrilled that he had asked. And, since I had never carried mascara in my purse, beforehand, I considered it a sign of kismet.

Several days later, he called! When I had told him my phone number, he hadn't written it down, so that meant that he had *memorized* it! Wow! (It never occurred to me to wonder why an older guy would be trolling for a young, inexperienced, impressionable, high school girl.) I was both pleased and flabbergasted that he had taken a liking to me. Ignorance is bliss!

It took two weeks of dating before he kissed me, which I viewed as a sign that he respected me. *What a total gentleman*, I thought, *so caring and considerate.* Wrong again. He then immediately pushed for exclusivity, which I took to be a declaration of undying devotion. He, of

46

course, was just reeling me in. We then progressed to the handholding stage. I couldn't believe my incredible good fortune, in finding someone whose ideas, values, and outside interests were *exactly* like mine. (Note that a stalker will agree with all you say, and in the manner of a chameleon, will reflect your values, morals, and judgments.) I had never heard of mirroring before.

Don't trust everything you see.
Even salt looks like sugar.
—Narges Obaid

All is not necessarily what it seems to be
at first blush.
—Robert H. Hopcke

Trust, but verify.
—Ronald Reagan

Life is what happens to you
when you're busy making other plans.
—John Lennon

Find growth from the "bad luck"
of meeting Mr. Wrong.
—Robert H. Hopcke

NOW I ASK YOU . . .

Have you noticed any Red Flags in your relationship? They are warning signs. They may be subtle, at first, so they are not always recognized. Red Flags indicate unhealthy, manipulative, or erratic behavior, leading to toxic and abusive conduct. Substance abuse, jealousy, and anger issues are clearly Red Flags, as are the lack of trust, isolation, and disrespect. Constant lying, or a lack of communication, are clues. Does he/she lie about family, education, or job history? Or criminal or arrest records? What or why does he/she have something to hide? Know that feeling pressured, threatened, or controlled are outright Red Flags. Don't make excuses for another's behavior. Get out before the blood starts flowing.

BENEFIT OF THE DOUBT

An odd event happened the first night I met Chuck's family. As I prattled on (as is my wont), relating several recent experiences, his oldest sister finally asked, "Who is this *Chuck* you keep talking about?" while the rest of the family members nodded in agreement, also showing their confusion. So I pointed at him. It turned out that the family had always called him by his given name, *Charles*, or a diminutive of his middle name, *Fred*erick, and had no idea that he had told me his name was Chuck. Abruptly, the room fell silent as everyone turned to stare at him, while he showed *no emotion, or guilty conscience,* whatsoever. (A clue, had I paid attention, but ignored it.) Meaningful glances were exchanged during this awkward moment, making me feel vaguely uneasy. I wished I understood what the heck was going on. Clearly there were underlying subtexts here that I didn't understand. Mentally giving him the benefit of the doubt, however, I decided that Chuck was just embarrassed about trying to make a fresh start of some sort—a new beginning, perhaps—and that a new name represented a way of overcoming some difficulty in his recent past: a tragic lost love, or a long-term friendship gone sour, I romanticized. *Little did I know.* I was simply a lamb to the slaughter. It turned out that Chuck had a long history of beating women, which landed them in the hospital. (Me, too.) This is the guy who stalked me for 50 years!

When you're in love, you put up with things
that when you're out of love,
you cite.
—Judith Martin, AKA Miss Manner

NOW I ASK YOU . . .

Have you ever seen someone faint? What did you do? Have you ever passed out? Were you embarrassed? Or were you scared or concerned? Fainting is a sudden drop in blood pressure, which reduces the blood flow and oxygen to the brain. There are many reasons why it may lead to a temporary loss of consciousness, including heat, pain, being upset or angry, hyperventilating, not eating or drinking enough, being in a too crowded space, overusing liquor or drugs, weddings, passing out while watching a birth, and funerals, not to mention medical conditions. An episode generally lasts for a few seconds or a few minutes. Most fainting spells are nothing to worry about.

IS THERE A DOCTOR IN THE HOUSE?

My wedding with Chuck was over an hour late to start, because the preacher was stuck in an earlier wedding that had gone off the rails. The groom—a psychologist—was having a hard time making a commitment. Every time it came to the point when he was to say, "I do," he would promptly faint. His buddies would dutifully haul him out the side door, slap his face around, and light him a cigarette. They would give him a private pep talk, until he finished smoking. When they thought he was composed enough, they would bring him in to try again, and again, and again. It obviously never occurred to the groom that he had a problem. *Physician, Heal Thyself!*

How southern belle of her.
—Kelly Marie Moning

NOW I ASK YOU...

I always thought fainting
showed an inherent weakness of character,
but I understand it now.
It is an act of self-preservation.
Confronted by emotion too extreme to handle,
the body shuts down.
—Kare Marie Moning

No commitment equals no results.
—Grant Cardone

NOW I ASK YOU . . .

How may weddings have you attended? Had you been to weddings before your own? Did you know what to expect? Some weddings seem to be perfect, while some have one problem after another (those are the weddings that are remembered the most). A dozen or so things going wrong (from petty annoyances to outright soap operas) shouldn't overshadow the hundreds of things going right. Embrace the imperfections with good humor. Smile, smile, and smile again.

THE TIE THAT BINDS

On the day of our wedding, there was a window of opportunity—well over an hour—that presented itself, in which I could have called the whole thing off. But I didn't realize that I needed to. Feeling somewhat superior in that commitment was not a problem for us, I was somewhat relieved when the ceremony before us was, at long last, completed, and we could finalize our own vows. So there I was, walking down the aisle, just strolling on down the railroad tracks, blissfully unaware of the freight train racing at full throttle right towards me. Our wedding went off without a hitch, and I figured that we were off to a good start. (Cue: "When I Fall in Love," sung by either Nat King Cole or Michael Buble.) I was happily unaware of anything unusual.

While driving back to my studio apartment, however, Chuck, my brand new husband of only an hour or so, delivered a one-two punch that left me reeling:

(1) He claimed that he lost his wallet, so we couldn't

go on our honeymoon, as planned. (Say, *what?*) Yeah, right. But who wants to start their marriage with a king-size argument, that would be remembered forever after? (One couple I knew preferred not to recall their wedding day, as they had a major shouting match, and that's all they could focus on). Since I was never too confrontational with anyone—being reluctant to give offence—I gave him a long, dark look, but said nothing, while trying to *understand* this turn of events.

(2) Further on down the road, Chuck informed me that he had quit his job, to play the horses full time. I was stunned. Not only could I feel future waves of disapproval coming from my staunch anti-gambling family, but I was now the sole support for the two of us, and everyone knows that teachers are underpaid. *What to do? What to do?* I couldn't decide whether he'd been fired, and just said that he quit to save face, or if he actually turned in his resignation on his own initiative. I simply didn't know how to respond.

Then, while I was trying to come to grips with these revelations he followed with the knockout blow. His third statement paled the first two into insignificance, and changed my life forever:

(3) Chuck gravely announced that if I ever had a baby, he would drown it in the bathtub. After hearing this chilling news—catastrophic, devastating, and terrifying— my brain became a series of short-circuits that rendered me incapable of processing what I'd just heard. I was struck dumb, unable to respond. My heart leaped into my throat and blocked my breathing, my head felt kicked in by a buffalo, and my vocal chords seemed paralyzed. My mouth opened and closed like a beached whale, making

no sound whatsoever. I couldn't breathe, I couldn't think, I couldn't talk, I couldn't cry. It was impossible to absorb. I searched for a response to a situation that was completely incomprehensible to me. How could anyone reply to such a statement? With that one sentence alone, I suffered an instant compound fracture of the heart, realizing that I had married a man with a head full of bent spaghetti wiring, while *my* head exploded like a Jackson Pollock. I had made the biggest mistake of my life.

A few weeks later in this ghastly marriage, Chuck announced—in no uncertain terms—that he would *kill* my whole family, if I ever left him. In great detail, he said that he would kill my father, my mother, my brother, and his wife, and their new baby. And that he would make me *watch*, while he did so, because, after all, it was my choice. And I believed him, totally. He reminded me often, whenever I was upset about something.

If a situation is going down at Point A,
why stand around at Point B?
—Nelson DeMille

. . . when sorrows come
they pass not single spies
but in battalions.
—Shakespeare

There are wounds that never show on the body
that are deeper and more hurtful
than anything that bleeds.
—Laurell K. Hamilton

NOW I ASK YOU . . .

How well did you know your boyfriend, girlfriend, or significant other, before you decided to move in together, or tie the knot? Unfortunately, many people who are in a committed relationship still don't know a whole lot about their partner.

Have you noticed any addictive behaviors in your partner? Some obsessive behaviors seem pretty tame and normal (social media, Internet, shopping, video games, binge eating, coffee or sodas, and even thumb sucking (which is isn't socially acceptable, but in private, who cares?). But many addictive behaviors are dangerous and life-threatening: tobacco, drugs, and alcohol. Even over-working (a workaholic), excessive plastic surgery, and thrill-seeking activities are considered dangerous. Ex-addicts can become addicted to something else: sex, bodybuilding, extreme tanning, body piercing, and tattoos, all in which one sacrifices his/her personal life to focus on an addiction.

Is an unstable job history evident? Are unsuitable role models obvious? Is there a fascination with violent people in the news? Does there seem to be an irresistible attraction with weaponry? Does he/she overlook or override other people's feelings? How does he/she interact with pets and children? Do you feel smothered? Are mood swings involved? Is he/she trustworthy?

So you think you have a pretty good idea of your sweetheart? And that you have a totally open communication? Granted, you portray each other in a positive way; you both see yourselves as "we"; you are highly satisfied with each other; you tolerate each other's quirks, as simply weird or amusing; you respond to each other's physical and emotional needs; and you make sacrifices for each other. So you think you know all about each other? Think again:

UNKNOWN PROBLEMS

(1) One woman hadn't seen her fiancé for several days, and couldn't connect with him via cell phone or email. So she went to his place of work, to talk with him, only to find that he had been fired six weeks prior. She discovered that he had been stealing from the company, in order to finance his gambling addiction. When he finally returned from Las Vegas, he couldn't understand her reaction to his "little" problem.

(2) Upon hearing that her fiancé was in major hock to the IRS, the bride called off the wedding. She explained that she wouldn't marry him until his debt was paid off. She refused to help him pay for his monumental prior mistake, as the consequences were his to bear. She wanted no part of the comingling of money, as it was his responsibility to take care of it alone. It took several years, but he finally paid off what was owed, and the couple was finally married, and are now happily raising their four children.

(3) The American bride and her Scottish groom made a gorgeous couple. The posh wedding featured his clan's plaid, in a number of creative, beautiful ways. The ceremony and reception went off without a hitch, but the same cannot be said for their ill-fated marriage. He was from a tradition in which wives did not work at any outside job. They stayed at home and took care of the house and

children, like it or not. Period. This came as a complete shock to the bride, as she was an educator, and loved to teach, and no one could keep her from her students. The marriage was over before the honeymoon.

(4) And in my case, Chuck and I hadn't been married long, when one day, I had to drive Chuck to a dental appointment for major root canal work. I didn't even know that Chuck was having problems with his teeth, as his mother had made the appointment for him. I was expecting a wait of several hours duration, and had settled in with a big, fat book, in the waiting room. Apparently, he was all set up in the dental chair, when the dentist told him that he was going to use sodium pentothal. Chuck leaped out of the chair, and strode into the waiting room, and rushed me outside. He kept shouting that "truth serum" was being used.

"*So?*" was my immediate response. "What kind of secrets could you possibly have, that anyone else would be interested in?" I was thoroughly irritated with this turn of event. I assumed that he was afraid of the possible pain involved, and was just using the knock-out drug as an excuse. *What a big baby!* I groused, to myself, of course. Wrong again! Not only did he have fantasy secrets, but *real* secrets, as well. (Chuck's heroes were gangsters in general, and in his delusional state, he was convinced that he was a hit-man for the Mafia).

It turned out that Chuck had *many, many* secrets. He was a psychotic schizophrenic, handing out physical, sexual, and emotional abuse, whenever his mood dictated it. Later, I went to the *Press Telegram's* newspaper morgue, and looking through all those old articles, I found that he had a habit of putting women in the hospital. I wanted out of my short marriage, of course, from day one, but I had never even heard the word *annulment* before, and even the term *divorce* was considered a dirty word, back then. But I would have left him in a heartbeat, except for his threats. He said that if I ever left him, he would kill my whole family (my father, mother, brother, and his wife, and new baby). But that I would stay alive, knowing that I could have saved them all, and that the extreme guilt I carried would be severe. So his punishment was two-fold. And I totally believed him, considering his behavior from the very first day we were married.

> *All secrets become deep.*
> *All secrets become dark.*
> *That's the nature of secrets.*
> —Cory Doctorow

> *Three may keep a secret,*
> *if two of them are dead.*
> —Ben Franklin

> *Learning to trust is one of life's*
> *most difficult tasks.*
> —Isaac Watts

> *When you finally trust someone without any doubt,*
> *you finally get one of two results:*
> *a person for life or a lesson for life.*
> —Unknown

> *It is not what you look at that matters,*
> *it's what you see.*
> —Henry David Thoreau

My friends tried to ignore my quirks,
since they didn't have a clue
as to what to do about them.
It didn't seem hard on them though.
They were already trained to ignore
their parents' alcohol abuse, constant bickering,
serial marriages, and nonsensical advice.
—Torry Spencer Hosser

Does your job require that you continue to take university classes to keep your skills up-to-date? Do you do so? Or can you take classes out of your field (underwater basket-weaving, perhaps)?

CLASSIC BEHAVIOR

While taking the Abnormal Behavior class, I first heard the term *psychotic schizophrenic*. Imagine my surprise when the classic behavior presented was exactly the same kind of behavior that Chuck had been displaying. For instance, on several occasions, Chuck loudly maintained that the trouble with our marriage was my *wardrobe*. So he would announce that he was going to rip my clothes into shreds, to save our relationship. At which point I would physically charge into him, holding him away from the closet doors, in order to save my clothes. After all, how could I work, and bring home a paycheck, if I didn't have anything to wear? A pushing and shoving match would then commence, with us wrestling around, until he got tired of the effort. Sometimes late at night, when he was in such a mood, I would sleep on the bedroom floor, with my back against the closet doors, so I could jump up and protect my clothes, if need be.

Then one night, after he started the same routine again, he suddenly reversed his position. "No! I'm not going to *rip* your clothes up! I'm not going to rip up your clothes! People would think I was *crazy* if I ripped up all your clothes. They would think that I was having some kind of *fit*; that I was out of *control*, or something. NO! I want everyone to understand that I'm serious about our love. So I'm going to take these scissors, and carefully *cut* your clothes into little squares." (How's that for logic?) Brandishing sharp scissors in his hand did not have a calming effect.

While the rest of the class was laughing hysterically about similar examples, it seemed I could hear the distant echo of a train. I was stunned to realize that Chuck's strange behavior not only had a name, *psychotic schizophrenic,* but was formally recognized as a mental illness. This course revealed a truth that I should have tumbled onto much sooner: Chuck was not just *sick*, he was *certifiable*.

The heaviest burdens that we carry
are the thoughts in our head.
—Unknown

The schizophrenic mind is
not so much split as shattered.
I like to say that schizophrenia
is like a waking nightmare.
—Elyn Saks

There is no difference
between acute schizophrenia
and a world at war.
—Gary Zukav

People are always selling the idea
that people who have mental illnesses are suffering.
But it's really not so simple.
I think mental illness or madness

can be an escape also.
—John Nash

One small crack does not mean you are broken.
It means that you were put to the test,
and you didn't fall apart.
—Linda Poindexter

Don't compare your life to others.
You have no idea what they have been through.
—Sam Cawthorn

NOW I ASK YOU . . .

Have you ever come across anyone with risky sexual behavior, or a sexual deviant? Someone who seeks erotic gratification through means that are considered odd, different, and unacceptable by most people? What did you do, or would you do, if something similar happened to you?

SEXUAL DEVIANT

Sex with Chuck was not a loving experience. There was no snuggling, no cuddling, and no canoodling involved, and no swooning afterward. It was of the Wham, Bam, Thank you, Ma'am, variety, which was actually much more desired than his violent sexual offences.

The worst was when he would bring out a blanket, and spread it on the living room floor. Then I knew that I was in for a disgusting, degrading, and violent experience. He was into some heavy S and M. His personal role model was Fatty Arbuckle. *Who knew?* He would shove bottles up inside me, and then beat on my stomach, trying to break them. He knew that the doctors wouldn't be able to retrieve all of the pieces of glass, and looked forward to the day in which he would see me in great pain, and that there was nothing anyone could do about it. Feeling dirty, both inside and out, my Snow White image was tarnished. So I took two baths a day. *Rub-A-Dub-Dub.* Sometimes I wonder how I survived it all.

*Our lives begin to end
the day we become silent
about things that matter.*
—Martin Luther King, Jr.

*I can be changed by what happens to me,
but I refuse to be reduced by it.*
—Maya Angelou

*She was powerful,
not because she wasn't scared,
but because she went on
so strongly despite the fear.*
—Atticus

NOW I ASK YOU . . .

Do you remember your dreams? Do you think dreams are a confusion of nonsensical images; just so much brain-lint? As such, do you resist, or ignore them, or reject them? Do you know that more of your brain is awake when you're asleep, than when you are awake and conscious? Do you see the symbolism in your dreams as a cornucopia of information, signals, or messages? Do you act upon such insight?

THE WORMS CRAWL IN

Long ago, there came a time when the Night Train chugged into my life, and my vaguely threatening anxiety dreams graduated into full blown nightmares. Heretofore, the dreams of my youth had been beautiful, life-enhancing experiences, from which I awakened renewed, refreshed, and revitalized. Now, the creepy-crawly terrors of the night took hold, and I slid into the world of Hieronymous Bosch. Later, I dreamed of a series of operatic dramas, including voice-overs, flashbacks, and fantasy sequences —two or three each night—in which I was *murdered* in the culminating scene. Each in a different manner. By Chuck, my husband. These dreams were brilliantly intense and gloomy, with accompanying sound effects, while the disturbing strains of Chopin's Opus no.35 (March Funebre") played solemnly in the background: Dum, dum, da dum, dum, dum, dum, da dum, da dum. It was all too gothically spooky.

Although each dream was creatively different from the next, the final scene was *always* the same. My coffin was slowly lowered into the ground, and after thumping to a stop, I could hear the dirt being shoveled on top of it: thud, thud, thud. Jolted wide awake, freaked out and jittery, with my heart hammering wildly in my chest, a warped recording of "The Worms Crawl In," ominously scratched into my awareness. Of course, with 31 flavors of fear flowing through my mind, I was afraid to go back to sleep. It was most disturbing. *Wasn't it enough that my days were in shambles?* I continuously asked myself. As my existence seemed barren beforehand, it simply didn't seem fair to add nightmares to the mix.

So now I had something new to stew about: *What was the message that I was missing here? What was this repeated nudging from my neural wiring all about? What was the night-side of my brain trying to say*? I suddenly had a new interest. Never having been one to do things in moderation, I became a champion researcher. I plunged heavily into the subject of dreams, in a determined effort to scratch this mental itch.

Like a junky on a binge, I absorbed every printed word I could find on the subject, reading dozens upon dozens of books and articles, in an attempt to understand my situation. (I collected 69 books on the subject, that are stacked one on top of the other, in a 7-foot-high column, next to my bed.) It was writ so large you could have read it from the Skylab, but I ignored the obvious, of course. The most useful for my immediate purposes were:

(1) Dreams tell us not only what we want or desire, but what we *need*, as well.

*(2) Dreams involve showing what we many not be seeing: directing attention to whatever we are most in danger of ignoring, or rejecting, in our everyday affairs.

66

(3) When our outcome becomes too rigid or limited, dreams give us the other side of the picture.

*(4) In a crisis, when our lives are threatened by outside circumstances, we will have the most vivid and meaningful dreams.

Aha! Eureka! Excelsior! And because one dream often throws light on another, experts suggest that far more satisfactory results can be obtained by trying to interpret them in groups, rather than looking at each one in isolation. Realizing that I had a problem of not seeing the forest for the trees, I decided to start recording my dreams in a diary, which I maintained for several years thereafter.

Consciously, I hadn't a clue as to what was going on, but luckily, instinct and intuition lent their guidance. Thank goodness I was picking up information subliminally, so I finally got the message: I was being sized up for a chalk outline. Chuck was literally plotting my imminent death.

Then I start reconsidering all of the near misses, and the variety of unusual incidents I had encountered over a number of months. For instance, Chuck would drive like a maniac, taking foolish chances, getting within inches of creaming dogs and cats. Was he hoping to scare me to death via a heart attack? He would speed and stop, speed and stop, repeatedly slamming me into the dashboard (this was in the days before seatbelts). He followed this with a series of deliberate near misses. He would aim for a telephone pole, street lamp, parked vehicle, tree, or whatever, driving as fast and as close as possible, before jerking away at the last moment. Of course, the object in question was always on the *passenger* side. I just thought he was a *sicko*, playing chicken with inanimate objects, and didn't see a more sinister plot.

For a number of weeks, he worked at hoping to make me think I was losing my mind, but he couldn't pull it off. I wasn't going for it. He'd make statements out of the blue, apropos of nothing, as if we'd been in the middle of a long conversation, or having no relationship whatsoever to what we'd actually been discussing, acting like I couldn't remember what had just transpired. *Give me a break, Wacko*. He finally gave up that plan, since I couldn't be convinced.

One night, as I was getting out of the bathtub, always an intensely modest experience for me, he barged into the room, and *unintentionally* bumped my radio into the bathwater. I was more concerned with the lack of privacy than the fact that I had just missed being electrocuted. My car brakes were tampered with on another occasion. And so forth and so on.

Taking another look at the string of bizarre *accidents*, and putting them together, the light finally dawned. Duh. One needn't be a member of Mensa to guess his intentions, but I'm obviously a slow learner. (Or I didn't want to admit the possibility.) As the cold breath of reality sank in, the background beat of a headache began, that rarely went away thereafter. I'd never been afraid of dying, but dying before my time, at the hands of another, was an entirely different matter. I realized that under the circumstances, caution was definitely in order from here on out.

At length, I accused him of planning to murder me. Breaking into a malevolent grin, Chuck happily answered in the affirmative, taunting me in exuberant glee, *"A wife can't testify against her husband!"* This sentence became a mantra to him. I heard that spousal privilege line, over and over again, delivered with undisguised hilarity. Those seven words were etched on the front of my mind, like the carvings on Mount Rushmore.

*Bad dreams have
the most important messages.*
—James Redfield

*The scarier the dream,
the more urgent the need
to figure it out, and
do what needs to be done.*
—Robert Moss

*I have had bad dreams and I've had nightmares.
I overcame the nightmares because of my dreams.*
—Jonas Salk

NOW I ASK YOU . . .

Are you just going through the motions of living? Have you received any abuse from a father, mother, step-parents, boyfriend, girlfriend, husband, wife, or partner? Rarely is abuse only a one-time experience, unless it is from a stranger. Know that the Post-Traumatic Stress Disorder found in war veterans is essentially the same as that for battered women, victims of child abuse, rape, and stalking, in civilian life. PTSD results from massive trauma that causes intense fear, helplessness, and horror, involving immense danger. If your trauma is/was severe, frequent, and repeated, know that you are at risk.

CONDITION RED

Late one night, while speeding down the street, almost three years into this ghastly marriage, Chuck finally snapped. Big time. Acting crazy and disoriented, wildly waving a gun around (*a gun? when did he get a gun?*), he informed me in no uncertain terms, that it was to be *my* decision as to which family member he was going to kill: my mother, father, my brother, his wife, or new baby daughter, since he didn't care which. He was simply in a trigger-happy mood. Do it or die, his eyes suggested.

This was it! The time was now! He'd finally gone off the deep end of the pool. When I shrieked that I couldn't make such a decision, he showed his displeasure by throwing his gun on the dashboard and backhanding me, while shouting, "Make a choice!" POW! "Make a choice!" POW! "Make a choice!" POW! Various colors exploded in my head, as my cheek and mouth went numb, and began to sting. Blood gushed from my nose, as it began to swell.

"Make a choice!" he chanted out of control, continuing to strike my face. The resulting bump on my nose is an indelible reminder of this experience. Although he was yelling right next to me, his voice seemed to come from a great distance, as if from the end of a long tunnel. "It's up to you! Make a choice!" SMACK!

Refusing to take further part in his mental derangement, I opened the car door to jump out. Unfortunately, Chuck grabbed the back of my blouse. So there I was, with my right hand holding onto the car seat, my left hand holding onto the open door, and my shoes dragging along the street pavement. Finally, my long blouse zipper broke, and Chuck lost hold of me, as I fell onto the street. Rolling over and over, I cracked my head. As a thousand excruciating pin-lights of pain lit up my brain, I momentarily blacked out. I revived after he managed to hit the brakes, and was roaring back in my direction, with tires squealing. My brain alarm began blinking *Condition red!* CONDITION RED! I shook my head to clear it. *Don't lose it!* my inner voice demanded. *Not now, not now!* Realizing that I had the life expectancy of a fruit fly, I finally understood the acronym FEAR: Fuck Everything And Run, as every functioning brain cell in my head screamed at me to vacate the premises. Spinning into action mode I jumped up and ran for cover.

I crouched behind some bushes in front of a house, teeth clenched, neck craned, muscles rigid. My heart felt like a kettle drum. When Chuck didn't feel the expected bump as he rolled over the spot where I had been laying, he got out of the car, and looked underneath it, his expression a perfect blend of confusion and incredibility. I could almost see the question marks dancing above his head, as he stood up and slowly scanned the area, his features reeking of homicide. (*Come out, come out, wherever you are!*)

I was so scared, my chest heaved in great gasps of air, and I was certain he'd be able to hear the rasping of my breath if he got any closer. With an air of icy determination, he returned to his car to park it, as my panic reflex kicked in. I took the opportunity to flee: feet flying, arms pumping. My heart beat in triple time, as I hightailed it around to the back of the house, and pounded on the door. But in the quiet of the night, the noise was magnified a millionfold, and I knew Chuck could easily find me. So I left, and ran to the next backdoor. I hammered on the doors of several houses, but I was so spooked by the echoes, that I wouldn't wait for anyone to answer them. I was utterly out of my mind.

You will have bad times,
but they will always
wake you up to the stuff
you weren't paying attention to.
—Robin Williams

You have to fight through the bad days
in order to earn the best days.
—Unknown

So far, you've survived 100% of your worst days.
This Too Shall Pass.
—Unknown

NOW I ASK YOU . . .

Have you ever found yourself in an unwanted situation, in which you were the odd man out? Awkward! How did you feel? What did you do? Did you or could you rectify the experience?

SAFE. KIND OF.

At the end of that row of houses, I ran into an overly tall chain link fence. My heart continued to throttle up, realizing that I was trapped, as a hundred thoughts streaked through my brain. My breathing was fast, hard, and becoming progressively more erratic. The phrase "Armageddon: The Final Frontier," neoned in my mind. I closed my eyes. *Slowly breathe in, breathe out*, I ordered myself, recognizing that as long as I was alive, I still had a chance to see another day. Digging below the terror for elements of rational thought, I hastily surveyed the area, and focused on the chain link fence at ground level, quite a distance away, where the dirt seemed somewhat uneven and disturbed. Upon closer inspection, I was elated to find a humongous hole directly underneath one section, resembling a tunnel to China, that had obviously been freshly dug by a very large dog. I was so thankful that no one had taken the time to fill in the crater. Desperate times call for desperate measures, so I didn't even have to think about it, as I automatically scrambled under the fence, and sprinted down another street.

Seeing a light on in the last house, I headed straight for it. When I got to the front door, I grabbed hold of the doorknob with one hand, as I began to knock with the other. Imagine my surprise as I went barreling through the unlocked door, right into a living room! My peripheral sight registered an older couple, with eyes round, mouths open, and faces blank with amazement, sitting on their couch together, watching TV. Hysterical at this point, I turned back, slammed and locked the door, sobbing, "Don't let him in! Don't let him in!"

Leaning against the door, and gasping like a landed fish, it finally registered that the couple was frozen in disbelief. Here was a totally wild-eyed stranger, in their house, unannounced. At length, with a scowl on her face, the woman slowly shuffled across the room. "Honey," she said disapprovingly, "*Put your clothes on*," as she yanked my blouse up over my shoulders. *I beg your pardon?* This was the first indication I had that after my full-length zipper had broken, my blouse had fallen off, held only by the long sleeves which were simply hanging inside-out from my wrists. So I had been essentially running around the neighborhood with my bra on display. This bothered me more than the fact that I had been bleeding profusely. When I shimmied under the fence, the blood mixed with the damp dirt, bark chips, and minced vegetation, forming a kind of mud that clung to my body. I looked horrible: like an escapee from an insane asylum or some sort of swamp creature. No wonder they seemed reluctant to help.

It became immediately apparent that I was interrupting their TV entertainment for the evening. They were in the midst of watching the classic *Red River*, starring John Wayne, and I was causing them to miss part of the dialogue. I felt terrible to be intruding, yet I refused to go back outside; this place represented sanctuary to me. Not knowing what else to do, I sat down beside them on the couch, and as my pulse and breathing slowed, finished watching the movie. Of sorts.

Yippy-ti-yi-yay, I thought. *I need to circle the wagons around my life.* I wasn't concentrating on the film, as silent tears blurred my vision, and I was alert to every little outside sound, straining to identify each potential threat. I was afraid that any minute, Chuck might crash in, and all Hell would break loose. *There are no Happy Trails here,* I noted.

During one of the commercials, the woman gave me a washcloth and a Band-Aid, and pointed me toward the bathroom. As I went through the door, I was frightened to see myself in the mirror. Yow! (*Mirror, mirror, on the wall . . .*). My face was Kabuki white, my eyes seemed to be popping out of my head in the manner of a cartoon character, and my tangled hair was in total disarray, giving me the look of Medusa. I thought it best to avoid the visual. I tried to wash off the blood, but the washcloth was instantly dyed red from the first wound I tried to clean. I felt terrible about ruining it. The only injury that was small enough for the Band-Aid to cover was a place at the bottom of my thumb, about the size of a quarter.

I was thankful that this was a two-bedroom house, and that the couple offered me the extra room for the rest of the night. I was wide awake all night, listening to every little sound, trembling in fear. My heart pounded like a jackhammer. Intermittently, I tried to use the bathroom. Unfortunately, that required that I pull down my pants, which were matted with blood, and stuck to my body. When I tried to peel them off, I fainted from the effort. Twice. The first time, I was surprised to find that I had slid down, when I awakened on the floor; the clue being the wide swath of blood left behind on the wall, looking like a macabre Rorschach test. The next time I toppled into the tub, headfirst, my body draped over the side. Although it represented a state of blessed anesthesia that kept me out of harm's way for a little while, I decided to leave the room. I was hurting too much, making too much noise, and worried that I might waken my hosts. This convinced me to control my bladder by whatever means necessary. I was in agony.

But I still can't get over the fact that the woman was a dispatcher at the police department, and didn't consider my problem worthy of official attention. She probably dealt with similar situations all the time, just not inside her own house, on a Sunday night, her time off. Kind of like a busman's holiday. In the morning, after she left for work, I called my school secretary, to tell her I wouldn't be there that day, and hung up before she had a chance to tell me that everyone was looking for me. And then I called my closest childhood girlfriend (because Chuck didn't know her), to come get me.

I then planted myself on the front porch, because my lecherous male host had blatantly suggested a romp-in-the-hay, and was staring at me with less than a wholesome interest. I guess that once a Dirty Old Man has seen your bra and some bare skin, he thinks you *want* him. Sure. "You old coot! You old perv!" I muttered under my breath. Now his wife's initial reaction to me made perfect sense. *Horny ol' goat*, I huffed and puffed. As if I didn't have enough to deal with.

Reaching out to rescue one another
under any condition is an eternal measure of love.
—Ronald A. Rasband

You are your last-line of defense in safety.
It boils down to you.
—Kin Repp

When you reach the end of your rope,
tie a knot in it, and hang on.
—Franklin D. Roosevelt

Our prime purpose in this life is to help others.
And if you can't help others,
at least don't hurt them.
—Dalai Lama

NOW I ASK YOU . . .

Have you ever been in an unbelievable situation, that you had only seen in movies, and didn't think such actions would ever touch your life?

IN THE MEAN TIME

Unbeknownst to me, Chuck got tired of looking for me, and went seeking my brother, instead. Knowing that Terry, his wife, and new baby, lived in one of the three apartment buildings next to a bowling alley, Chuck began his search. Looking in all the attached parking lots for their car, circling around the front and sides of the buildings, he was scanning the area for a distinctive vehicle: a mint-green 1955 Thunderbird convertible hot rod. It shouldn't have been hard to find. It wasn't there.

Unfortunately, as he drove back up the alley. Terry was driving down the alley, returning from a late movie. Pleased to see Chuck, thinking that he thought enough about them to come over for a visit, Terry rolled down the window. That happy thought was short-lived, however, as Chuck shouted that he had just *killed* me, and had come to kill them also. Shoving Maureen's head down, in anticipation of flying bullets, Terry stomped down hard on the gas pedal, and laid rubber through the parking lot. Pulling into the carport, he sent her running into their apartment, to lock herself in, and call the police. Being nineteen and hot-headed, he sped over to our parents' house, and grabbed an old hunting rifle. Mother freaked when she saw Terry load it, and storm off. She and our father also called the police, hurriedly dressed, and zoomed over to my apartment.

Arriving at my place, Terry found the apartment door already open.

Chuck was calmly sitting in a chair inviting him inside. "Hey there, Terry, how good it is to see you! Come on in," he gestured, with a big smile on his face, as if nothing in the world was wrong.

Upon seeing this odd behavior, Terry refused to go in, suspecting a trap of some sort. "*Where's Sherry*?" he demanded. Chuck widened his grin. "*Where's my sister*?" Terry reiterated, as Chuck gave have him a smile that should have put him on penicillin. After shouting back and forth for a bit, the first squad car pulled into the parking lot.

In a last ditch effort, still trying to lure him inside, Chuck matter-of-factly said, "Come on in and I'll kill you!" As Terry was about to enter, two policemen had slowly walked up behind him. Terry was happy to see what he considered to be backup, reinforcements coming to help him. Not so. Terry was knocked unconscious by the first officer, who upon seeing the rifle, surmised that *he* was the bad guy, and confiscated the gun.

The police then engaged Chuck in conversation, who feigned perfect innocence, and lied without compunction, spreading his hands in a practiced manner, palms up, eyes wide, saying that he didn't know why his young brother-in-law had come after him. He calmly explained that yes, he and I had had an argument, but that I had taken off in a hissy fit, so he didn't know *where* I was. He then attacked my family's credibility, *complaining* that my whole family was weird, and all this nonsense was finally getting to him. He just didn't know how to *deal* with them, he added, just as my parents arrived on the scene. Of course, my mother and father were hysterical, seeing Terry on the ground, and not finding me anywhere. Their reactions fed right into the storyline Chuck had been fabricating, so it was easy to see *who* the officers believed. The good news is that they did not arrest Terry; the police released him to our parents' care.

Later, when Mom and Dad finally got home, they called all of my teacher friends, who got dressed, and went outside to places they thought I might be, and literally beat the bushes. Here I had deliberately not called anyone— why put everyone in a tizzy?—and they were all out in the middle of the night looking for me, anyway.

Then the phone calls to my parents started coming. Chuck just wouldn't let the situation alone. Every time my mother or father answered, he used insulting and repulsive language, calling them foul names, taunting them by saying he had killed me, and there was nothing they could do about it. The minute they would hang up, he would call again. Dozens upon dozens of calls came in, one after another, in a matter of minutes. My parents were afraid not to answer the phone, in case I was trying to call for help. So they felt they had to endure his ranting.

Chuck's Academy Award performance had been so believable that the police actually became concerned about *my* crazy family. He had laid it on so thick, after Mom, Dad, and Terry left for home, that the officers actually *believed* my father had a vast gun collection in the house, stockpiled with tons of ammunition, and that he vowed to kill Chuck! The officers sped into the driveway, and rushed into my parents' house with their guns drawn! My mother kept pleading with them to listen to Chuck's vile and threatening phone conversations, and then they would know who to believe. On cue, the phone rang again, and she answered, immediately handing the receiver over. The first officer blanched, upon hearing such an explosive burst of obscenities, as he passed the receiver on to his partner, who had the same reaction. Both seemed stymied and unsure of the situation. Stunned into silence, they left shortly thereafter, shaking their heads in confusion.

I've got thoughts
more tangled than
my headphones.
—Unknown

The mere attempt
to examine my own confusion
would consume volumes.
—James Agee

The more I think
the more confused I get.
My life has become
this one big
I DON'T KNOW.
—Unknown

Anyone who isn't confused
really doesn't understand the situation.
—Edward R. Murrow

I'm more confused than a chameleon
in a bag of Skittles.
—Unknown

If confusion is the first step to knowledge,
I must be a genius.
—Larry Leissner

NOW I ASK YOU . . .

Do you have many friends? Of those, do you have a true-blue friend (loyal, faithful, dependable) that you can count on, rain or shine, day or night, year after year?

TRUE-BLUE FRIEND

I hadn't seen my true-blue friend for several years. Terrell had married right out of high school, and had three daughters, while I had gone on to the university, and then taught school for a couple of years. When I called my closest childhood friend to come get me, I told her that I didn't know the name of the street, or the address, but I gave her directions, as best as I could. She said "Yes, of course" without any hesitation. Since I obviously hadn't stressed that I needed help, and that this was a matter of some urgency, she leisurely took her daughters to their different schools, and went to a couple of stores, before picking me up. The wait seemed to go on forever: oceans rose and fell, continents formed, dinosaurs died. And I desperately needed to use a bathroom.

Upon her arrival, Terrell got out of the car to meet me, as I gingerly stood up from the steps to greet her. The pain was nauseating. She took one look at me, and knew that something had hit the fan somewhere. Putting her hand out in front of her like a traffic cop, she yelled "STOP!" and dove back into her car, and took two Valiums. She brought me one, and when I refused to take it (never having heard of Valium before), she gulped that one down, also.

Figuring that my parents were at work, and not wanting to take the chance that Chuck might be waiting at their house, Terrell took me to her house. She immediately put me in her bathtub, to soak my clothes off. It was heaven, just to be able to use the toilet again. Then she cleaned my scratches, scrapes, and gaping wounds, putting some kind of salve all over them, applying gauze over that. When she was done, I looked like something akin to a mummy. She dressed me in one of her muumuus, since all of my ripped and bloody clothes had to be thrown away. I was so thankful for her efforts on my behalf, but don't know if I ever expressed those sentiments at the time. Probably not, given my state of mind.

My shock was genuine and bone deep. I definitely wasn't thinking clearly about what to do next. Later that afternoon, Terrell and her husband, Bob, both suggested that I check into the hospital, but I didn't think that was necessary. And, discounting the ache in my head, back, arms, shoulders, chest, stomach, and legs, I *was*. "Fit as a fiddle, top-drawer, first class, hunkey-dory, thank you very much," I assured them, tightening my jaw so they wouldn't see the pain, while nodding to show how fine I was (fine is a four-letter word for denial.) "Especially since you've taken such good care of me," I added for good measure. Truth be told, I'm not a fan of hospitals. The sharp smell of formaldehyde alone sends me right over the edge. As such, I will not willingly place myself in such unpleasantness. "I'm all right. I'm fine, really. Everything is just peachy keen." I was a million miles from fine, unless you consider the acronym: Fucked up, Insecure, Nervous, and Emotional. But I felt fortunate just to be alive. Not once did I think that I was inconveniencing anyone (which should have told everyone how far off the beaten path I was).

I still had no idea that everyone was worried about my whereabouts. I just wanted to lay low where Chuck couldn't find me. So I stayed overnight in their guest bedroom. I was unaware that my brother had spent that Monday night, as well as Tuesday night, on the CSULB campus, looking for me, and interviewing other students, or that friends, family members, and colleagues, were frantically searching for me.

Tuesday afternoon, my mother finally figured out that I was hiding out with Terrell. Blowing in like a hurricane, she was understandably furious that I hadn't called. When she finally wound down, she took a good look at me, and said, "Get in the car. We're going to the hospital." *Excuse me?* I'd had enough of being ordered around, and I had determined that I was never again going to do anything until I was damned good and ready. I really wasn't able to discern the difference between loving concern and controlling behavior, at that point. My brain seemed to be functioning with all the agility of sludge.

Since I had already gone through this conversation with my friends, I was adamant about not going, and stuttered and sputtered as we argued a bit. Then, in a voice of reason, she said, "You know, Sherry, it will help you get a *divorce*, if you have to stay in the hospital." Aha! With those magic words, I was out the door in a flash. (Cue the Rolling Stones: "You can't always get what you want . . . You get what you need.") My friends piled in their car, trailing ours.

*Best friends are people who make
your problems their problems,
just so you don't have to go through it alone.*
—Unknown

I get by, with a little help from my friends.
—The Beatles

NOW I ASK YOU . . .

Have you ever spent any time in a hospital? As a patient, or visitor?

Was everything hunky-dory, or did you have some complaints?

HOSPITAL BLUES

Although I was slowly shuffling along, stiffly and carefully, we four (Terrell, Bob, Mother, and I) walked through the hospital door together. The nurses, as well as those manning the check-in counter, took one look at me and yelled, "STOP!", "Freeze!", and "Don't move!" in unison. "Hold it right there!" another nurse yelled, as she quickly pushed a wheelchair up to me. I couldn't figure out how everyone knew that *I* was the prospective patient. I kept protesting that I was fine, and that the staff was overreacting. Disregarding my objections, they placed me in the chair, and wheeled me away, leaving my mother to fill in the forms, and my friends to explain the situation.

Of course, it turned out that I was still in shock: my eyes seemed to be bulging out of their sockets like Ping-Pong balls. The hospital personnel insisted on checking me very carefully, to make sure that I didn't have any broken bones or other injuries, and administered a number of x-rays and tests. One doctor didn't like the look of my brain x-rays—concussions are tricky—and I was told I would probably have a two week stay for observation, so he could keep an eye on whatever it was that was bothering him. It all sounded like so much mumbo-jumbo to me. "Oh," I said intelligently. I definitely wasn't processing things clearly.

Finally, their pushing and prodding over, I was placed in a room with a carnival-like atmosphere, alongside three other patients. A veritable parade passed by to visit them, rattling on like castanets. There was a sense of barely restrained frenzy in the air. Words sprayed around the room like a loose high-pressure hose, while the volume constantly changed. But all meaning was lost, as everyone appeared to be speaking some unfamiliar language: Old Norse, Gaelic, or Susquehannock. Raucous laughter, snippets of gossip, and good-natured teasing came whirling across the beds like a confetti tornado.

What I needed was a place to lick my wounds in private; to be comforted in quiet, with a good slug of endorphins. I was tired. Bone tired. I found it hard to concentrate, much less rest, what with all the merry-making going on. Especially, when those around the furthest bed began drinking champagne, and clinking their glasses together. I don't know *what* they were celebrating, but they sure were happy. I knew on some level that I should be celebrating along with them; rejoicing that I was convalescing, instead of decomposing, but no, not yet. I wondered if I would ever get to be that joyful again. I doubted it. In the extreme.

For the first time, the police were supportive, the *Bellflower Police*, that is. A squad car was parked outside the room's window during the night. It made me feel safe and secure, at last. I fell asleep, almost overwhelmed with nostalgia for plain vanilla boredom.

The next morning, a different set of nurses came on duty, and it was clear that I had entered the Red Queen's world. The supervisor pitched a fit, when she saw that I was supposed to be placed in a private room; and then, to make matters worse, when she saw the bandages that my friend had lovingly administered two days prior, she went into orbit. It was "off with their heads" time, since no one had changed my bandages since I checked in. As a result, they had to *tear off* all the gauze that was now matted to my wounds. Talk about hurt! My physical healing had to start all over again. I was not a satisfied customer.

Later that afternoon, Bob came by, to check on my progress, on his way home from work. I could hear many raised voices in the hallway. Recognizing his voice, I crawled down to the bottom of my bed, and looked out the doorway, to see if it was really him. He walked by my room in a frantic state, and I called out to him. He doubled back, took one look at me, and yelled back over his shoulder, "Here she is! I *told* you she checked in yesterday!"

Bob walked right in, and asked how I was doing, so he could report my current situation to Terrell. As he stood at the bottom of the bed chatting with me, about a dozen doctors' and nurses' heads jammed in the doorway, like olives in a jar, watching us. Never realizing that they were concerned for my safety, and that they thought Bob was Chuck. I considered their behavior to be rude and intrusive. "Can't anyone get some privacy around here?" I complained. I couldn't fathom why everyone was being so ill-mannered, which just goes to show that my thinking still wasn't up to par.

A week or two later, my mother checked me out of the hospital, against the doctor's wishes. She had her station wagon packed with everything I would need to stay in Las Vegas for six weeks. That was the time required to establish residency in order to obtain a *quickie* divorce. She and my father had a tough time getting my things, because Chuck wouldn't let any of my family in the apartment. They finally appealed to the manager, who allowed them to take *only* my clothes, nothing else, because of the legality of the situation. They had to leave my car, and personal items, but I didn't care. I was outta there! With a whoop of uncensored gratitude, I was almost overwhelmed by a sense of freedom and escape.

And so we were off! I imagined Chuck in my rearview mirror, getting smaller, and smaller, and smaller, until he was permanently out of my life. The Hallelujah Chorus rang out in my head, as my heart did a little dance, which was extremely unnerving, but I was filled with euphoria: sheer, uncut, unabashed euphoria, thrilled with the notion that at last, at long last, I was definitely packing up, getting out, and moving on. And I would never have to see Chuck again. Famous last words.

A hospital is no place to be sick.
—Samuel Goldwyn

The good news is that we managed to save your life!
The bad news is that you are going to spend
the rest of your life paying for the good news.
—M. Lemac

Medicine is a science of uncertainty
and an art of probability.
—Unknown

A hospital bed is a parked taxi
with the meter running.
—Groucho Marx

NOW I ASK YOU...

To do what nobody else will do,
in a way that nobody else can do,
in spite of all we go through,
that is what it is to be a nurse.
—Rawsi Williams

NOW I ASK YOU . . .

Frightening experiences can have long-lasting consequences. Have you had any scary events happen to you? Were you panic-stricken, tense, and terrified? Did you ever tell anyone about them? Experts say that there are ways to cope: telling someone, making a plan, feeling your feelings, asking for help, accepting support, having a positive mindset, and not giving up, are ways that will help your situation.

PREDATOR ON THE PROWL

The passing desert appeared harsh and brutal. This was not the world of Georgia O'Keefe. Unusual plants insisted on living where it seemed impossible to survive. The color green was largely absent. The oppressive heat, odd creatures, desolate rocky plateaus, and endless sand, seemed an apt comment on my life. Everything seemed poised to prick, sting, bite, or kill me, while the ground continually shifted underneath my feet. *Just like home*, I observed silently.

In the midst of a triple-digit heat wave, Mother and I arrived in Las Vegas, steamed, baked, and deep-fried. After spending all day looking, we finally found a reasonably priced apartment for me to reside in, just off the strip, behind the Sands Hotel and Casino. Unfortunately, the electricity couldn't be turned on until Monday, so to escape the 110 degrees at midnight, we found ourselves in a local drugstore, enjoying the air conditioning. I was bedraggled, but hopeful. I had been sprung from the prison of marriage, and in my mind I did a whirling dervish routine. The relief was exhilarating.

The apartment manager had assured us that he would testify in court that I had established the requisite state residency for a quickie divorce. *Six weeks*, I thought happily, *six weeks!* I wanted this marriage over and done with, finished and forgotten, dead and buried. Kaput. So, this seemed to be the fastest and the safest way to go. After Mother was convinced that I was settled, she left.

I was detached from the world I understood. I no longer stood within a shared cultural belief system. I was emotionally cut off, estranged, and totally out of the loop. I felt as separate from the crowd as if we were a different species, while the words from a childhood song, "The Farmer in the Dell" repeated, "The cheese stands alone . . ." It played over and over in my head. Everything felt odd, strange, and rearranged. I was simply drowning in depression. In between bouts, however, I was able to glimpse a new beginning: a fresh start; another chance to get it right. It was a considerable comfort.

Then somehow, Chuck found out that I was staying in Las Vegas. Somehow, he was able to obtain my address. So he embarked on a journey to find me (In *my* car). In kamikaze mode, he apparently was driving too fast, crossed over the centerline, and collided with a cement truck in the middle of a bridge. He ended up in the hospital. Somehow, his family was able to obtain my phone number, and the calls started coming in, one after another. I became jumpier than a basket of grasshoppers, as they pleaded for me to return home. They cited an ungodly number of broken bones, and multiple injuries, itemizing them in gross detail, and emphasizing that Chuck was soon to die.

Well, boo and hoo. I just couldn't seem to work up a decent regret, and lacked the depth of character to offer much sympathy. Truth be told, I just couldn't even scrape up the grace to feel *concerned* about it. Needless to say, I bypassed the Hallmark cards. I'd been around his dysfunctional family far too long, and didn't believe a word they said. They wanted me to visit Chuck in the hospital, because it was his one last wish. Failing that, they wanted me at the funeral. As trustworthy as the Borgias, I had the sneaking suspicion that they just wanted me to break my Nevada residency, so I remained in exile. (*I'll get you, my pretty, and your little dog, too!*) Finally, the calls tapered off.

It later turned out that Chuck had apparently come through the accident with barely a scratch. Why was I not surprised? *My* car, however, was a total and complete loss, with photos to prove it.

After copious amounts of sun, sand, and Coppertone, I returned to California with divorce papers clenched tightly in hand, resisting the urge to turn a self-congratulatory somersault. But, in the mid-sixties, the times were still restrictive. Marriage was considered to be a *forever* experience (hum along with Diana Ross and Lionel Richie, singing "Endless Love"). There was a large-scale cultural prejudice against divorce. The word itself was considered "dirty," and was only spoken in hushed whispers. In the eyes of polite society, a divorcee was a hussy, a fallen or scarlet woman, used or damaged goods, tainted, and so forth. I was not prepared for the ostracism I had to endure—like a leper or pariah—feeling that I was walking around with a Hester Prynne-like tattoo emblazoned on my forehead. Heads turned and whispers followed wherever I went. It was as if people mentally took a step backward, to remove themselves from such wickedness. You'd have thought that I had a contagious condition, or I'd been fraternizing with the enemy. It was a flaming wonder that they hadn't run we out of town, or tried to stone me. ("Before You Accuse Me" by Eric Clapton, could have become my personal theme song.)

What I couldn't fathom was the clear, if subtle, change in those I knew *well*, as I walked a daily gauntlet of disapproval. My friends and colleagues' tones turned businesslike, at arm's length, without personal warmth, in a kind of guilt by association attitude. The women seemed to edge away, distancing themselves more each day, as I was clearly a daily reminder of their own vulnerability, and what *could* happen to them. Most appeared afraid to have me around their boyfriends or husbands. They were fearful, I suppose, that I was suddenly a rival, and that I might leap upon their guys, tempting them down the garden path, or luring them onto the rocks, in the manner of Sirens from days of ole. What rubbish! I needed another man like I needed a brain tumor. An emotional porcupine, I all but *bristled* with Do Not Disturb, No Trespassing, Stay Away spines. Why couldn't they see that? So much for sisterhood.

I eventually began to make my recovery. Yahoo! With time and effort, my mind stopped sizzling in its habitual static. The knockdown doll was bouncing back.

When the new school year began, I started teaching in a new school, and my life finally returned to something approaching normal. The jubilant strains of

"Zip-a-dee-do-dah" happily encircled my mind and heart each day, as I looked forward to a new life without Chuck.

But the fun had just begun. Unfortunately, Chuck didn't take rejection well. He wouldn't let go, and refused to be ignored. (Sing along with Sting's lyrics, "Every breath you take, Every move you make, I'll be watching you.") Chuck found my new school, and would show up just before the class was over for the day, and wait in his car. Intermittently, other teachers would walk me outside as a group, casting dirty looks at Chuck, waiting until I got into my (new) car, before disbanding. A mad chase would then ensue. Whenever he'd catch me at a signal light, he'd shout out, "*I love you!* Don't worry! You have nothing to be concerned about! I would *never* hurt you!" and similar words, none of which inspired confidence in what he was saying.

Thereafter, whenever Chuck would follow me, I'd head for the local Sheriff's Department, to wait in their parking lot, until he would get tired and go on home. (Cue Whitey Huston singing: "AND I-I-I-I-I-I WILL ALWAYS LOVE YOU-OU-OU-OU-OU-OU-OU"). Long after he departed, I would leave in the opposite direction, and take a circuitous route going back to my new apartment. It was flat-out scary.

Life is full of scary things.
The trick is not to let your fears
get in the way of living.
Whatever else you do,
don't settle for a life half-lived.
—C.S. Harris

Making a big life change is pretty scary.
But, know what's scarier?
Regret.
—Zig Ziglar

Focus on where you want to go,
not on what your fear.
—Tony Robbins

Life shrinks or expands
in proportion to one's courage.
—Anais Nin

Fear is only as deep and the mind allows.
—Japanese Proverb

F-E-A-R has two meanings:
Forget everything and run, or
Face everything and rise.
The choice is yours.
—Zig Ziglar

Courage is being scared to death . . .
and saddling up anyway.
—John Wayne

NOW I ASK YOU . . .

Have you ever asked for help, and none was given? How did that make you feel? What did you do about it? Did you know that 13.5 million people are stalked every year in the United States (SPARC)?

A MATTER OF SOME URGENCY

My concern was approaching critical mass, while both the Long Beach Police Department and the Los Angeles County Sheriff's Department continued to maintain that they couldn't do anything until Chuck actually, physically, did something to me. In those days (the sixties, as well as the seventies, eighties, and early nineties), according to the law, constantly following me, harassing me, phoning me, threatening me, looking through my windows at night, sending me long letters, and leaving unwanted gifts on my front porch (Charlie perfume), did not count as criminal behavior. I was left with the burden of unexpressed rage at all those who failed to help me, and remained indifferent to my plight.

I would hear remarks like: "A pretty girl like you? Who wouldn't want to follow you around?" or "With your good looks, what do you expect?" or *"What did you do to upset him?"* or the ever popular, "You should feel flattered!" Similar sentiments were delivered with mental pats on the head. There, there. They just couldn't see why I was so uncomfortable, or what the fuss was all about. (Over three decades later, my primary physician said to me, "Don't you wish your husband paid as much attention to you as your stalker?" Proving once again, no matter how highly educated, there are people who *still* don't get it.) Talk about a blind spot.

This had been going on for years. Terrified, and out of my depth, I didn't know what to do. The police again refused to get involved over a "family matter," even though we were no longer a family, and his stalking behavior started *after* the divorce. I couldn't convince anyone of the seriousness of the problem. No one wanted to see my divorce papers or my restraining order. (Cue: "Bad Moon Rising," by Creedence Clearwater Revival.)

Then he actually, physically *did* do something! Growing weary of our game of hide and seek, Chuck decided to escalate matters. After wildly chasing my car down the street one late evening, he plowed his car into mine. I felt like I had been rammed by a runaway freight train, as he shoved my car across two lanes of oncoming traffic, over the curb and into a parking lot, slamming it into a short cinderblock parking block. (There were no cell phones in those days!) He jumped out of his car, ran around it, ripped open my door, and grabbed me (my fingers still clutched in a death grip on the steering wheel). He dragged me out by my hair, tearing hunks out of my scalp in the process. Dazed, I was kicking, screaming, and fighting, although somewhat incapacitated by the blood streaming into my eyes. I probably did little more than thrash and flail both arms around, due to dizziness from the knock on my forehead. As my strength waned, he threw me into his front seat (think: Grade B movie), tore around to the driver's side, leaped in, and stomped on the gas pedal. The car backed out, and lurched onto the main street, fish-tailing and burning rubber, as we shot off like a rocket. It all happened so fast, it was hard to believe it had actually taken place.

Craning my head over my shoulder, I could see my car windows and driver's door were left wide open, and the radio was on. My purse was lying open inside the car, and a few miscellaneous items had spilled out and were rolling on the asphalt. Chuck had abducted me right off a major street, and nobody could do anything about it.

As we caromed down the street, a la Mario Andretti, Chuck leaned over, and retrieved two bottles of liquor from the floorboard in front of me. He opened both, placing a bottle of whiskey between his inner thighs, and gripping a bottle of vodka in his right hand. He commenced to chug-a-lugging liquid courage, as he drove. Having never seen him take even a sip of alcohol before, I was astounded at the number of bottles of all shapes, kinds, and brands, that were rolling around under my feet.

My head was thundering as little twinkle lights spread across my field of vision. Since I was unaware that head wounds bled copiously, often looking far worse than they really are, I was more than a bit concerned about the status of my physicality.

With pinwheel-like eyes, and a demented "Here's Johnny!" look about him, Chuck informed me that he knew I *still* loved him, and wanted to continue our relationship. He knew that I *really* didn't want the divorce, and that I had been *forced* into getting one by my family. He maintained that they had *poisoned* my mind against him, and that he was proving the depth of his love for me, by *rescuing* me from the clutches of my family. Un-huh.

He appeared to truly believe his projection, and trust me, I didn't contradict him, knowing that arguing was not in my best interest. I wanted both his hands on the steering wheel, and his eyes on the road. Chuck then explained that we were heading for Mexico, where we could just be by ourselves—without any interference from others—and we would live happily ever after. He continued to rattle on about what we were going to do after crossing the border, how we were going to live, and so forth. He said he couldn't wait until I cooked and cleaned for him, without someone else to bother us. (Me? *Surely you jest*. My kitchen is a minimalist masterpiece, as I am rarely in it. I only have a kitchen because it came with the house. I do not cook or bake. And I have housekeepers. This guy didn't know me from Adam's ox.) His dream, my nightmare.

While visions of domestic bliss danced in his head, I was in emergency mode, knowing that if we ever crossed the border, I'd never live to tell about it. For the first time in my life, I appreciated the infinite series of traffic signal red lights, seeing them as providing more opportunity for escape. My heart seemed to be trying to thump *out* of my chest, as I was red-lining in the adrenaline department.

Finally, after traveling a good length of time, I spied a black-and-white, idling off the highway, hidden back amongst some enormous bushes. I figured that this might be my one and only chance, and that I had to get out of the car. *It's now or never*, I thought. But remembering the *last* time I tried leaping from a moving car, I wasn't keen on doing it again. Luckily, a set of railroad tracks crossed Pacific Coast Highway and like a good driver, Chuck actually stopped. I was out that door in a second!

Instantly, I switched into GO mode, kicking into a turbo charge, shouting and gesturing for the police, when with unbelievable timing, the police unit shot across the road, lights swirling, siren shrieking, and headed back in the opposite direction. They didn't even *see* me, and I knew my chances of being saved ranked right around zero.

Chuck had, by now, also jumped out of the car, and was chasing me, leaving both doors wide open, with the engine running, sitting in the middle of Pacific Coast Highway. He was fast gaining on me with his long legs, and lunged forward, only to grab the heels of my shoes. I stumbled, but managed not to fall completely, and regaining my balance, I shot on down the road, with adrenaline pumping into my system at warp speed. He hit the ground heavily, and slid. I could hear him howling for me: "Come back! Come back! I love you! COME BACK!" A high-pitched keening followed, providing an eerie sound track for the scene.

A pick-up truck traveling in my direction, sped across the opposing lanes of traffic. Angry horns blared on all sides, as the driver pulled in front of me, shouting, "Get in! Get in!" I ran around, ripped open his passenger door, and found three small children frozen on the seat, their eyes as big as beach balls. My no-nonsense teacher voice instantly took over, as I ordered, "Everybody up!" They stood up, I slid in, they sat down, and we were off.

"I saw you trying to get to the police car!" the driver yelled. "Don't worry! We'll catch up to it!" He blasted back across the opposing traffic, ignoring the cursing, gesturing drivers, as we sped on up the road, in an apparent effort to break the sound barrier. We finally caught the squad car, as it no longer had its siren on—the emergency being over—and explained matters to the officers. They said they would gladly help me, so I thanked the good Samaritan, said goodbye to his children, and they left.

The police spent some time, looking for Chuck, while I, in a state of high anxiety, cowered, hiding below the window level. Both he and his car were gone. Then the officers drove me back to their city line. The Seal Beach Police officers were so nice and courteous. They were genuinely caring and helpful, while I displayed the upset, devastated, confused demeanor of a person in crisis.

Unfortunately, when they called the Long Beach Police, all public service came to a screeching halt. Now this was the city in which I was raised, and continued to live, and taught, and paid taxes, and the response of the police that had sworn "to protect and to serve" was: "*We aren't a taxi service!*" They refused to help.

The Seal Beach officers were aghast. I was obviously shaken, wigged out, and disheveled, resembling a bad Picasso imitation: my complexion was the shade of Cream of Wheat, my make-up was smeared with streaked mascara and blood, my hair was ripped out in places, looking as though I had jammed a wet finger into a light socket, my torn blouse was missing several buttons, my hose were in shreds, and my high heels were mangled. Clearly, I'd been through an ordeal, and couldn't walk miles home, in total darkness (as there were no city lights or buildings in that section, then). In addition, I had no money to even call for a cab.

The Seal Beach officers were clearly shocked by this turn of events.

They called the LBPD a couple more times, to no avail. They profusely apologized to me, explaining that they weren't allowed to drive into another city's jurisdiction, so they did the next best thing, and called a cab for me. Then they waited with me until it came, just in case Chuck came back on the scene. I had the taxi take me to my friend's house, and Terrell and Bob put their change together, and paid for the taxi, and I slept there overnight, in their guestroom.

After everyone calmed down, we all went to bed. In the dead of night, their cat leaped upon the bed, landing on my stomach. I thought Chuck had found me, and I screamed bloody murder, fighting for my life. And woke up their whole family, Terrrell and Bob, their three daughters, and the cat. Again. Boy was my face red.

It took two days for me to get up the nerve to go back and retrieve my car. I was reluctant to return to my vehicle, unless accompanied by a Sherman tank or Special Forces of some kind, such as a heavily armed platoon of Green Berets or Navy Seals. My parents drove me to my car, with obvious apprehension, since there was no hope of police involvement anywhere on the horizon. I found my car basically unchanged, although the radio was turned off, and the door was shut. I don't recall if my purse or wallet was still there. On the driver's seat, however, was the white shirt that Chuck had been wearing during my abduction. It was ripped and filthy, embedded with dirt, oil, and grime (when he had skidded across the pavement on his chest). Safety pinned to the front of his shirt, was a torn note that said: **See what you made me do!** He obviously was still NOT taking credit for any negative thing he did (deliberately causing a car accident, and kidnapping me, not to mention drinking and unsafe driving). Round and round it goes, where it stops, nobody knows.

A restraining order is a document
about as useful as a parasol
in a hurricane.
—Stephen King

Memorize the Big Three:
(1) You are not to blame,
(2) You deserve support,
(3) You are not alone.
—Unknown

Life is full of second chances.
When they come, be more
intentional, courageous, and
appreciative.
—Brendon Burchard

Everyone needs a second chance.
Some of us need a third or a fourth chance.
—Catherine Depasquale

NOW I ASK YOU . . .

Have you ever dealt with an insurance company? Did something happen to your vehicle or house? Was hospitalization involved? Were you paid what you thought was a reasonable settlement? Or not? Do you get upset just thinking about it?

INSURANCE

Chuck was very open about trying to get my insurance death benefits. Again, I knew I'd get no help from the police, because, after all, *planning* a murder didn't count. Truly, I understood that intentions don't always translate into action, but it seems to me that a *pattern* of behavior was apparent. He had a *history*. The intensity of his thoughts and schemes should say something. What was I supposed to do, just stand around, twiddling my thumbs, waiting for the Grim Reaper to arrive? I always seemed to be circling the drain, racing toward oblivion, with one foot planted in Forest Lawn. Continually anticipating my final exit was not conducive to good mental health. And, trust me, the wedding vow phrase, "til death do us part," came to have an altogether new meaning for me.

The insurance situation left such a lasting imprint that I have purposely refused to carry life insurance on myself since that unhappy experience well over 50 years ago. Years afterward, when I was a corporate director for an international business, the president of the company suggested an increase in the board members' individual insurance coverage from one million to two million dollars, whereupon I considered resigning, rather than deal with the temptation issue in a logical manner.

There was a very cautious man.
Who never laughed or played,
Her never risked, he never tried,
He never sang or prayed.
And then he one day
passed away,
His insurance was denied,
For since he never really lived,
They claimed he never died.
—Unknown

NOW I ASK YOU . . .

When you see a neighbor struggling down the street, during inclement weather, do you stop to pick him/her up? Wind, rain, sleet, snow, or mud, do you ask if anyone you know needs a ride?

RAIN, RAIN, GO AWAY

Whatever the weather, there is always something new to learn. When I was a brand new teacher, it had rained for two solid weeks, with no end in sight. The streets were not only flooded, but the water lapped over the front door steps. It was dark, and the storm was fierce, when I saw three of my third grade boys slogging in water up to their knees, struggling in the torrent to get to school. I stopped my car, and they hopped inside, as the water crested the running board. Now the inside of my car was wet, too, as they thanked me profusely for the ride. I slowly maneuvered down the street—that was akin to a flowing river—and we finally got to school in one piece. After the fact, I was told, in no uncertain terms by the principal, to never, ever, do that again, due to insurance concerns. Really? *Who knew?* I just thought I was helping.

Rainbows apologize for angry skies.
—Sylvia Voirol

A rainy day is a special gift to readers.
—Amy Miles

NOW I ASK YOU...

When life throws you a rainy day,
play in the puddles.
—Winnie the Pooh

The way I see it, if you want the rainbow,
you gotta put up with the rain.
—Dolly Parton

Life's not about waiting for the storm to pass . . .
It's about learning to dance in the rain.
—Vivian Greene

NOW I ASK YOU . . .

Have you ever had an unusual, unplanned, and unexpected experience, that took you by surprise? Did the odds seem incalculable? Unlike coincidences, synchronicities are *meaningful* events, that have an *emotional* impact, involving incredible odds, that stagger the imagination. Individuals who have been involved in such a unique event, have called them gifts from the Universe, godwinks, small miracles, post-it notes from above, nudges from heaven, and such.

WHAT ARE THE ODDS?

Having been an educator for over 50 years, it has been my observation that administrators sometimes make decisions, not realizing the havoc that will ensue down the line. One such decision happened in the old Norwalk/La Mirada School District, in which my mother was a teacher. One summer, a boss had made the decision that all the newly built schools should use the old furniture, and the older schools would use the new furniture. It sounded fair to him (whereas, obviously, neither the aesthetics of the situation, nor fit, nor match, were of concern to him). Unfortunately, no one bothered to tell the teachers of this turn of events.

At the time, I was attending CSULB for a teaching degree, and was working as a recreation leader during summer vacation, at a newly built school in the city of La Mirada. One day, I just happened to walk off the playground, on my way to the office, and took a different sidewalk that I hadn't ever used before. Then I passed two burly workmen, who were moving a huge, long, extremely heavy, chest of drawers. As the guys struggled on, one started to lose his grip, and as the chest tipped forward, the top drawer slid open, spilling charts, posters, artwork, and numerous papers at my feet. The chest was quickly set down, as I ran over to help pick up the mess, as papers were flying in the wind. As I retrieved each item, I became confused and concerned, recognizing that the items belonged to my mother, who taught second grade at another school, in the city of Norwalk. I even came across a couple of charts, and art project examples that I had made!

I asked the movers what they were doing with the chest, and they explained the recent directive from on high. I ran to the office, and called my mother in Long Beach, to explain the situation. She, in turn, called all of her colleagues (who lived in various cities), who then descended upon the new school en masse, to retrieve all of their teaching possessions. What a disaster!

If I hadn't been walking past the workmen at that particular moment, none of the teachers would have had any idea in September, as to where all their personal school charts, posters, lesson plans, books, maps, and realia had gone. Timing is everything!

After the whole experience was over, I pondered the precise, split second timing that involved three cities. The mathematical odds of this happening are astounding. This even seemed to defy explanation. A minute either way, or taking the usual sidewalk, would have completely changed the outcome. The timing involved is staggering, and simply takes my breath away.

The fact that just the right people
appeared at just the right time
in just the right place
is a dazzling synchronicity.
—Dr. David Richo

You have to realize
in this life and your life
that timing is everything.
—Paul Orndorff

Most of what makes a book 'good'
is that we are reading it
at the right moment for us.
—Alain de Botton

Never let the odds keep you from doing
what you know in your heart you were meant to do.
—H. Jackson Brown. Jr.

Never tell me the odds.
—Han Solo in *Star Wars*

NOW I ASK YOU . . .

Have you ever had a persistent, disturbing, preoccupation with someone or something? Did your obsession keep you thinking about it, finding it difficult to think about anything else? During the early seventies, I was obsessively into art. I spent my free time in museums, art galleries, art shows, and art festivals. My walls were covered with original paintings and reproductions. I even became a docent at the CSULB Art Museum. I mostly lamented the fact that I couldn't afford the pieces that really spoke to me.

ARTWORK

One year, I was looking for a second job. So I showed up for a modeling interview, but realized that the opportunity would conflict with my teaching schedule. The modeling agency interviews were being conducted in a large back room staging area, which could only be reached through a large front room. It had been rented for a short period of time, as an art showroom, for a rising, talented artist: Kirwan.

I was stunned upon realizing that I had stumbled into something totally unexpected: a private art party. Oh, boy. This was my kind of place! The room was packed with people roaming around, drinking champagne, while intensely discussing the various works on display. I made the tour, with the extremely intricate paintings on display. Wow!

I could hardly contain my enthusiasm when I came upon a huge lithograph, titled *Mr. Dark*, which is based on the character in Ray Bradbury's book, *Something Wicked This Way Comes*. I immediately bought a copy (#38/100, 1973) from Kirwan, himself. I later had it framed, which was extremely difficult and costly to do, because of its size (four foot by seven foot), as well as the thin paper involved. This particular drawing took Kirwan three months to complete, as the full-sized figure of a man has 317 separate images tattooed on his body, as seen through his suit. (Bradbury's head is shown on the lower left leg, and Kirwan's head is shown on the lower right leg. Very unusual. It has been an outstanding conversation piece, all these years hence.

Six or so months thereafter, I drove from Long Beach into Los Angeles, where a yearly art fair was taking place. Several streets were closed to traffic, in that area, to accommodate the crowds. Artists set up shop on sidewalks, grassy areas, and in the middle of the streets, showing their various wares and talents. It was quite a colorful event, with balloons and bubbles galore, and a happy, energetic crowd.

As I wandered about, I came to a sudden halt in front of a huge pile of small pictures, one showing two feet. It looked like one of Kirwan's I had seen. I then asked about the picture, since no artist's name was signed. None of the other pictures in the pile were autographed either. I quizzed the elderly couple as to the name of the artist involved, and was not satisfied with their answer. I left with a bad taste in my mouth.

On the long drive home, I agitated about it, and decided to call Kirwan, in Culver City, although I figured it was a lost cause. This meant that I was going to have to take some time to find his phone number (if I still even had it).

In addition, if we did connect, I might have to suffer the indignity of feeling foolish for bothering him, if nothing was wrong. But I overrode my misgivings, and persevered.

Luckily, I found the number, and luckily Kirwan answered. I nervously introduced myself, starting with, "You won't remember me, but I was at your show in Long Beach, over half a year ago, and . . ."

"Oh, I remember you!" he interrupted, and proceeded to describe the outfit that I had been wearing that day, which shocked me silly. Then I haltingly spilled out my story. He freaked at that, and in a mad rush, told me that, several months prior, his art studio had been broken into, and sixty thousand dollars worth of his paintings had been stolen. He said he was going to call the police right that minute, and he'd call me back at a later date, when he had news.

A couple of weeks later, Kirwan did call me back, to tell me that the elderly couple had been so nervous about my questioning, that they quickly packed up their belongings and left the fair, soon after I departed. But the organizers of the event had their names, and information, so the police were able to retrieve most of his stolen artwork. He was so grateful, he promised me a painting as a reward.

So again, I had arrived in the right place, at the right time, with the right solution. And again, three cities were involved. *How weird is that?*

I never paint dreams or nightmares,
I paint my own reality.
—Frida Kahlo

NOW I ASK YOU . . .

Do you think you have a good vocabulary? In either a school, or a work setting, or even in a normal conversation, have you ever heard any words that you never heard before? Or words that you have never even seen before? Or words that you've heard, but didn't understand? Have you found any words in books or articles that you were unfamiliar with? What did you do? How did you react? Did you immediately go to your dictionary or computer? Or did you think about it for a while, and then decide to check it out later? Did you follow up in your search, or did you forget about it all together? How did that make you feel?

RUDE AND MOCKING REMARKS

As a junior in college, I was not paying an ounce of attention in the philosophy class that day. It was hot, and I was not focusing on the dull and boring delivery on the subject at hand. I was simply zoning out—in a dreamlike state—when I heard the instructor say, ". . . and of course, there is *reincarnation*," whereupon the entire class began to jeer and derisively laugh. That sure caught my attention. *What was that word again? Why did everyone else know about it, and I hadn't a clue? Why was the whole class being so negative? What was so unusually odd about it, that would cause such an instant uproar?* So, being curious, I later moved my inquiring mind to the library, where I began researching the subject. In the days before computers and the Internet, you couldn't just Google it. It was difficult to find any such information in libraries or independent bookstores, but I persevered. As the result of such questioning about one unknown word, my study of reincarnation has taken over 63 years to date, and I now own several hundred books on the subject. I find the concept to be incredibly fascinating!

As far back as I can remember, I have consciously referred to experiences of a previous state of existence.
—Henry David Thoreau

Genius is experience. Some seem to think that it is a gift or a talent, but it is the fruit of long experience in many lives.
—Henry Ford

NOW I ASK YOU . . .

Do you have a distinguishing quality or characteristic that you might want to drop kick? I certainly do. I recognize that I am a *prude*, and I do try to combat that trait whenever possible. However, I continue to use alternative swear words: Dagnabbit! Holy Cow! Rats, Rats, Double Rats! and Fudgecicles! to express my anger or strong emotion. (After all, I was a teacher and professor for 50 years, so I had to watch my language). But after all these decades, I still have trouble talking about specific body parts, and maintain that there are certain things that should remain unsaid, especially while one is eating. For example, when we were first married, my husband, Wayne (who worked in a hospital) wanted to discuss his daily experiences at the dinner table. Whereupon, midstream, I would quickly stand up, and run to the bathroom, fighting a gag reflex. So he learned to save his stories until later in the evening, and omit the gore.

GENERATION GAP

One night, my husband Wayne, and I, went to dinner at a local restaurant. As the 16-year-old hostess was walking us to our table, she loudly exclaimed, "You guys smell just like baby butts!"

Say what? "I beg your pardon?" I strangled in reply, as diners turned to gawk.

"You guys smell just like baby butts!" she loudly reiterated, as my husband and I exchanged shocked looks and raised eyebrows,

Hmmmm. "You mean like talcum . . .?" I tentatively asked, treading lightly, although fearing the worst.

She quickly interjected, "No, no! It's not a *bad* thing. You know, like after a baby's bath, you sprinkle powder."

Ahhh, it finally became clear: Baby powder she understood, talcum powder she didn't. It all boiled down to a simple generation gap. Just another linguistic confusion.

Old Generation are using
walking sticks,
New Generation are using
Selfie sticks.
—Unknown

NOW I ASK YOU . . .

Have you had any interest in parapsychology? Are you curious about any of those subjects? Have you actually dabbled in some (hypnosis, ESP, telepathy, precognition, clairvoyance, psychokinesis, near death experiences, spiritualism, mysticism, alternative medicine, crystals, and such)? Do you find any, or all, of the unconventional, supernatural, woo-woo subjects fascinating, captivating, and compelling? Or do they seem to be unscientific, ridiculous, and nonsensical?

EYE OPENER

During the late sixties and early seventies, I was totally enmeshed in all the "new" metaphysical subjects, that are so prevalent in the general public today. Very few books were written about such topics back then, and those that were, were hard to find, so I had a really difficult time doing personal research. But I was undeterred. I found such psychic phenomenon subjects to be so exciting that I gave speeches about them to various groups, to share my newfound knowledge. (I was a teacher, after all.)

As such, I was asked by the head of one group, if I would give a talk at the next month's meeting. I was slated to be the first speaker, and then, after the break, a special guest professor from New York City was going to give the major presentation. (New York was about as far as you could get from California!). Of course, I was thrilled to be the warm-up speaker! I couldn't wait to hear the pearls of wisdom from a real professor from afar!

When I asked about the topic, I was told that I could speak on any subject.

"Any subject?" I reiterated. "But . . ."

"ANY SUBJECT!" she forcefully interrupted. (I ignored her tone of voice, and thought, *So, Wow! Okay then, What to choose, what to choose?*).

Every subject was so riveting to me, it would be a tough choice. At length, after a couple of days of indecision, I finally chose to present on a brand new word that I had just become acquainted with: Synchronicity.

When the date rolled around, I was ready: I had my stories, facts, and charts prepared. The audience was thoroughly engaged in my presentation. The material was all so new to them, that the resulting interactive question and answer period went way beyond our allotted time limit. Then we broke for our shared potluck meal, with many happily discussing the topic, as we ate. When everyone was assembled again for the main event, the guest speaker was introduced, with much fanfare and applause. He stood up, and powerfully barked, "My subject was to be Synchronicity, and SHE (jabbing his finger at me), said it much better than I ever could!" And he promptly sat down. He was NOT a happy camper. Confused faces were looking around, as lots of whispering was going on, as one lady loudly demanded, "Is this a *joke*?" But I was just as shocked as everyone else. Eventually, the synchronicity of the situation was not lost on the audience, as everyone erupted into laughter, and excited chattering. *What fun!*

AFTERWORD: Years later, I, too, became a professor, and was invited to speak to various clubs and organizations, conferences, conventions, and for various school districts in different states. And, I was featured on two TV stations in New York City. This eye opening experience clearly shows what Dr. David Richo says: "Synchronicity happens so that we can advance toward our destiny."

I will not commit
the fashionable stupidity
of regarding everything
I cannot explain as a fraud.
—Dr. Carl G. Jung

It's time we speak about
our natural psi abilities
as easily as we discuss the weather.
—Elly Molina

The day science begins to study
non-physical phenomena,
it will make more progress in one decade
than in all the previous centuries of existence.
—Nikola Tesla

NOW I ASK YOU . . .

Have you ever received a sign that you think is given directly to you? True, you see signs each and every day, in a million different ways, but I'm talking about a sign in which it has given you some kind of understanding, insight, or direction.

BLIMP

I was always beseeching the Universe for a sign, to tell me if readers were going to like my latest book. "Give me a signal! Give me a sign!" I would rail.

So around 9:30 one morning, I turned onto Woodruff, a large four-lane street, with middle turn lanes, and bicycle lanes, to find not one vehicle on the road, coming or going. This was highly unusual. And spooky, as the fog was particularly dense, and much lower than usually experienced. Portions of the fog were swirling about, in such a way that I never had witnessed beforehand. And I was mesmerized by the soundless atmosphere, as it appeared that I was the only person left in the whole wide world. Very weird.

So as I was staring at the low-hanging fog, I was shocked to see the nose of a blimp piercing through the fog bank. I couldn't believe my eyes, as it slowly materialized, and seemed to be heading down at an angle, straight towards me! I figured that the pilot hadn't realized the fog was so low, and was looking for some landmarks. As I white-knuckled the steering wheel, scenes of police and hospitals instantly filled my mind, even as I recognized that neither the pilot nor I would survive the crash.

Seemingly, at the last minute, the blimp jerked up, and slowly moved across the street in front of me, barely skimming across the rooftops, as it headed for the nearby Long Beach airport. In large letters, painted on the side of the blimp, it said: GOOD YEAR. I happily decided that this was a big thumbs-up from the Universe, which meant that my books were going to do well that year, and I could live to write another day.

Sometimes the sign will be subtle. Sometimes signs will jump out at you with its message, like a knock on the noggin. In my twenties and thirties, when I would walk down the aisles of various bookstores, I might find a book on the floor, or a misplaced book, or a book would suddenly fall off a shelf, landing at my feet. When I would pick it up, my whole body would tingle and ripple. Knowing that this was a sign from the Universe—that the book had not come into my awareness by accident—I would immediately buy it, as I knew it had a special message for me.

Sometimes signs will simply take you by surprise. One day, I had lunch with a friend at a Mexican restaurant. I knew better, when I ate a bunch of salsa, because it doesn't always agree with me. But it sure was good, so I overate it anyway. Alas, much later, on the way home, my stomach started gurgling and growling and churning. Big Time. And I was suddenly in a race to get home to my bathroom in time. I lost the race. Yikes! And adding insult to injury, the license plate on the car in front of me read: U IDIOT! *Can you believe?* I definitely won't pull that stunt ever again. Oh, woe is me. Lesson learned.

I have a large wooden sign in my library that says: If

you're waiting for a sign THIS IS IT! It always makes me laugh.

The Universe doesn't answer questions.
It simply gives you signs.
—Lukas Boyer

You won't miss a sign from the Universe.
It will keep getting louder and louder
until you get it.
—Unknown

You can ask the Universe for all
the signs you want, but ultimately,
we see what we want to see
when we're ready to see it.
—Craig Thomas & Carter Bays

If something happens that strikes you
as totally odds-defying,
chances are the Other Side
has just worked its magic.
—Laura Lynne Jackson

NOW I ASK YOU . . .

Have you ever been involved in casual or unconstrained conversations about other people? Have you ever talked about the personal or private affairs of others? Dishing the dirt? Do you know that negative gossip is twice as common as positive gossip? My husband, Wayne, would stop gossiping people in midsentence (whereas I always wanted to know what gossip they had to share). He was the better person. I never considered that I was gossiping (criticizing, complaining, or faultfinding), when talking about experiences in which *I* was involved. But I learned my lesson:

SHHHH!

I was scheduled to give a presentation to a school district in Colorado. I flew into the Salt Lake City International Airport, in Utah, through a heavy, driving rainstorm. I was met by two principals, who would drive me to their destination. As we were total strangers, killing several hours, we talked to while away the time. Late in the conversations, grasping for subject matter, one man said: "Oh, I hear that you received your doctorate at BYU." When I answered in the affirmative, he said that he also graduated from BYU, and started quizzing me as to who I knew at the university, name by name. "No, no, and no," I responded (after all, it had been several years since I had been on campus.) Then he started asking me about specific professors. Only a few names were familiar to me. Then, seemingly as an afterthought, he asked about one in particular, which I knew well, as he was a professor of a required class for my doctoral group.

Even though we students were all longtime educators or administrators, we all raced to the back row in his classroom. The room was small, and closed in, with no air conditioning, and our instructor could sweat, BIG TIME! In addition, he had terrible body odor. Every time he'd raise his arms, the front row would be practically wiped out.

Deodorant versus antiperspirant became *the* topic of discussion at night, regardless of what we should be studying. What we learned from that class had little to do with the subject at hand: deodorant keeps you from smelling bad when you perspire, whereas antiperspirant attempts to keep you from perspiring at all. We covered the pros and cons, facts and myths, commercial versus natural deodorant, dry-cleaning problems, and whatnot. "At least the class wasn't a total loss!" I said with a flourish. An uncomfortable silence inserted itself, before he announced, "He's my brother-in-law."

Good grief! So there I was, in a car with two total strangers, in a different state, and out of millions of people in California, Colorado, and Utah, I had to tell my tale to him. *What are the odds?* Talk about a bell that you can't unring! Boy was my face red. Right then and there, I determined to never say anything about another that I wouldn't say to his or her face! Later, after I twisted in the wind for a while, he admitted that his whole family felt the same way about the professor. But the damage was done.

Words spoken
can never be recalled.
—Wentworth Dillon

If you must slander someone,
don't speak it—but write it—
Write it in the sand
near the water's edge.
—Napoleon Hill

Gossip dies when it hits
a wise person's ears.
—Unknown

Be careful with your words.
Once they are said,
they can only be forgiven,
not forgotten.
—Unknown

If you didn't HEAR it with your own ears,
or SEE it with your own eyes . . .
don't INVENT it with your small mind,
and SHARE it with your big mouth.
—Unknown

NOW I ASK YOU . . .

Are there some things, some people, or some places you need to release? It is said that breakups are one of the hardest experiences you go through in life, even when things didn't go well beforehand. After a breakup of some sort (a long friendship, boyfriend/girlfriend, partners, or a divorce), have you ever felt that your latest experience had ruined you forever? In so far as future love relationships are concerned, not to mention sexual situations? Did you think that any romance in your life was as dead as a doornail, the passenger pigeon, or the dodo bird? Do you desperately want to feel normal again? Do you wish to feel up-close-and-personal again, but thought that would never ever happen? "Get over it, and move the fuck on," a friend advised.

MOVING ON

After obtaining my divorce from Chuck, I moved into a brand new apartment building that was beautifully furnished. Many individuals had filled the units in record time, so I felt better: safety in numbers, as well as comfort. The ping pong table was situated right outside my door, so I met a lot of young adults that were moving in. Each apartment had a glass front wall, with an overly-sized glass door within it, so I could see everyone who played. One fine looking man, Jerry, and his brother, often played there, so I saw them as they came and went. We nodded in acknowledgement of each other's existence, but we didn't exchange any chitchat. Later, we had seen each other at the weekend roaming parties in various apartments, as he would flash me a gigawatt smile, as he passed by. He looked at me like I was a seven-layer cake. (*Lordy, Lordy, Lordy!*).

For the record: I am not a fairytale princess who needs saving. I'm not into drama. I am not high-maintenance. Nor was I looking for a Good Time Charley. I was definitely not interested in taking a walk on the Wild Side. But there it was again, as unwanted electricity was charging through my nether regions. My entire body was sending me yes, yes, yes signals, while by brain was saying no, no, no. Whew!

At one party, Jerry latched onto me, taking me around and introducing me to all of his friends. He was sooooo good looking—one supercharged mass of hunky masculinity—but, even so, I called it an early evening, as I wasn't YET used to all that fun and frolic. I always excused myself early. I couldn't believe that I might even be slightly interested . . .

The following Friday evening, I was sitting on my couch, doing schoolwork, when Jerry opened my front glass door, barging right into my apartment unannounced. "What are you doing sitting here all alone on a Friday night?" he asked, clearly incredulous, as he looked around at the piles of papers surrounding me, in disbelief. "Uh, are you writing a book, or something?" he added as an afterthought.

"No, uh, I'm grading homework," I stammered.

"Well, no one should be alone on a Friday night," he continued, shaking his head at the lunacy of it all. "Come on," he pleaded, "Come with me!" Explaining that he was just walking a couple of blocks down to the Rusty Rooster, and that he'd love to accompany me. He assured me that if I didn't like the atmosphere, he'd walk me right back home. "I think you'll really like it!" he coaxed. "Please come," he added. "*Please!*"

His offer held the promise of being diverting, and so, our first date began. The Rusty Rooster on Lakewood Boulevard was *the* local place to be, in those days. It was a *huge* nightclub, with dozens upon dozens upon dozens of tables placed around an immense dance floor, with a raised stage for live entertainment. The place was packed sardine-like, standing room only, with everyone obviously having a super fine time. (I didn't tell Jerry that I had never been in a bar or a nightclub before, given my upbringing, so this was a whole new experience for me. I was moving into uncharted territory. I felt like Dorothy in the *Wizard of Oz*).

We sat down at an empty table, next to the dance floor, that had a reserved sign, and when I was concerned about it, he said, "Don't worry about it," even though tons of people were standing. I thought we might get kicked out. But just then, the band concluded with a climactic fanfare, and left the stage for its break. Suddenly, the crowd starting chanting, "We want *Jer-ry*! We want *Jer-ry*!" Everyone began wildly clapping, and stomping their feet in cadence. The noise was tremendous! I turned around in an effort to see who this fabulously popular fellow was, but could not spot anyone getting up. Disappointed, I turned back to the table, and found the seat across from me empty. My first thought being, *Geez, he's left me already?* I looked up in time to see my date casually making his way across the dance floor and climbing onto the stage, as the crowd went bananas! Gawking like a schoolgirl, I watched in amazement as Jerry delivered stand-up comedy off the top of his head, zinging one-liners left and right in response to the audience. He then launched into a couple of show tunes, and ended his routine by wielding a giant-sized pair of drumsticks on the drum set and cymbals. Va-va-voom! The room erupted into loud shouts, whistles, and thundering applause.

I was stunned. And impressed. What a talent! Now here was a guy who knew how to laugh, joke, and enjoy life: Mr. Personality Plus, with a cock-of-the-walk attitude. And he seemed to have tons of friends and admirers. This was just what I needed! I was starry-eyed, already deep into mindless devotion and hero-worship mode. Talk about going ga-ga! So, like a berry in a blender, I was a goner. (We all have our weak moments.)

All is not necessarily what it seems at first blush,
and the significance of what occurs to us,
may only be obvious later on.
—Robert H. Hopcke

Live for what today has to offer,
not for what yesterday has taken away.
—Unknown

Six letters, two words,
easy to say,
hard to explain,
harder to do:
MOVE ON.
—Unknown

NOW I ASK YOU...

It's a scary thing moving on,
part of me wishes life were more predictable,
and part of me is excited that it is not.
I think it's impossible
to tell the good things from the bad things
when they are happening.
—Chris Crutcher

Life is about making mistakes, learning, and moving on.
—Shamity Shetty

We need to have the commitment
to do what we need to do to heal and move on.
—Anne Wilson Schaef

Don't feel any guilt when you let somebody go.
You're not leaving them behind. You're just moving on.
—Pieter Elsen

NOW I ASK YOU . . .

Have you ever witnessed poor sportsmanship? As a teacher, I have seen plenty over the years, so I would schedule what I called "graceful losing skills," that were to be used in place of the most childish poor sportsmanship (name-calling, spitting, biting, hair-pulling, sucker-punching, tripping, hitting, kicking, etc.). Sportsmanship has to do with how people play games, not if they win or lose. So I was always surprised, when I would see adults acting out.

UNCONTROLLABLE RAGE

On this first date with a guy, as we walked through my apartment, he saw my chessboard, and wanted to play. I said that I was just beginning to learn the game, but he insisted. We played for a bit, but he wasn't really watching the board, as he was checking out my unusual wall art and household decorations. At one point I said, "Uh, I think I won." This guy couldn't believe what he saw. And he started yelling, as he jumped up, and charged back and forth in total disbelief, talking to himself. I couldn't believe what I was witnessing, as he said, "How could I lose to a *girl*?" And I responded with, "First off, I am a woman, and what does gender have to do with it?" as I pointed him toward the outside door. I never saw him again, thank goodness. His temper tantrum caused such a negative display, that I have never played chess since. (It is said that you play checkers for fun, and you play chess for keeps.)

Much later, shortly after meeting Jerry, he and two of

his friends and I, went bar hopping. I don't drink, so I had no interest in this, but they were looking for a specific friend, so the four of them could play pool together. At the same time, I was just beginning to be introduced to his friends. So we wondered through several bars, and finally gave up looking for their friend, and settled in a large bar with many pool tables. Then they called upon me to be their fourth, so they could play against another four men. I kept saying that I'd never played pool before, and wouldn't be any good at it, but they said that three couldn't play, only four. And it didn't matter that I couldn't make a shot, because they could. So the game began, and money changed hands. Finally it was my turn. And, wonder of wonders, I ran the table! I was hyperaware of all the dropped jaws in the room. (I thought it was my short dress, and fancy high heels, while everyone else was dressed in Tee-shirts and tennis shoes). But even Jerry and his buddies were staring at me. Then it got really quiet, as everyone continued to stare. Talk about shocked! I couldn't do it again, if my life depended upon it. "What's wrong?" I asked. "I thought I did good." But suddenly, everyone in the room started shouting, and gesturing, as they *ran* us out of the building and into the parking lot. We were lucky they didn't tar and feather us. They kept calling me a shill. "What's a shill?" I wanted to know, since all of this was new to me. Later, a dictionary told me that a shill is an accomplice of a gambler or swindler, who entices or encourages others to bet or become involved in whatever the game is. So pool is another game that I will never play again.

Victory is in the quality of competition
and not the final score.
—Mike Marshall

It is your response to winning and losing
that makes you a winner or loser.
—Harry Sheehy

Good sportsmanship goes beyond the game;
it starts with respect.
—Tommy Hilfiger

I was pleased with both games.
Our sportsmanship was outstanding.
—Wade Clark Mackey

What you are as a person is far more important
than what you are as a basketball player.
—John Wooden

The most important lesson I've learned from sports
is how to be not only a gracious winner,
but a good loser, as well.
—Amy Van Dyken

NOW I ASK YOU . . .

How long does it take to get to know someone? How long does it take to *really* get to know someone? Some say that you should wait two months, before becoming exclusive. According to *Psychology Today*, the rule of thumb is not to get engaged for at least six months, and to wait another year before getting married. Of course, factors, variables, and patterns are identified, but experts all say the longer the better, and that you will *never* stop getting to know your partner.

BIG MISTAKE #2

We became instant companions, truly inseparable. Whenever I was around Jerry, my good sense seemed to be conspicuously absent. For instance, at night, when he would remove his jacket, he'd find dozens of slips of paper, with women's names and phone numbers in his pockets. He was so indifferent to them, tossing them in the trash without further ado, that it never crossed my mind that I might need to be concerned about this, at some time in the future. So much for connecting-the–dots. Needless to say, he was quite a ladies' man. All the women wanted Jerry, and he wanted *me*. What an ego trip! He went out of his way to be attentive, and show how much I meant to him, making me feel like HOT STUFF. Sizzle, sizzle. (Sing along with Tina Turner: "Steamy Windows" or "Rock Me" by Muddy Waters.) And being so emotionally starved, I happily lapped it up. We had absolutely *nothing* in common, but that fact was conveniently placed on the backburners of my mind—where it simmered away—as

Jerry never ceased to flip-flop my heart, and turn my brain to Silly Putty. I was simply too besotted to notice.

It was like my brain went on permanent vacation until it was too late. And so, after a whirlwind courtship of a whole six-and-a-half weeks, without a flutter of apprehension, we got married. (And the dish ran away with the spoon.) It wasn't one of my brighter decisions. We married with more optimism than insight, and didn't have a snowball's chance.

In my defense, however, it wasn't as if I hadn't considered the obvious; *obvious* being the operative word here. Wanting to profit from my previous mistake with Chuck, I paid heed to the popular saying, "Unless we learn from our history, we're doomed to repeat it." I felt that I had learned something about choosing a partner. So I was looking for someone who was diametrically *opposite* from my first husband. In my mind, I compared Chuck to Jerry, and there was no contest between the two: the former was a cold fish, while the latter was a hot tamale.

This was my "Getting To Know You" period (from The King And I Broadway musical, by Rogers and Hammerstein), wherein I compared thirty items, and it all looked good to me (listed in *The Bogeyman: Stalking and It's Aftermath*). *What's not to like?* Jerry appeared to be a new and improved version. I couldn't see any way in which these two guys were the same. I thought I was being selective. However, I was still concerned with superficial considerations, never getting to the real meat of the issue. Again I saw the package, not the contents, the frame and not the picture. I was looking at nothing of substance, failing to ask the more important questions, regarding deep-seated values, dreams, and goals. I didn't factor in the *inner* being, nor did I see alcohol and drugs looming high on the horizon. I didn't recognize that both Chuck and Jerry had a pretty cavalier attitude toward the truth. I was in a great expectations mode.

My thinking was that out of a virtual smorgasbord of women, Jerry picked *me!* And I was deeply flattered. So he obviously *loved* me (Say, *what?*), and by marrying Jerry, I'd be getting rid of Chuck in the process, *forever*: a sort of two-for-the-price-of-one deal. So there I was, simply confusing ego, sex, and convenience, with true love. Swell. It was a dumb idea, that was clearly destined to fail; another huge mistake that had the potential for misfortune written all over it, in flashing neon. *Out of the frying pan, and into the fire.* This was my second bad decision about men.

No need to sugarcoat it.

Oh, my. When worlds collide. Instant trouble in paradise. Once again, I had degenerated into something less than perfect. Suffice it to say that Jerry was not the tons of fun that I imagined him to be. This was not what I had expected. In the extreme. But to be fair, living with *me* on a 24/7 basis, was not what *he* expected either. We disagreed on everything. Our basic attitudes and viewpoints on life were at loggerheads, and we had yawning differences in social outlook and responsibility. Studly Do-Right, he was not. My enthusiasm for his lifestyle had rapidly waned. In addition, our schedules interfered—I worked days, and he worked nights—providing an added wet-blanket effect. Nor was he particularly funny, without a full audience to play to. It became abundantly clear that we were not singing from the same hymnal. And it hurt.

His temper became a danger zone. It was extremely

unnerving to watch charming, hilarious Jerry morph into King Kong, yelling or lashing out, or complaining, at a moment's notice (a Jekyll and Hyde experience). I had no idea that drugs were involved. (No one talked about drugs, in those days. It was all about alcohol.) Ours became an ongoing Punch and Judy show. (Sonny and Cher's "The Beat Goes On," came to have a whole different meaning for me.) For instance, during one argument, he picked up my jewelry box, and heaved it at my head with such force that it tore a huge hole through the closet door, leaving wood splinters, the broken box, and my destroyed jewelry scattered all over the floor. If it had connected as intended, I might not be telling this tale. Luckily, I instinctively ducked, and it just missed my head by a fraction of an inch. Another time, he grabbed me by my long hair, and dragged me around the apartment, like a cave man. I had rug burns to prove it. Hair stylists refused to do my hair, thereafter, because it was falling out in clumps, and they thought I had some kind of infection or disease. I was too embarrassed to tell them what actually happened. I cut my hair short, thereafter, so *that* would never happen again. It was safe to say that my bruised and battered life plan had officially disintegrated.

Arguing became our *only* form of communication. We both took Phyllis Diller's advice to heart: "Don't go to bed mad. Stay up and fight." The lyrics to Ira and George Gershwin's "Let's Call the Whole Thing Off" ("You like po-ta-to, and I like po-tah-to, you like to-ma-to, and I like to-mah-to") exactly matched our situation: total knee-jerk behavior.

And, adding insult to injury, Chuck's intrusiveness did not abate, as I had expected. His continued interference in my life definitely affected my new marriage. Whenever I mentioned his latest contact, Jerry would withdraw, becoming emotionally distant. All Jerry heard were my complaints, and he never actually *saw* Chuck, so he couldn't really *do* anything about the situation. This was tough on his ego. Jerry was a banty rooster-type character, that required *action*. So he felt somewhat less of a man—powerless, helpless, and impotent—due to Chuck's continuous contact, and his own ineffectiveness. In time, Jerry began to question whether Chuck might simply be a figment of my imagination, which, of course, didn't sit well with me. At all! Chuck was a definite drain on our lives.

Actions speak louder than words.
—St. Anthony of Padua (1200 AD)

Actions speak louder than words, but not nearly as often.
—Mark Twain

Actions speak louder than words.
And sometimes inaction speaks
louder than both of them.
—Matthew Good

NOW I ASK YOU . . . .

Has your presence ever been demanded at a sit-down with the Big Boss, and you didn't know why? Were you mad? Sad? Glad? Afraid?

SUMMONED

I had a day job, as a teacher, whereas Jerry had a night job. He was the manager for 12 bars and nightclubs in Long Beach. He had substitute bar tenders, as needed, whenever the regular bar tenders were absent. But on this particular night, he ran out of subs, and as such, he had to do the bar tending himself at one bar. He called me a little after 1:00 AM, to say that his car wouldn't start, and that I needed to pick him up around 2:00, when all the bars closed. So I leaped out of bed, and changed my clothes, combed my hair, and drove down to pick him up. I was a little early, so I sat at the bar. He fixed me a coke (with a red cherry on the top), and we chatted and laughed, as he was closing up the bar. There was only one couple that was still sitting at the huge horseshoe bar, directly across from me on the far side. They seemed to be staring at me, but, after all, there was no one else left to look at. At 2:00, we all left.

The next day, after the elementary school closed at 3:10, the principal fairly ran into my classroom, telling me that I had to go see the Superintendent of Schools right away!!! Like *NOW!* "Uhhh, okay, but why?" I asked, but he only said, "Go, go, go!" So I went. I couldn't imagine what the problem was all about. It was absolutely *scary*, and it felt like I was walking into the Lion's den.

When I was seated, the superintendent asked what I did last night. Aha! So that was what all the commotion was about! I told him that I do not drink, and I do not smoke, nor do I do drugs. And that everyone who knows me, knows that Pepsi is my drink of choice. It turned out that the couple that was at the bar so late, recognized me as their son's teacher. (I had never met them.) So they told both my principal and the superintendent that I was out *carousing* in a bar late at night. Oh, boy. (I, in turn, wondered *what they were doing in a bar, so late on a school night, when they had children at home. Did they depend on my third grade student to babysit the younger children?* But, of course, I never asked.) Both my principal and superintendent were satisfied with my answer, and it was never mentioned again.

Sometimes the questions are complicated,
and the answers are simple.
—Dr. Seuss

NOW I ASK YOU . . .

Have you ever had occasions in which it looked as if you had bought the farm (whether by accident, health issues, or by the hands of another)? Did you see yourself pushing up daisies? Have you had any near misses, when you thought you were a goner, just short of saying the BIG ADIOS? Did you see yourself already crossing the rainbow bridge? Did you think you got a second chance, at death's door, to better your life, and make better choices?

DEATH AVOIDED

Miracles surround my life. It appears that I have more lives than cats! It is strange that I haven't yet kicked the bucket, since I have had many opportunities to bite the dust (I never thought that I would live to be forty (I am 84 now!). In my nightmares, I had often seen myself as six feet under (in a coffin, looking up from the other side of the grass). I will only list one example of skirting death here:

One day, Jerry and I were getting dressed in the morning, and we both needed the small bathroom mirror at the same time. We were trying to see over, under, and around each other, while carrying on a king-size shouting match, at the same time. He finally lost it, and grabbed me around the neck with both hands, and choked me out. (It only takes 10 seconds to cause unconsciousness.) It happened so fast, that I didn't know what hit me. I fell on the floor, and didn't move for so long, that he thought he had *killed* me. (Brain death can occur in 4-to-5 minutes). At length, I was bit by bit awakening, by hearing a far-away noise. It finally registered as crying. Then I recognized that it was *Jerry* crying. And I realized that he needed help. (I wasn't the least bit concerned as to why I was on the floor. It never even crossed my mind.) So I slowly, steadily, turned around, and crawled out of the bathroom, then inched down the hall on all fours, and finally looked up into the living room. "Jerry, what's wrong? Why are you crying?" I asked, in a raspy, hoarse voice (I could hardly talk.) The look on his face was that of total shock. He froze, and just stared at me. Finally, he smiled a big smile, and came over and picked me up off the floor. I had no idea what had happened, and he didn't tell me, of course. And I didn't know enough to ask. It took several days before I *realized* that I had been strangled. I was in a state of stunned disbelief. (Often, a crime victim has details of the event emerge hours or even days after the experience, after blocking it out at first. Strangulation can even cause memory issues.)

Jerry's choking episode made such an indelible impression upon me, that I no longer felt confortable wearing choker necklaces, turtleneck sweaters, or scarfs tied around my neck. In the same manner as earlier side effects to Chuck's behavior, I eliminated silver jewelry (reminding me of handcuffs), and sleeveless blouses (which couldn't cover bruises). I didn't want to remember any such violent behavior.

Strangulation has been identified as one of the most lethal forms of domestic violence. There are around 300 murders each year, in the United States, that are officially categorized as suffocation/strangulation/ asphyxiation. And half of those involved a lunge for the throat, to end a domestic disagreement. Losing consciousness indicates at the very least a mild brain injury. Statistics show that a woman who has been strangled by her partner just once, is *eight* times more likely to be killed by that partner.

It's amazing how stupid you can be, when you're in love.
—Lucy (Charlie Brown's friend)

Anger doesn't solve anything. It builds nothing,
but it can destroy everything.
—Unknown

The brain protects itself by switching to essential
life support in a time of physical trauma.
Only after safety returns do the full details
of the trauma start to come back.
—Michael Connelly

So, when you hear 'He choked me,' now you know.
You are at the edge of a homicide.
—Casey Gwinn

Trauma has a way of damaging memory.
In some cases, victims
never get their memories back.
—Lucy Score

NOW I ASK YOU . . .

Have you ever contemplated suicide in jest, or pulling the plug for real? You are not alone. According to the World Health Organization, approximately 800,000 people die by suicide each year worldwide (nearly 50,000 in America in 2022, according to the CDC). And who knows how many others survived their suicide attempts? Know that anything can happen to anybody. Every now and then, a little rain can turn into a hurricane. And a nonstop series of disasters can follow. In such a case, it is normal to burnout via extreme mental or emotional stress (feeling fear, anger, sadness, grief, obsessive thoughts, aloneness, no support system, helpless, trapped, exhausted, and defeated). All this puts too much pressure on your capacity to handle things in a normal fashion, and you see no upside to your problems. Don't do anything rash to yourself. It is often said that a few weeks from now, things will be different. A few months from now, you will have forgotten your problem. And a few years from now you will wonder why you worried so much. The solution to your problem may be just around the next corner. Understand that it takes more courage to live, than to kill yourself. Plough on!

BREAKDOWN

I was adrift with only one oar in the water. Prolonged depression inevitably creates chronic exhaustion. In those times of great stress, strain, and sorrow, thoughts of suicide had taken up a very assertive residence at the front of my mind. I seemed to be losing my marbles. All I wanted was to dematerialize into the either, to simply vanish from the screen. Death appeared to be cozy, comforting, and inviting. I longed for the deep sleep of Sleeping Beauty, or at least Rip Van Winkle. Each morning began with Chicken Little shrieking that the sky was falling. A funeral dirge played loudly in the background of my mind—a constant presence—engendering thoughts of getting my affairs in order: making out a will, and listing burial suggestions. But even *that* took too much effort. I was too tired to even write a note. I thought long and hard about such an act. I was in serious meltdown mode.

My life appeared to be an open wound that couldn't be stanched. Chuck was seriously mentally deranged (and still constantly following me and harassing me), whereas Jerry's life was now completely overtaken by drugs (his fun personality had turned into Attila the Hun, coming at me with hammer and tongs, throwing everything in sight at me). And my emotions took even more of a swan dive when I had a miscarriage (all traffic had stopped on the freeway, because of a major accident, and we couldn't get to the hospital for help). So the "Rock-a-Bye-Baby" blues also got to me; an experience I hadn't even fully processed yet. Severe postpartum depression took a stranglehold on my life, and wouldn't let go. So, alongside sleep issues, as well as PTSD and PPD, and my out-of-whack hormones, all seemed to be issuing me a double-dose of everything. In addition, an oppressive weighted blanket of gloom and doom, seemingly surrounded me. With my sense of loss, and despair, I just didn't have it in me to keep on going. I was saying goodbye to violence and dysfunction. The Rolling Stones' "19th Nervous Breakdown" would have been especially appropriate at that time.

So I bought two bottles of sleeping pills. That Sunday

night, I started swallowing the pills (Sing: "Suicide is Painless," the M.A.S.H. theme song.) It was a rough row to hoe, as I kept gagging. But I persevered anyway, with visions of permanent sleep on my mind: my very own poppy field. I was finally closing the door on chaos, ready to sink into a deep, deep sleep, nestled all snug-like in Baby Bear's bed: J-u-s-t right!

Oh, great. Just great. For once in our married life, Jerry came home *early* that night. What timing. Talk about synchronicity! Yelling obscenities the minute he charged through the door, as per usual, his fury was always disproportionate to the crime (whatever he thought the crime was). I was so thrilled that I wouldn't have to hear it anymore, or deal with it ever again, that it didn't even bother me. It must have been apparent that something was amiss, since I wasn't responding with my usual verve. Shortly thereafter, he found the empty bottles and packaging in the trash can in the bathroom, and went ballistic. Throwing me over his shoulder, while holding me in place, he raced out to his car, shoved me onto the seat, and roared off to the emergency hospital.

While my stomach was being pumped, Jerry stood at the end of the gurney, holding on to my feet, with tears coursing down his cheeks. I was enraged. I didn't want him even *touching* me. I considered his crying to be of the crocodile variety. *All for show*, I thought, *all for show*. But I couldn't say anything, what with the tube running down my throat, while the doctor gave me a lecture, in no uncertain terms, that what I did was against the law (which was certainly news to me!). This was not a pleasant experience, and I wouldn't recommend it to anyone. I was trying not to be overwhelmed by the absurdity of it all: I wasn't even a success at suicide. *Oh, this was a great idea! I fumed. I am such a genius.* Talk about a downer!

Suicide is a permanent solution to a temporary problem.
—Phil Donahue

People who die by suicide,
don't want to end their lives, they want to end their pain.
—Unknown

Most happy, successful people, at one time,
have considered suicide. They decided against it.
—Richard Bach

The hardest thing I ever did was continuing my life
when I wanted to die.
—Juliette Lewis

But in the end, one needs more courage
to live than to kill himself.
—Albert Camus

The man who, in a fit of melancholy kills himself today,
would have wished to live had he waited a week.
—Voltaire

Don't you dare give up on tomorrow,
because of the way things look today.
—Neale Donald Walsch

Never let a stumble in the road be
the end of your journey.
—Unknown

Success is not final, failure is not fatal,
it is the courage to continue that counts.
—Winston Churchill

AFTERWORD: Years later, when I was married to Wayne, I was able to help those people who were considering suicide. For instance, a teenage girl, who lived across the street, had a rough family life. She'd come over in the evenings, to sit on my front porch steps, and talk about her suicide longings. She later went on to the university, and became a *psychologist*, and was able to help others in the same manner.

NOW I ASK YOU . . .

Have you ever been in a courtroom situation? Were you a jury member? Or were you a witness for the prosecution or defense? Was it like watching trials on television or the movies? Was it boring or exciting? Would you like to experience another court trial?

COURTROOM DRAMA

I had switched schools because of Chuck, and due to our changing financial condition (a reverse Midas-touch, thanks to Jerry), we moved around a lot; which I decided, were reasons enough for Chuck to be out of the picture for awhile. I didn't have time to give Chuck much thought, however, as I had become pregnant again. (*How had that happened? I was on the Pill!*). Sometimes life just sucked.

I gained sixty pounds (eating mostly eclairs and pickles), and had a severe case of toxemia (I no longer had observable ankles), with other assorted health issues. I was extremely uncomfortable. And because of our money situation, I had only two maternity blouses and one maternity skirt to wear. I did not look or feel my best: fat and dowdy. My glamour quotient was approximately zilch. So much for being vain, fashionable, and sophisticated. And, in my mind, there was a bevy of beauties waiting in line for Jerry's attentions. Which wasn't the best ego boost for me.

You can imagine my shock and amazement when the district attorney called me, asking if I would be a surprise witness against Charles, at an upcoming trial. Of course, I fairly jumped to the chance, hoping that this would be the last time I would ever have to deal with Chuck. When I met with the DA, there was another woman—a few years older than me—in his office. She turned out to be his first wife (*wife?*). Once I had absorbed that shock, she informed me that they had a child together (*child?*). Apparently, she was so afraid of Charles, that as soon as her testimony for her divorce was over, her father—*a policeman!*—whisked her away to some other town, where she was living in hiding. Good grief. If her *father*, who was trained to deal with such matters, was afraid of what Chuck might do, what recourse did I have? My thoughts were reeling, as another epic headache began.

So now, at long last, Jerry believed all my off-the-wall stalking stories. Having a common enemy, we were at peace during the duration of the trial. So he escorted me to court, consoled me, and sat with me through the ordeal. During the trial, he basked in his role of the *good guy*, the protector of *his* woman, and so forth.

What could possibly go wrong? I was looking forward to *my* day in court. When we arrived for the trial, the large courtroom was crowded wall to wall. Three classes of high school students had taken up most of the seating, and I was worried that I might have to discuss sexual abuse in front of possible former students. This did not bode well. Not only that, but I was close to giving birth, and I was *huge*, and hardly fit into my clothes. I simply looked horrible.

To make matters worse, the only seating available was right behind the defense table. Not good. Of course, Chuck and Jerry were exchanging hard looks (Cue: "The Good, the Bad, and the Ugly" soundtrack, by Ennio Morricone). It was all male ego and posturing. Very primitive. Then,

I was shaken to the core to see both my parents seated not far from us. Talk about shock! I hadn't told them about the trial, not wanting to further disturb them about Chuck. Oh, boy.

It turned out, that without me to harass, Chuck had been keeping himself busy by terrorizing other women. He was originally arrested and charged with kidnapping, aggravated assault, rape, and the attempted murder of *five* women on separate occasions. But the DA felt he had a better chance of conviction by focusing on the latest victim, showing Chuck's over-the-top violence: She had been (1) plucked off a street corner, then (2) driven to his house, (3) where he had savagely beaten her, (4) and stabbed her *twenty-seven* times with a knife, (5) next he took a beer bottle, smashed it in half, and gouged out her stomach, and (6) *then* he raped her. Proving himself to be an extremely dangerous, sick, and demented individual.

I testified in the court trial, but was unable to say anything that really mattered, because of the Spousal Privilege Exception Statutes. Both the DA and the lawyer said that I couldn't discuss anything that happened *during* our marriage. Chuck's threats against my family and myself never made it into the trial. Neither did his murder attempts, nor his bizarre sexual abuse. His lawyer summed up my questioning by concluding that it was *my* fault that Chuck went around kidnapping and raping other women, because I had the audacity to *divorce* him! If we had remained married, he announced with ill-disguised hostility, the women of the city would have been safe (conveniently sidestepping the matter of what would have happened to *me*). *Can you believe it?* He *sneered* at me, as he concluded his questioning. So I became the patsy, the scapegoat, the fall guy, for Chuck's horrendous behavior. Talk about displacement! Yet again, a lawyer was criticizing a victim for instigating the violence, blaming the prey, not the predator, judging the injured, not the perpetrator. And, of course, I was not allowed to respond on the stand. It was an unfair and unnerving experience, to say the least.

I was shocked to hear that my mother was called to the stand. She testified that Chuck had kidnapped *her* one evening, when she was in her nightgown and robe. He lured her out to his car, to speak privately about *me*, shoved her in, and roared off. She talked a-mile-a-minute, always having had quite a way with fast and furious words, and he eventually brought her back to the house, and let her go. Chuck didn't want to deal with her nonstop yacking; it just wasn't worth the effort. He had always been fascinated with a mother-daughter ménage a trois. But never in my wildest imagination would I have thought that he might be *hinting* that my mother and I should indulge in such behavior. Oh, gross! It makes me sick even to think about it. Good grief! Mother was *mortified*, not just by experiencing the situation in the first place, but by having to relive it, and *talk* about it, in open court. She obviously wanted to disappear into the ether, and I felt guilty for bringing this added negative experience into my parents' lives. (We never once mentioned this court experience thereafter. We all acted like it never happened.)

During the lull, as Mother left the stand, Chuck glared back at me once again, hissing that he was going to *kill* me for all the lies that I told on the stand. (*What?* I wasn't able to say anything damaging, more's the pity. *What was he talking about?!*) Upon hearing the threat, Jerry heatedly leaped over the little guardrail, and the two of them grabbed each other, becoming involved in a noisy no surrender no retreat battle. It was all guy-testosterone nonsense. It would have deteriorated into a full blown dog fight in the middle of open court, if the bailiff and others hadn't quickly intervened, to the tune of the judge's gavel banging away, "Order! Order!" So much for courtroom decorum.

How very male of you, I stewed. This display was about territorial rights, all over again. Guys and their raging macho-driven turf wars were really getting on my nerves. *What is this? My classroom? The playground?*

I was humiliated. None of this was helping matters. Both sorely needed adult supervision, and I longed to send them to opposite corners for a time out. Instead, I recited a ditty to myself, by Lewis Carroll:

Tweedledee and Tweedledum
Agreed to have a battle,
Cause Tweedledee said Tweedledum
Had spoiled his nice new rattle.

My embarrassment did not end there. Oh, no. By the time the two were pulled apart, *I* was ordered out of the courtroom for causing a disturbance. (Me? Surely you jest. *Chuck* threatened me! *Jerry* started the fight! *What did I do?* I didn't scream, yell, or cry. I didn't say anything! I watched this spectacle in frozen disbelief and astonishment, along with everyone else. I sputtered and spewed, but no articulate words came forth. My loss of dignity was complete. Stunned, I couldn't even think what to do as a symbolic gesture, just to keep myself from a major meltdown. (Sing along with Albert King: "If it wasn't for bad luck, I'd have no luck at all.") My life seemed reduced to a Three Stooges routine. It made me feel like retching.

At the close of the trial, Chuck was finally sentenced to the Atascadero State Hospital for the Criminally Insane (now called the Atascadero State Hospital, for obvious reasons), where he was to spend the next seventeen years of his life. Thank God. Chuck would finally get a check up from the neck up. I was ecstatic, turning somersaults in my mind. I had to exercise the utmost self-discipline not to jump up and down like a pogo stick, yelling, "So long, farewell, auf Wiedersehen, hasta la vista, goodbye and good riddance!" *And that's that*, I said to myself, while mentally dusting my hands of the situation. *I will never have to deal with him ever again*. Dream on.

Chuck continued to send letters to me throughout his years behind bars, so he was always in the background of my mind. He received an early release for *good behavior* (of course, because there were no women there to harass!). Then his stalking behavior continued in earnest.

*Money will determine whether
the accused goes to prison or walks a free man.*
—Johnnie Cochran

*The defendant wants to hide the truth
because he's generally guilty.
The defense attorney's job is to make sure
the jury does not arrive at that truth.*
—Alan Dershowitz

*It takes a long time to learn
that the courtroom is the last place in the world
for learning the truth.*
—Alice Koller

NOW I ASK YOU . . .

Have you had a baby, or adopted a baby? How did the baby change your life? Did your perspective of life change? Did everything take longer? Did your choice of entertainment change? Were your days more hectic, busy, and complicated? Even so, was it worth it? Did your love expand?

BABY JAY

Jerry and I had approximately two weeks of a marital truce during the trial, but our union remained a one-way ticket to disappointment. After the big reconciliation scene was over, and my worries about Chuck were over, Jerry and I were back to square one, squabbling continuously. Nothing had changed in our situation. The theme music for that period in my life was clearly, "The Thrill is Gone," by B.B. King. It became evident that what little had held us together had quickly eroded and completely disappeared.

Every night, Jerry would ask, "Are you going to have the baby tonight?" And I always said, "No, the doctor said I have *two* more weeks to go." And off he went to be with his buddies. The problem was that three doctors had a joint practice, so I saw three different men—months apart— and two said the same thing, "You have two more weeks to go." They didn't know me, and I didn't know them, so I never really knew what was going on with my pregnancy. I didn't even know enough to ask intelligent questions.

So I went to see three different friends that day, and each told me that I was going to have my baby that night! One was very adamant, saying that she had been tracking my contractions, and she knew what she was talking about. But I didn't believe them, because of what the doctor said. So, of course, Jerry left, and I went into the bathroom, and I didn't know what was going on, because my water broke, and I didn't know what that meant. So, I was standing in the bathtub, thinking I was urinating for a long time (having never heard of amniotic fluid), and was freaking out. I finally called down to the gal who lived in the apartment below me, who had just had a baby. And she told me that I was ready to give birth. Since Jerry wasn't there, her husband took me to the hospital.

A guy ran out with a wheelchair, and I was saying that this was probably a false alarm (that's all I had ever heard about the birthing situation), and the guy proceeded to give me an angry lecture: "Then why are you here?" and so forth. He was majorly ticked! So he wheels me into a room that was packed like sardines. About 20 or 25 women (it looked like more!) were on beds and gurneys, with their husbands standing beside them. While I began to throw up the cheeseburger (with onions), fries, and a malt, that I had eaten for dinner, at the same time that I suddenly had diarrhea. Both ends were involved. *Talk about gross!* So the nurses cleared the room of all men, who were not happy about the situation, and let me know their feelings, in no uncertain terms; like I was in control, and was deliberately inconveniencing them. I was dying of embarrassment. So I was the last to arrive, and the first to give birth.

It was apparent that the staff was being run ragged, since so many pregnant women arrived at the same time, and were not expected. So there I was, as Jay was almost completely delivered into the doctor's arms, when an anesthesiologist rushed in to give me a spinal (which is to prevent pain). I didn't want it (I hate shots!), and I was yelling, *"No, no!"* as my doctor was yelling, *"No! No, that's not needed!"* But the man shot me with the spinal anyway. I was not a happy camper, as I was then focused on *him*, and not my brand new son, Jay.

Of course, Jerry was nowhere to be found during the BIG EVENT. I was pretty shocked to see my Mom and Dad. *How did they know?* They were thrilled to see Jay through the nursery window, and were furious that Jerry was nowhere to be seen. They asked where he was, and I said that I didn't know, but that he might be in a house, sitting on the sandy beach, all by it's lonesome. They went searching for Jerry, and actually found him (!), and dragged him back to the hospital. *Can you believe?*

A new baby marks the beginnings of all things—
wonder, hope, and
a beautiful dream of possibilities.
—Unknown

Having a baby is a life-changer.
It gives you a whole other perspective
on why you wake up each day.
—Unknown

A grand adventure is about to begin.
—Winnie the Pooh

NOW I ASK YOU . . .

Have you ever been involved in an unforeseen, serious, and dangerous situation? One that required immediate action? Did you or a family member need emergency service of some kind? Did you need the police, or medical attention, or property damage experts? Or all three? Did you receive such help, as quickly as possible? Were you satisfied with the results?

EMERGENCY!

My parents had never visited my apartment (they did not approve of Jerry, nor his lifestyle or behavior). So it was quite surprising when my mother dropped by one hot July day. I was proud to present my brand new two-week old baby to her, as I placed Jay in her arms. Of course, she and my father had seen Jay through the hospital glass windows, but didn't get to hold him. At once, she became concerned about her grandson, asking me about his soft-spot. (*Soft-spot? What the heck was that?* I knew next to nothing about babies, having never been around them for any length of time, so it was a whole new experience for me. I was clueless.) It turned out, I learned, that a bulging soft spot may be a sign of brain swelling or fluid buildup in the brain, which can damage the baby's developing brain. If untreated, permanent brain damage or even death can occur, in severe cases. Mother took immediate charge of the situation, and called the local hospital, and was told that we couldn't wait for a doctor's office appointment; that we had to go to the nearest emergency room, forthwith. Mother explained that we would bring Jay immediately, while the doctors cleared their schedules, to make way for an emergency operation.

Mother informed me that she would follow me to the hospital, and leave from there to drive home, after the situation was taken care of. I then explained that my car had been stolen a couple of days prior, and that I had no way to get to the hospital. (This was our third car that was stolen!) So she took us there. (Jerry was at work on a late shift, and had had to rely on friends to drive him to and from the site, since the loss of our only vehicle, so he was unavailable, also.)

When Mother and I arrived at the hospital, everything had been cleared for the operation. Other operations had been canceled, and specific personnel were ready and waiting. Then I was asked for my insurance, and everything skidded to a complete stop. I told them that my insurance was through the school district. I was then informed that said insurance didn't cover women on pregnancy leave. *Say what?* (This was in the sixties, and things were different then.) And furthermore, since it was summer vacation, I wouldn't go back to work until September, so they were unsure of any future income. (They said that I could easily quit my job, and move to another state. Again: *Say What?*) Jerry wasn't insured through his job either, so the hospital refused Jay's admittance because, to all intents and purposes, we were dead broke.

I was in some kind of a shocked state, in total disbelief that a hospital would refuse to admit a child in an obvious situation, as Mother called around to other hospitals, to no avail. They all required insurance. Jay was finally admitted to a hospital in Torrance, that dealt with the indigent and charity cases. And, since we had no car, we couldn't visit

163

him every day. Luckily, Jay was only a few weeks old, and wouldn't feel that his parents had deserted him.

Medical professionals,
not insurance company bureaucrats,
should be
making health care decisions.
—Barbara Boxer

To appropriately respond to an
emergency requires a very clear
mind to cooly analyze what the
observations are and how to fix it.
—Buzz Aldrin

Care shouldn't start
in the emergency room.
—James Douglas

By failing to prepare,
you are preparing to fail.
—Benjamin Franklin

NOW I ASK YOU . . .

Have you ever had questions about your relationships? Questions that no one else could answer? It is said that the Ouija board (also called a Spirit board, or a Talking board) can answer your questions. (It is supposed to communicate with "the other side.") Have you ever used one before? If so, were you satisfied with the answers you received?

TUMBLEWEED

One afternoon, a so-called friend and I were having such a good time, playing with a Ouija board, at her apartment. Unexpectedly, the board said that she was *not* my friend. And I started laughing. Furthermore, it stated that she was having an affair with Jerry. *No, surely not,* I thought. But I heard her catch her breath and hold it. When I looked up, the blood had drained from her face, as she stood up on wobbly, unsteady legs, knocking her chair over backwards in the process. She backed across the room, holding her hand over her mouth. Her stricken expression and demeanor told me more than I wanted to know. The raised hair on my arms and the prickling up my spine—from my tailbone to the base of my skull— confirmed the message. Alarm bells, flashing lights, and loudspeakers went off in my head, as I tore outta there in a heartbeat. *Take a wild guess here, Ace.* I had been denying what my subconscious, my intuition, and my babysitter, had told me from the start. (I am reminded of a quote by Diane Sawyer, "I think the one lesson I have learned is that there is no substitute for paying attention." I had not yet learned that lesson.) It took me some time, but finally, Jerry's casual affairs—heavy on the *s*—became so obvious that I could no longer ignore the situation. So much for being true-blue. His attempt at monogamy fell short of the mark. Way short. Way. Such self-deception spelled IDIOT in my mind: neon-flashing, in huge, bold uppercase letters. I pondered the vast difference between trust and stupidity, as "Your Cheatin' Heart" (by Hank Williams) ricocheted wildly around in my head. *"This is the last straw!* I yelled. Best to get this part over, like ripping off a bandage. *"This marriage is sooooo over!"* There was nothing left to salvage.

Still, I was shocked right down to my shoes. Now *why*, when Jerry had such an impressive rep as a swinging dick and a hoochie-coochie man, was I so crushed, shattered, enraged, and devastated to find out it was true? Why did I think he would be so big on commitment, simply because *I* was in the picture? It was just tough to acknowledge that, like the old saying, I'd been treated like a dictionary; useful when Jerry needed me, but any one would do. The betrayal was overwhelming. The hurt was incredible. It was hard coming to terms with the fact that I had been only the Flavor of the Week, as "Chain of Fools" (by Aretha Franklin) blasted away on my inner stereo. I swear, Jerry had stampeding infidelities out the wazoo. Remembering all those pockets full of phone numbers, my suspicious mind concluded that if all the women he'd known in a biblical sense got together, an arena the size of Staples would be needed. In my rich imagination, he had populated half of Southern California.

Believe me, I had a raft of emotions I'd give anything to deny. Although I'd briefly considered a *Have Gun,*

Will Travel approach to revenge, I knew it was not for me. I was ashamed of even *thinking* that. I could never instruct someone to inflict pain upon another (even though two men—a mafia guy in New York and a California policeman—offered to "take care of Chuck" for me), and I considered it. But it would have resulted in a degree of guilt and remorse that would have been unbearable. *I am not handling this well*, I observed. And although a bullwhip, a cattle prod, and Lorena Bobbit's method of justice held a certain appeal, I knew that our love or companionship had gone with the wind, a long time ago. In any case, I had no energy to follow through with any revenge plans. Lucky for him. Needless to say, this episode took the last layer of shine from our relationship.

Skidding into the parking lot, and charging into the apartment much *earlier* than expected, I found a red-eyed Jerry sitting at the kitchen table behind a humongous beach-ball sized mound of marijuana. It looked like a huge tumbleweed! We both froze, bug-eyed and slack-jawed. It was a *WTF!* moment. In that split second, that seemed to last for eons, everything came together in perfect clarity. It became obvious that I had married a flim-flam artist: a small time, dime-bag, Tango king, who obviously had been sampling his wares. And that my so-called *friend* was keeping me occupied, so Jerry could roll a ton of joints.

OhmyGod! Lost in a time-blur, the events of our short life together ran through my mind like a slide show on speed. No wonder he could talk a blue-streak. No wonder the guys all called him Slick. No wonder he was so energetic. No wonder he had so many friends. No wonder they came over, at all hours of the day and night!

Well, duh. Everything instantly made sense: the mood swings, the paranoia, the escalating violence, the odd hours, the whispering conversations, the numerous phone calls, the loss of his jobs, and his sudden disappearances. It felt like the tectonic plates were shifting beneath me, as I considered my options (Think: Paul Simon's song, "Fifty Ways to Leave Your Lover").

"How could you have placed me in this situation?!" I raged. Studly- Do-Right, he was not. All I could think of was my third grade classes: I constantly ranted to my students the equivalent of "Just Say No!" only to find that my very own husband—the father of my newborn—was a small-time dealer! How could this have happened? *How could I not have known?* I was obviously looking out for other characteristics: Jerry's great looks, sparkling personality, and talents provided perfect misdirection. The only thing that held us together was that we looked great as a couple. That just wasn't enough. *"Get yourself and your tumbleweed out of here! NOW!"*

Since both of my marriages were laced with conflict— during which I lost my independence, self-control, and self-esteem—I thereafter became more inwardly discriminating about what I committed myself to, and why. And I made a solemn vow, shaking my fist at heaven in the manner of Scarlett O'Hara, "As God is my witness, I'll never get married again!" Famous last words.

Happily, once all of this nonsense was over, I realized that having Jay was a blessing in disguise. Rearing a son enriched my life in ways I'd never dreamed possible. I turned into a new person overnight, totally absorbed, and fiercely protective, of this new addition to my family. My father's exasperated response to my second divorce, however, was, "Now that you have a child, no man will ever want to marry you!" (He was Old School.) Like I needed a husband to be complete. To which I responded, "Don't worry about it, Dad. We're a package deal." ("A woman without a man is like a fish without a bicycle." Gloria Steinem.) And that was that. Subject closed. End of discussion.

Sometimes your heart needs more time to accept
what your mind already knows.
—Unknown

Cheating is a choice. Period.
—Charles J. Orlando

I'm learning to love the sound of my feet
walking away from things not meant for me.
—Unknown

NOW I ASK YOU . . .

Have you ever said something without knowing all the facts? Were there unexpected repercussions (physical, psychological, economic, or social)? Were there unintended and unwelcome consequences? Were you surprised?

UNANTICIPATED RESULTS

"That little bug isn't going to hurt you!" I announced in my most judgmental voice, as my third grade students were quickly shifting positions to get out of its way. We had been sitting in a circle on the rug, quietly reading our textbooks together, when a beautiful, iridescent, emerald-green beetle (the likes of which I had never seen before or since), arrived out of nowhere. It interrupted our lesson, and caused every student to disengage. It irritated me that a little insect, the size and shape of a ladybug, could command so much attention, even if it *did* move in such a speedy fashion.

No sooner than I had made this unfounded statement than the bug circled around and made a beeline right for me. It leaped upon my ankle, and bit me before I could even attempt to move—CRUNCH!—and the pain came in Technicolor. Ouch! (I refused to cry in front of my students, as I didn't want them to worry.)

Immediately, my ankle and foot swelled to such unbelievable proportions that it became difficult to pry off my shoe. The infected area was beet-red, extremely hot to the touch, and started to throb with a rhythm roughly approximating the rate and intensity of a jungle drum.

After school, I hobbled over—with one shoe on and one shoe off—to see the nurse, who gave me a list of addresses for specific district-sanctioned doctors to see on my way home. (Naturally, one doctor was on vacation, and another—situated clear across town in the opposite direction—had moved. It took me quite a while to find a doctor on the list, and then, because I had no appointment, I had to wait for a good length of time to see him.

Suffice it to say that I was out of commission for three days, taking anti-venom shots and swallowing anti-inflammatory pills. As a result, this experience taught my students NOT to believe everything a teacher says, and I learned to keep my mouth closed about things I know nothing about. Needless to say, this was a very painful lesson for me to learn, both figuratively and literally.

Every kid has a bug period.
I never grew out of mine.
—E.O. Wilson

Bugs never bug my head.
They are amazing.
It is the activities of humans
which actually bug me
all the time.
—Munia Khan

I'm empathetic to a fault.
I really do—embarrassingly enough—
tear up when someone
squishes a bug right in front of me.
—Kristen Bell

I ate a bug once.
It was flying around me.
I was trying to get it away.
It went right in my mouth.
It was so gross!
—Hilary Duff

We owe bugs gratitude for everything
from pollinating plants to
supporting the decomposition
of animal waste.
—Unknown

I loved being outside. We'd hold
lightning bugs in our fingers
and pretend they were diamond rings.
—Loretta Lynn

NOW I ASK YOU . . .

Do you like to watch television? Do you monitor your children's viewing? (There are over 100 TV series for children.) Have you ever used television as a baby sitter? Did you feel guilty about it? Even with all the negative discussions saying that watching TV will rot your children's brains, do you believe it? Know that TV for children can become their most reliable teacher, companion, and friend. (Consider: *Mr. Rogers Neighborhood*, which ran from 1968 to 2001, 912 gentle and thoughtful episodes, in 31 seasons.)

CHARLIE BROWN

On February 15th, 2002, the day after Valentine's Day, my third graders—who were always so happy about anything and everything in life—were quietly lined up *before* the school bell rang to start the day. They weren't into playing games that morning, as per usual, as all were seemingly thinking their own thoughts, and not interacting with each other. A gloomy mood had settled over the entire group. *What in the world?* I thought, as they entered the classroom, without the usual amount of rambunctious energy, smiles, and happy greetings.

So I chucked the beginning morning exercises, and asked them what was wrong. Very little response was forthcoming. Finally, after some prodding, they explained that Charlie Brown didn't get any valentines. *Say what?* The now classic, *Be My Valentine, Charlie Brown* TV cartoon, had premiered the night before, and the whole class was touched by the story. All of the students showed a caring concern about the situation, and all had a soft spot in their hearts for Charlie Brown. Empathy was strong. Suddenly, as if a dam had broken, they all offered their feelings (sad, angry, disbelief) on the subject.

So the morning lessons went out the window, as they all wrote heartfelt letters or cards to Charlie Brown (something they *wanted* to do, as opposed to an impersonal assignment). Afterward, they made original valentines, happily coloring, cutting and pasting. Thereafter, I showed each valentine to the group, as they oohed and ahhed over their classmates' artwork. The students watched as I placed all of them in a huge envelope, addressed to Charles Schulz. I mailed it that evening, and promptly forgot about it.

Several weeks thereafter, a huge envelope arrived at the school for Room 21. Within it, we found a long personal handwritten letter from Charles Schulz, and a large glossy photograph of the Peanuts Gang, with each of their signatures (a nice touch), and a set of coloring pages for each student. Wow! That impromptu lesson was meaningful in many more ways than one.

We must not fail to recognize that
television can be a hugely positive influence
in children's lives.
—Robert Winston

It's not whether children learn from television,
It's what children learn from television . . .
because everything that children see
is teaching them something.
—Joan Ganz Cooney

*Never underestimate
the importance of small things.*
—Matt Haig

*Sometimes the smallest gestures
can have the biggest impact.*
—Lama Surya Das

*No act of kindness, no matter how small,
is ever wasted.*
—Aesop

NOW I ASK YOU . . .

Have you ever had any TV commercials that you loved? Or ones that you couldn't stand? (In the olden days, televisions had no mute button.) Lots of women preferred Hallmark commercials. Me, too. Some of my old favorites are: M & M's candy "They Do Exist," Wendy's "Where's the Beef?", Life cereals' "Mikey likes it!", Coca-Cola's "Mean Joe Green," and my all time best-loved was the California Raisins' "Claymation R & B Raisins," singing Marvin Gaye's, "I Heard it Through the Grapevine."

COMMERCIALS

When Jay was around four-years-old, he would carry around his bucket of Hot Wheels, so he could play with his little cars wherever he went. One day, it was way too quiet, so I went looking for him. Upon slowly opening his bedroom door, I saw that his bucket was empty. Opening the door further, I saw that Jay had placed all of his Hot Wheels lined up in straight rows. When the door was completely opened, Jay clamped on his old battered cowboy hat, as he looked up, and happily shouted, "*Howdy!* I'm Cal Worthington, and this is my dog, Spot!" as he gestured to his lion plush animal. With an ear-to-ear grin, he said, "Want to buy a car?"

I was astounded, to say the least. Jay had the whole, wacky, off-beat TV commercial down pat: the cars, the hat, the unusual pet, and the big smile before the hard sell. Each commercial had a different "dog, Spot" (a *live* lion, tiger, elephant, hippo, bear, gorilla, camel, bull, penguin, chimpanzee, anteater, iguana, goat, goose, many snakes, a boa constrictor, a skunk, and even a killer whale), but never a dog. Children loved his commercials, while many adults said his saturation advertising drove them crazy.

So I wrote Cal Worthington a letter, telling him that he was a true television *super star*, as young children were singing his jingles, and imitating him, and I used Jay as a model. And surprise, surprise, he wrote back! Cal said that he would hire Jay, any time, because he knew that Jay would be a great car salesman. *How fun is that?*

The relentless wild commercials ran from the 1950s for almost half a century. Sometimes as many as 100 90-second commercials a day, were seen on the West Coast, with its "Go see Cal, go see Cal, go see Cal!" jingle, selling over a million cars. Oddly, the most recognized dealer ever, never owned his own car. He would just borrow one from the lot, as needed. He had 29 dealerships.

The verses were different for each commercial, as Cal played around with his "dog, Spot." A few are listed below:

If you want a better buy, go see Cal.
You're the guy we satisfy, go see Cal.
Give a new car to your wife,
she will love you all your life,
Go see Cal, Go see Cal, Go see Cal.

If your axle is a saggin', go see Cal.
Maybe need a station wagon, go see Cal.
If your wife has started naggin',
and your tailpipe is a draggin'
Go see Cal, go see Cal, go see Cal.

If you need a great big truck, go see Cal.
If you need a little truck, go see Cal.
Get a camper, change your luck,
buy a van and save a buck,
Go see Cal, go see Cal, go see Cal.

If you're a little short of cash, go see Cal.
Doubled over in a flash, go see Cal.
If other dealers have you cussed,
here's a dealer you can trust.
All you have to do is just
Go see Cal, go see Cal, go see Cal.

All of the jingle lyrics are said to be written by Cal Worthington, to sing to the tune of "If you're happy and you know it, clap your hands."

NOW I ASK YOU . . .

Have you had the experience of coincidence before? Everyone has, but not everyone acknowledges it or admits it. The common variety includes thinking of a person, and the phone rings, and that particular person is calling you, or bumping into a long-lost individual that you were thinking of, or getting a letter or email from him or her; or two people saying the same thing at the same time; or sending emails to each other at the same time. Have you enjoyed such instant connections? Or have you dismissed it, overlooked it, shrugged if off, or ignored it? Or simply laughed at the oddball experience, and then promptly forgot about the encounter, since there was no direct cause and effect relationship?

VISIT

My aunt and uncle came to visit us in California from Texas. We took them to see Knott's Berry Farm, a 57-acre amusement park, with a famous restaurant, over 165 rides (including 10 roller coasters), dozens of shows, and various attractions. It is a hugely popular entertainment site, with the average number of five million visitors a year. While in the park's crowded Old West Gold Town section, in that whole mass of strangers, my uncle accidently bumped into his neighbor (who owned the ranch next to his). Neither knew that the other was also visiting California. "What a coincidence!" everyone laughed. "It's a small world after all."

Such coincidences simply affirm that we are all connected in subtle and wonderful ways; that we are on the same wavelength. It is said that chance encounters don't really exist. When people cross your path, there is always a reason, and there is always a message for you (and/or them). Afterwards, stop and give your unexpected meeting some thought. Know that every such event has significance.

When you live your life
with an appreciation of coincidences . . .
you connect with the underlying field of
infinite possibilities.
—Deepak Chopra

NOW I ASK YOU . . .

Have you ever had the experience of a repetition of events? A cluster of occurrences, like a chain, or a beaded necklace, or a connected pipeline? When seen separately, a trail of happenings may appear to have little or no comprehensible significance. But it begins to make sense when the episodes are viewed together. Then the cumulative effect becomes as bright as road flares, calling attention to something important in your life. It is meant to underline something that can't be ignored.

THE ECHO EFFECT

Shortly before I received my cancer diagnosis, out-of-the-blue, in one week, I read two books, and saw three TV movies, in which cancer was the subject matter. (The word wasn't mentioned on the books' cover flaps, or in the TV preview ads. I never would have read or watched them, had I known.) *How weird is that?* What a coincidence! And I didn't give it another thought. I didn't even have an inkling. It was only after the fact, that I saw the clues. What seemed random and meaningless turned out to be quite important. I had an emergency operation, in which a five-pound cancerous tumor was wrapped around my kidney, so both were removed.

Shortly thereafter, a student teacher was heard to hiss at a high school student: "You are a cancer. Cancer is bad!" Now I ask you, how does his help? That comment rather startled me, and I felt duty bound to have a discussion of what *not* to call students, and how to set a good example.

*A stand alone experience may have
little or no comprehensible significance.
However if it begins to make sense
when seen in the context of similar experiences,
it can then be regarded as
but one piece in a larger mosaic.*
—Frank Joseph

Cancer is a word, not a sentence.
—John Diamond, M.D.

*You can be a victim of cancer, or a survivor of cancer.
It's a mindset.*
—Dave Pelzer

NOW I ASK YOU . . .

Have you ever had a birthday party? When growing up or as an adult? Have you ever hosted a birthday party? For a youngster or an adult? Did they feel the same? Which was your favorite? Birthdays are the best! You get cake, with candles, and ice cream. Balloons and decorations and friends surround you. And you receive calls, cards, and emails. And often, gifts are given. My birthday is January the 1st, New Year's Day, so I also get fireworks, a parade, and football games. I always look forward to my birthdays. (I'm shooting for 100 years!)

BIRTHDAY PARTY

As an adjunct professor at BYU one summer, I was working off-campus with a number of student teachers, in their last required all-day, four week class, before certification. It was a show-and-tell experience, in which I presented tons of books and exciting projects to use in their own classrooms, to spice up otherwise dull subjects.

Everyone eagerly participated in whatever lesson I presented, with much laughter and gusto involved. All became close to each other, with the exception of one older gentleman, who kept a reserved, dignified distance. He was obviously retired, and teaching was to be his second career. Besides having gray hair, he always wore 3-piece suits, with long-sleeved white shirts, and formal-colored ties, while everyone else was dressed in colorful, casual summer outfits. So he not only looked, but acted, differently.

I was concerned that he hadn't jelled with the group,

as easily and quickly as others had. I suspected that he came from a supervisory position, in some other field, and was unused to such familiarity and frivolity.

So one fine, enormously HOT day, I happened to overhear a clerk mention that it was the gentleman's birthday. I decided to do something about it, in an effort to solidify his position in our class "family." Later that afternoon, I explained to the class that we were going on a walking field trip, and everyone enthusiastically followed me outside. They enjoyed the breezy walk (it was cooler outside than inside), and were quite pleased, as I led them to an ice cream parlor, several blocks hence. I then explained that we were there in celebration of his birthday.

Everyone clapped and happily congratulated him, in one way or another, and we all spontaneously sang "Happy Birthday" to him, as other customers joined in the festivities. The class was delighted when I said that each person was to choose his/her ice cream, as my treat, so we could all party together on this special day. It was interesting to see all the different flavor choices that were made, with much laughter and hilarity involved. As we were close to the end of our school day, the gentleman stood up before us, and began to thank us, but started *crying* instead. You can imagine how stunned we all were, to hear this older man say that he had *never* had a birthday party in his entire life, and it meant so much to him. You just never know how your actions will impact others.

Count your age by friends, not years,
Count your life by smiles, not tears.
—John Lennon

NOW I ASK YOU...

The older you get,
The better you get,
unless you are a banana.
—Betty White

I binge when I'm happy.
When everything is going really well,
every day is like I'm at a
birthday party!
—Kristie Alley

Today is the oldest you have been
and the youngest you will ever be again.
Make the most of it!
—Nick Gumbel

To quote Shakespeare:
"Party thine ass off!"
—Unknown

NOW I ASK YOU . . .

When a child asks you a question, do you always answer? True, the question may happen when you have a full house of guests, and it's not an appropriate time for a heart-to-heart. But, do you get back to the child and have a later conversation? Or do you let it slide, if it is something you don't want to talk about? If asked tough questions by neighbors or friends, do you lie, or avoid the questions? It all depends, I know. If someone asks you a personal, political, or controversial question, how do you respond? Do you actually answer the questions, or somehow manage to say that it is a private matter?

Something to think about *before* the questions begin.

TOTAL GROSS-OUT

As I waited for the third graders to straggle into line, the first one crowded so close, she ended up on my foot. As usual. *Why is it that students always stand on my feet?* I asked myself for the umpteenth time, as I bit back a shriek of pain. They seem to want to get as close as possible. It's no wonder my feet hurt so much when I get home.

While standing on my foot, waiting for the bulk of the class to arrive after recess, the first student looked straight up into my face, and made a shocking discovery. "Ms. Meinberg! Ms. Meinberg! You have *hair* up your nose!" she announced, in a voice that could be heard two blocks away.

Everyone immediately jostled around for a better view. *Oh, Geez, why me?* I silently implored the heavens. "Yes," I smiled. "*Everyone* has nose hairs."

"Say, *what?*"

"No way!"

"Not me!"

"Uh-uh!"

The group members yelled in ragged concert, spontaneously clasping their hands over their noses. They were all nodding in agreement: *No one* had nose hairs, but me.

"Why do you have hair up your nose?" they clamored. Repeatedly.

Do I really want to answer their questions? I asked myself. *That's a big N-O! Should I? Yes, No, Maybe so?* I deliberated.

But, seeing that I couldn't convince them that everyone had hair up their noses (it was just *too gross* to even consider!), as soon as we entered the classroom, I immediately launched into an impromptu health lesson about nasal hair, the purposes for, and so forth. The students found various science, health, and reference books, to compare and contrast information, but none addressed the issue of nasal hair. Nor did my large nose pictures and posters help. (My motto is: Strike while the iron is hot! I'm a great one to rearrange the schedule for *meaningful* learning to take place.)

Still no one *wanted* to believe that they had nose hairs. So I lugged out my coffee can full of small mirrors, and passed them out to each student. The children checked out their own reflections, as well as each others. Wow! It was like pulling teeth, but they were finally convinced that *everyone* had hair up their noses, whether they liked it or not.

The class finally understood that the function of nasal

hair is like a line of toy soldiers, *defending* their bodies. The nose hairs are ready to trap or catch dust particles, pollen, bacteria, and viruses, to keep them from *invading* their lungs and respiratory system. The nasal hairs are like a front line defense.

We drilled each other on the reasons for nasal hair, so they could later inform their family and friends of same:

"The nose hairs are defending your body."

"Dust sticks to nose hairs."

"Nasal hair sweeps away the bad stuff, like a broom."

"Just like eyelashes protect your eyes, nose hair protects your insides."

"Nose hair traps the bad germs, and viruses."

"Nasal hair keeps all the bad stuff from going into your body."

"The nose hairs trap the pollen and bacteria."

"The nasal hairs trap the invaders, so they won't cause an infection in your lungs."

The third graders couldn't wait to get home, to tell everyone that each person actually had such a horrible thing as hair up their noses.

There's nothing like a gross-out lesson to get the kid's attention.

If I can't horrify,
I'll go for the gross out.
I'm not proud.
—Stephen King

NOW I ASK YOU . . .

Have you experienced those dark and ugly days when nothing goes as expected? When one problem after another pops up, like a Whack-A-Mole? Have you dealt with overwhelming days, tiresome days, or dramatic days? Those are the sucky bad days. It's good to remember that both good and bad days are only 24 hours long. And you can handle 24 hours!

VERY BAD DAY

In 1972, the children's book, *Alexander and the Terrible, Horrible, No Good, Very Bad Day*, by Judith Viorst, was first published. I read a preview about it in the *Psychology Today* Magazine. When no bookstores had it in stock yet, I tried to order it. The owner of one bookstore laughed in a very unpleasant manner, telling me there was no such book with that *ridiculous* title, and curtly dismissed me. I was obviously wasting his time. Now I am not one to give up or give in easily, so I stood my ground. (The man was rude. *Is that any way to run a business?*) I politely argued with him, as a crowd of onlookers formed around us, listening to our conversation. I was well-known in the Long Beach Unified School District, as an expert in Children's Literature, as I was always presenting show-and-tell speeches in various schools and conventions. So the teachers in the crowd were enjoying our debate. (Years later, as a professor, I taught kiddy lit courses in two universities.) I finally convinced him to order one. He was amazed to find that there *was* such a title. And because I was ordering it, others did also. Later, when I went back to pick it up, the bookstore owner had a change of heart. He told me that every time I ordered a new title, he would order a dozen copies, because he knew they were going to sell. We established a good relationship thereafter, over the unusual title of a book. *How weird is that?*

All these decades later, *Alexander and the Terrible, Horrible, No Good, Very Bad Day* continues to be a best-selling children's classic. Over four million copies have been sold! And a movie was made, based on the book and title (2014), via the Walt Disney Pictures and the Jim Henson Company.)

> *Good days give happiness,*
> *Bad days give experience,*
> *Worst days give lessons,*
> *The best days give memories.*
> —Unknown

NOW I ASK YOU . . .

After your high school graduation, did you go directly to work, or did you continue your schooling? Do you give your thoughts a second chance? What's the rush? Can you stop, hold back, wait, and consider your options again?

ON SECOND THOUGHT

On week nights, I moonlighted at the Long Beach Unified School for Adults, which was held on the Wilson High School campus. I was working with those students who had either dropped out of school, or had been kicked out of school. For a time, they had all enjoyed not going back on a daily basis, but reality finally kicked in, when they couldn't get a job without a high school diploma. We teachers were helping them with GED preparation. One night, my class was startled to hear the crash of glass being broken, and car sirens going off. We all rushed to the windows, to see what was happening.

Outside our classroom windows, we watched as a gang member bashed out the front windshields of a line of parked cars, a dozen or so, leaving the jagged shards all over the surrounding area. When he got to the end of the line, he detoured *into* the building hall where we were. When he passed my class door, and ran out the front doors, I followed him at a dead run across the campus. He was fast, but I was gaining on him, in my heels, yet. Just as I caught up with him, a car careened around the corner, and screeched to a halt in front of the school, giving him barely enough time to dive in, before they caromed off, for a fast getaway.

No one could believe it, when I chased after the gang member who did so much damage. And to this day, I do not know what I would have done, if I had caught him. He was taller, heavier, and he had a *bat!* Obviously, I hadn't thought it through. I was operating on reflex action.

It is often said that the second thought is best.
So they are in the matters of judgment,
but not in matters of conscience.
—John Henry Newman

Second thoughts are ever wiser.
—Euripides

NOW I ASK YOU . . .

You do realize, don't you, that everything you do, and everything you say, is modeling behavior? Even if you no longer have children at home, do you understand that you are modeling behavior for youngsters in your neighborhood, in stores, parks, and so forth? Wherever you are, children are observing you, and imitating you.

MODELING BEHAVIOR

I was observing a student teacher in the first grade. She was presenting a lesson on ecosystems, and had brought a 26-gallon terrarium, filled with plants, worms, crickets, and a frog (named Fred). The students listened attentively to the lesson, and made their own Food Chain charts. As they finished with their follow-up activities, the children went to observe the terrarium inhabitants. They wanted to get a closer look at Fred, so the student teacher picked him up, and held him, as the students oohed and ahhed. Then, with a stricken look on her face, she suddenly yelled, "He peed on me! Fred peed on me!" Oh, the shock and horror of it all! Of course, the class followed along like a Greek chorus, "Fred peed on her! Fred peed on her!" Mass pandemonium, as she charged to the sink to wash her hands. Know that what you say, and what you do, will be mimicked by children, whether they are yours or not.

Model the behavior you wish
more people would display.
Lead first.
—Robin S. Sharma

I think a role model is a mentor—
someone you see
on a daily basis,
and you learn from them.
—Denzel Washington

Being a Role Model is the most
powerful form of educating.
—John Wooden

NOW I ASK YOU . . .

Do you know what to expect as your child becomes a six or seven year old? Have you noticed remarkable changes in his/her social and thinking skills? You may be surprised to hear what goals they already have in mind.

EARLY GOALS

On early morning recess duty one day (at my inner city school), I chanced upon a tiny second grader, who was beating up all the children who were wearing red, and teaching the "official secret handshake" to students wearing blue. He had already decided, at the early age of seven, that he wanted to be a member of the Crips gang. He was trying to make a name or rep for himself already, to ensure an early entrance to the social club of his choice. I remember thinking, *Now there's a kid who knows what he wants, and is going for it.*

Another second grader announced that his ultimate goal in life was to go to jail. The other children asked if he knew how to get there.

"Sure," he responded. "Jus' kill somebody!"

In response to my impassioned plea to help and support her third grade daughter's struggle for learning, the mother responded, "Why? She cute!" I was shocked to the depths of my feminist soul. *What century are we in?* I repeatedly asked myself.

In my third grade class, Destiny was saving her pennies for a *breast-reduction operation.* When I pointed out that, since her figure was straight up and down, it didn't seem to be something that she need concern herself with at this point in her life, she said that she wanted to be prepared— as she didn't *ever* want to be bigger than her mother, who was the perfect size.

Believe you can and you're halfway there.
—Theodore Roosevelt

Setting goals is the first step in
turning the invisible into the visible.
—Tony Robbins

NOW I ASK YOU . . .

Did you made any long-term goals as a child? Did they pan out?

LONG-RANGE GOAL

Scotty was a pasty-white, Sumo-sized third grader (nicknamed the Michelin Man, and also the Stay-Puft marshmallow Man, after he sat on a sink in the Boy's Room and broke it off the wall.) His whole life revolved around wrestling. All he wanted to do was wrestle, but none of the boys would wrestle with him, because of his size and ability.

Scotty was totally uninterested in learning to read. His mind was filled with fences, walls, and barriers. He vowed and declared that he had no reason to read, because his goal in life was to be a TV wrestler. And he had the strength and size to succeed at it. I told him that he needed to read, so he could read his future contracts. He said that he would hire a lawyer. I told him that he could be cheated out of his money, but he wasn't going for it, as he would be best friends with his lawyer.

Knowing nothing about wrestling (I didn't know that my father had been a 4-state college champion in his weight class, and had coached a wrestler for the Olympics), I researched the subject, and found that the only wrestling school in the country was in Northern California. So I contacted the school one morning, asking about the requirements, and requested an application package. "Are you sure that's what you want, little lady?" asked the man, in a jovial manner. "You don't sound like a wrestler, to me." So I told him about Scotty.

When the large package arrived at school, I gave the material to Scotty, explaining that the first requirement for entrance to the wrestling school was a high school diploma. So he had to learn to read, in order to complete his education, and achieve his ultimate goal. And besides, I reminded him, he'd need to read his contracts, lawyer or no lawyer.

Then I bought a little paperback book (5 x 5) about wrestling, as further motivation for him to learn to read. It had pictures of all his favorite wrestlers on the left-hand pages, with biographical information about them, on the facing right-hand page. I told Scotty that he could have the book, when he could read it aloud to me. He was totally stoked, and learned by leaps and bounds.

> *Never give up on a dream just because*
> *of the time it will take to accomplish it.*
> —Unknown

NOW I ASK YOU . . .

Are you able to adapt to any given situation, by having a range of responses? How quickly can you adjust to change? Are you able to respond to circumstances in the most effective way?

UNEXPECTED INTRUSION

As a student teacher supervisor, I was observing a tenth grade student teacher at Poly High School, and she was freaking out! She had apparently taken the wooden sign that read: THERE CAN'T BE A CRISIS TODAY: MY SCHEDULE IS ALREADY FULL, to heart. Her lesson was in shambles. She had barely begun her presentation, when the door slammed wide open, and six policemen trooped in, with a drug dog. The dog, and its trainer, walked up and down each row, checking out the students and their belongings. Then half of the class went outside to speak with the officers. When they came back inside, the other half went outside to take their turns. At length, two of the boys were hand-cuffed, and taken away, never to be seen again. The student teacher was most concerned about not finishing her lesson plan. Not to worry. That was the perfect time for a *meaningful* discussion regarding drugs, as every single student was focused on the subject. It was a great Life Lesson for her: Be flexible.

Stay committed to your decisions,
but stay flexible in your approach.
—Tony Robbins

Notice that the stiffest tree is
most easily cracked,
while the bamboo or willow survives
by bending with the wind.
—Bruce Lee

A rigid mind is very sure,
but often wrong.
A flexible mind is generally unsure,
but often right.
—Vanda Scaravelli

NOW I ASK YOU . . .

Has the subject of death visited you, yet? Death had never touched me personally, until my mother died, and much later, after my father died. The longer I have lived, however, the more friends, family, neighbors, and pets have died. Then my husband, Wayne, experienced a long, lingering death. We had been together for 54 years! The subject of death seems to visit inner city children sooner than the rest of the young population. A case in point: Ambrosia (my third grade student) was inconsolable. Her father had been shot and killed on her front porch, by his girlfriend's boyfriend. "Blood all over *everywheres!*" she wailed.

GOOD INTENTIONS

I was concerned about Hallelujah, one of my best third graders, that year. He was clearly upset. Several times during the hour, he came up to me, to whisper his grief about his pet bird that had died that morning. Thinking to console him, I rummaged through stacks of my personal children's books, and finally found *The Tenth Good Things About Barney*, by Judith Viorst. The book is about a little boy whose cat had died. I thought it might help Hallelujah to see how another youngster had handled a similar loss.

Later in the day, after I had presented a lesson about continents, and everyone was involved in the map follow-up assignment, Hallelujah came up to me, and slammed the book on my desk. "Well, I read it," he announced, "but I didn't like it!"

"But, why?" I asked, thoroughly shaken, while mentally flogging myself for my good intentions.

"Because it was sad, and it's too much like what happened to me," he explained. "You know, Ms. Meinberg," he continued softly, "Everyone has been so *nice* to me today. And everyone has tried so hard to cheer me up. But, you know, I just can't be happy today, no matter what. It's just too soon!"

I marveled at the wisdom of this child. I don't like to recall how many years it took me to discover that time, does indeed, heal all wounds.

And, in the end,
It's not the years that count.
It's the life in your years.
—Abraham Lincoln

NOW I ASK YOU . . .

Have you ever wanted to fight for people, or causes that matter? Have you ever seen problems in your workplace that are hard to ignore? Did you have direct, credible information of some kind of general or specific wrongdoing? Did your concerns involve a violation of law, rule, or regulation? Or mismanagement, a waste of funds, abuse of authority, or a danger to public health or safety? Were you motivated by a strong sense of professional, civic, or ethical behavior? Were your concerns serious enough that you wanted to do something about it, but you didn't know how to do it? Or were you worried about the potential fallout? Know that many states now provide Whistleblowers Protection Laws.

WHISTLEBLOWER

I never heard the word *whistleblower*, when I wrote my book. Perhaps it wasn't coined back then. (Not so! I later found that the first U.S. Whistleblower Law was passed in 1777, and then a tighter law in 1978). At least, the word wasn't mentioned in normal conversations.

My motivation was pure (my Kumbaya moment). I felt a moral responsibility to try to right the wrongs that I was seeing in my local public school district. As a result, I wrote my first book, *Into the Hornet's Nest: An Incredible Look at Life in an Inner City School* (1993). My innocent desire was that if the public was aware of the educational problems therein, we could all work together to fix them. Wrong. I was shocked and dumbfounded at the huge and lasting response. It had a divisive impact that I couldn't have foreseen: the book clearly divided the district.

The teachers thought I was the best thing since sliced bread (they told me so!), whereas the administrators thought of me as a traitor. And I was shunned, because, as one administrator put it, "I had held out the district's dirty laundry for everyone to see." *So why didn't they clean the sheets?* It was not a pleasant experience. Some principals even tried to convince their teachers to ignore the book, by not reading it. So, of course, they all went out and bought it (Thank you very much!). I couldn't believe that there was an effort to ban my book.

After thirty-four years in my school district, I retired. Then I became a core adjunct professor at National University, in a different county. Over my 16 years there, I had three adult students, who had checked out of my class on the first day, because their parents had been administrators in the district, when the book had been published. (I did not know their parents, but the taint still stood. And I sincerely doubt that those three students had actually read the book). Even though I considered my efforts to be righteous, the repercussions persisted. Over the decades, various individuals have suggested that I reprint my first book, which is certainly validating. But, even though I have written 23 other books since then, and have been honored with numerous awards, every now and then, someone from the good ole days, will say, upon first meeting me, "Oh, you wrote *that* book!"

Nothing strengthens authority
so much as silence.
—Leonardo da Vinci

*Speaking up . . . is one of the hardest acts
a person can do. It requires immense courage
and sacrifice.*
—Jennifer Fraser

*Every country needs whistleblowers.
They are crucial to a healthy society.*
—Fuad Alakbarov

*Speak out, as the future
of the next generation
is relying on you.*
—Steven Magee

*If you see something that is
not right, not just,
you have a moral obligation
to do something about it.*
—John Lewis

NOW I ASK YOU . . .

Have you had any good luck/bad luck stories, or any bad luck/good luck events in your life? There are as many good luck/bad luck stories as there are bad luck/good luck stories. Some times your good luck is shining through for days. And then something happens, and you have a streak of rotten luck; where it appears that you can't catch a break; that you're going downhill, and the world is against you. Then later, the tables are turned, and you have a lucky turn of events. Keep an open mind. It's important to not jump to negative conclusions about how things are, and how you think they should be. Timing may be involved; it might be awhile before you can get the whole picture.

BAD LUCK/GOOD LUCK

I taught school in the daytime, and moonlighted as a waitress in the evenings and on weekends. On this particular night in question, the Bob's Big Boy restaurant was packed, as usual, so servers were working in a whirlwind of activity.

I came out of the swinging kitchen doors, holding a large tin tray aloft, carrying three bowls of hot bean soup. Unfortunately, the floor area in front of the doors had just been mopped, and no one had been notified. My foot slid on the slippery surface, and I couldn't maintain my balance. And I went flying. Down I went, with the metal tray and broken pottery crashing all over the place, as hot soup splashed all over me. My white blouse turned instantly brown. Ouch! I was knocked out momentarily.

Every person froze, as they witnessed the noise and the mess. It was one of those moments, I suppose, when everyone hoped someone else would do something about the situation. Talk about BAD luck.

Only one person leaped to my aid. Suddenly, as I opened my eyes, there was the most handsome man, staring into my face. He quickly introduced himself, saying that he worked in a hospital, and that he was there to help me. So he gingerly pulled me up into a sitting position, and then helped me stand. The onlookers clapped, as he slowly led me through the swinging kitchen doors, and into the break room (where only workers are supposed to be.) We talked for a while, and made a date, before I went back to work. That unusual chance meeting of Wayne, on the floor of the restaurant, turned into marriage. And Wayne and I were together for 54 years, before he died. Talk about GOOD luck!

Find growth from the "bad luck"
of meeting Mr. Wrong.
—Robert H. Hopcke

Aren't I lucky to have survived
so much bad luck.
—Ashleigh Brilliant

Sometimes bad luck
hits you like a Greek tragedy,
and it's not your own making
when you have a plane crash,
it's not your fault.
—Werner Herzog

If a black cat crosses in front of you,
it doesn't mean bad luck.
It means that the cat
is going somewhere.
—Unknown

Some luck lies in not getting
what you thought you wanted,
but getting what you have,
which once you have got it,
you may be smart enough to see
is what you would have wanted,
had you known.
—Garrison Keillor

At my age, "getting lucky" means
finding my car in the parking lot.
—Unknown

You never know what worse luck
your bad luck
has saved you from.
—Cormac McCathy

NOW I ASK YOU . . .

Have you ever had trouble making a decision? Did you ever have good reasons both pro and con? Did your decision change things in many ways? Were you happy with the results?

RED HOT

Well, Wayne and I had difficulty deciding whether to get married, or not. You see, we had both been married twice before, and who wants to go down in flames a third time (if it didn't last)? And I had a son, and he had three sons (which only added to the confusion). We were conflicted, to say the least. When I wanted to get married, he didn't. When he wanted to get married, I didn't. (Think: "*Is You Is Or Is You Ain't My Baby?*" by Louis Jordan and Billy Austin).) We seesawed back and forth for four years.

Finally, I was washing dishes one evening—with suds up to my elbows—and he asked me again. "Right!" I answered, in what I thought was a pessimistic tone, but he took the word literally, and was thrilled about what he perceived to be a positive response. Hmmmm. *Well, why not?* I thought. We'd certainly dilly-dallied about it long enough.

So, like a fairy tale in which it always takes three tries to get things right, we went for it. Since it was a work night, we thought we could just fly into Las Vegas, get married, and fly straight back. But we soon realized that we didn't have enough cash on hand (this was in the days before ATMs), and we couldn't access any bank funds at that hour. So we opted to drive. We figured it would take four hours to get there, and do the deed, and four hours to drive home. Then we could get back to work. We could do it in one night. We were determined.

The weather, however, did not cooperate. A slight drizzle turned into a relentless pounding rain. And gale force winds made it hard to keep Wayne's little Volkswagen on the mountain roads, but we persevered. When the radio news station stated that a huge fire had broken out at the Las Vegas Airport, we took it as a good sign that we had made the right decision. We listened to the excited updates throughout our drive to Las Vegas.

When we finally made it into town (much later than the four hours we had anticipated), we went straight to the Las Vegas City Hall. But the whole area was pitch black, without a light in sight. We couldn't understand it, because we knew that it was supposed to be open 24/7. Oddly, when Wayne ventured up the stairs, and leaned on the door, it opened. He briefly wandered around inside, and came back outside, saying that the place had a smoky smell. We both thought it weird that the front door was unlocked, and no one was there.

We found a phone booth, and (while getting drenched in the downpour), pawed through the telephone book to find the closest wedding chapel. We boogied on over there as fast as possible. The chapel's employees clearly wanted to marry us, but said that we had to have a license from the city hall first. We said that it wasn't open. They said that it was. We argued back and forth, until eventually a woman called the number for city hall. Of course, a recorded message stated that it was open 24 hours. We trekked from chapel to chapel, trying to get married, but everyone sent us back to city hall. Not one person believed our story. In desperation, we returned to city hall, to no avail, as the place was definitely closed. Finally exhausted, and looking and feeling like drowned rats, we decided to throw in the towel, and get a room for the night—to dry off, if nothing else.

After spending much time and effort trying to find a motel that not only had a vacancy, but fit our budget, we finally found a room. Wayne was asleep the minute his head hit the pillow, but I was too wired on adrenaline and worry, to do anything but agitate all night long. To top it all off, there was a refrigeration truck parked next to our outside wall, with its noisy motor running the entire night, which bothered me, no end.

So I got little sleep that night.

When Wayne awoke the following morning, we hurriedly called our jobs to say that we would be absent, and then trooped back to city hall. This time it was open for business. The night before, there had been a fire on the premises, just before we had arrived, which gutted the building. The inside walls were totally black, and because there were no windows to speak of, the only light was from flashlights and Coleman lanterns, reminding us of old WWII newsreels of the Blitz, or later episodes of the X-files. Workmen were crawling all around the area, shouting back and forth, trying to follow phone lines, electrical wires, and fire hoses, while pushing through a slew of couples, who were milling about, waiting to apply for marriage licenses. What a chaotic mess!

After waiting outside in the pouring rain (neither of us had umbrellas), for what seemed to be an eternity, we finally arrived at the counter. A clerk typed our information on the license, and demanded the fee. We had just

211

enough money to pay for the license, but not enough to get married, which was extra. *Who knew?* We thought it was a package deal, and we hadn't planned on staying overnight in a motel, so we were out of luck.

So out in the rain we went again, to find a place that would cash a check. We slogged from casino to casino, but since we weren't guests at their hotel, they wouldn't cash my check. We finally got lucky at a check-cashing establishment (I'd never heard of one, before). What an ordeal.

We were thrilled to arrive back at city hall, with money in hand, so we could quickly get married by a Justice-of-the-Peace, and be on our way home. We were directed to stand in a little closet-sized room, with bars on its small window (which gave one the impression that marriage was quite literally a prison sentence). A judge swooped in, beginning his speech before we were even in position.

"Do you, Sherry, take . . ." whereupon I interjected, "I do, but aren't we supposed to have witnesses?"

The judge agreed that this was so, as he rushed out the door, to grab two strangers walking down the hall, and dragged them in to be a part of our nuptials.

He began again: "Do you, Terry, take this woman . . ." at which point Wayne interrupted by saying, "My name isn't Terry."

"That's my brother's name," I added, helpfully.

"*What?*" the judge said. "But it says so, right here," as he dramatically flapped the marriage certificate around."

"It's wrong!" both Wayne and I said in unison, shaking our heads back and forth. The judge checked our driver's licenses, and ran from the room, leaving the four of us to stare blankly at each other.

212

Shortly thereafter, the judge flew back in with the corrected paper.

(It looks so phony: big eraser marks can be seen, over which the name WAYNE is superimposed, typed in darker print, obviously from a different typewriter.)

Finally—ta-dah!—we were officially married. As we walked out the door, my new husband announced in a voice that carried to the back walls, "I sure hope this marriage lasts, having just met you last night!" All talking ceased, as everyone in the place stared at me, with me being extremely embarrassed. Wayne clearly thought it was wildly funny. (For the 54 years we were together, he thought his off-beat goofy humor was hilarious. I beg to differ). What a way to start our marriage!

Although it was still raining, we wanted to eat breakfast before we left town. So we stopped at Caesar's Palace. While we were eating, we heard several sirens, but didn't think much about it (since loud, shrill, warning signals are common among the background noise of our big city everyday. However, because my seat was situated directly across from the restaurant door, I could see people intermittently hurrying past in the hallway. Then a stretcher went by, and then another. Finally, a stampede of people charged past. *What on earth?*

As we finished eating, it became clear that a wing of the hotel was on fire. When the female guests of those affected rooms were evacuated, they were sent to the women's room directly across the hall, as it contained a *huge* rest area. I went to use the facilities before leaving for our long trip home. I found the women's stories so compelling, that I stayed to hear them all.

One elderly lady reported that, as she was attempting

213

to get dressed, while pulling on her girdle, the firemen begged her—while pounding on her door—to vacate the premises. "Lady," they pleaded, "You can always buy new clothes, but you can't buy new skin!"

"Why, honey," she explained, "I couldn't let those sweet young men see me without my clothes on. Why I have a scar from here to here, and from here to here," she gestured, making a big X across her stomach.

A very young woman (who looked all of sixteen), was totally traumatized by her experience. Apparently, she and her husband had just eloped, and climbed into bed to begin their honeymoon, when the firemen axed through their door. The shock of it all! She couldn't stop crying. "There, there," I was saying, while patting her ineffectually. She was understandably inconsolable.

While I was engrossed in other stories, Wayne periodically sent in women to find me. They, too, got caught up in the various plots, and stayed. So other husbands, too, began sending in emissaries. Eventually, however, I reluctantly left, knowing I needed to get started with my own marriage. The important thing in all their stories was the fact that everyone was alive and well.

While driving back to California, we agreed that those three major fires—in such a short time-frame—were communications of a sort, symbols or omens of our future together: a sign that we were going to have one sizzling red hot marriage. And so it was!

Happily ever after is not a fairy tale.
It is a choice by you.
—Fawn Weaver

AFTERWORD: We were involved in seven fires, during our marriage, none of which were blamed on Mrs. O'Leary's cow.

NOW I ASK YOU . . .

Do you read mostly fiction, or nonfiction? Or a little of both? As a child, I read mostly fantasy novels, because I could use my imagination. As a result, I called nonfiction books boring. Yet, all of the books I have written are nonfiction (how did that happen?), but readers tell me that they *feel* like fiction. Go, figure.

ASTONISHED

When my *Autism ABC* book was newly published (2009), I sent copies to family, friends, neighbors, and anyone who had someone with autism in their families. Oddly, strangers began to send me money, along with notes to keep autism awareness moving. So I would check the addresses of those individuals, and would place copies of the book in their closest neighborhood libraries. One man, who lived in Vacaville (where the heck was that?) also sent me money. When I checked for the closest library, all I found were three county libraries for that whole major farming area. So I send two copies each, to all three libraries, and forgot all about it, in the hustle and bustle of daily life.

One day, a young neighbor from the next block (about third grade), brought a visitor from Northern California (about fifth grade), over to meet me. I have a number of unusual paintings, plants, books, and colorful stones, crystals, and geodes in each and every room, so children always find something that interests them. When they went into my library, the newcomer picked up a copy of

Autism ABC, and happily announced, "Oh, I read this book!"

And I slowly shook my head, saying, "No, I'm afraid not. This book has only been out for a short while, and it has only been placed locally. So you must have read a similar book." We ended up arguing with each other. She finally told me that she and her girlfriend had gone to the library together, and she had checked out this book, and both read it together—because her friend has a little brother with autism. Then she told me what the book was all about. The impact was immediate: I was flabbergasted, realizing that they had found the book in one of those Northern California county libraries. And I quickly apologized. Needless to say, I was thrilled with the news that *Autism ABC* was actually being put to good use!

Sports entertain for a night;
a book can touch the world for years and years.
—Albert Clayton Gaulden

NOW I ASK YOU . . .

And, speaking about those who are autistic, I observed the following experience the day after I typed the previous page.

ANGER ISSUES

I was standing next in line, at a mail service shop. I brought a new book to send to my great, great grandson. The clerk kept motioning me backwards, with her hand motions, although she didn't say anything to me. So I moved way back, and other customers lined up behind me. The clerk was dealing with a woman, and a very tall, good looking, teenager. It was clear that she had dealt with these two before. The clerk kept taking photos of the boy, but the camera was causing problems. It was taking far too long to suit the young man, and he was getting antsy about it. He kept clenching and unclenching his fists, and staring at the clerk in a menacing manner. At length, he barked, "I'm going to *punch* you in the face!" His mother (or guardian) softly said, "Be nice now. Be nice," as the customers behind me exchanged raised eyebrows and dark looks. The clerk was clearly rattled, as the line was getting longer, and the camera was not working properly. After they left, she fairly shouted, "I don't care if that guy *is* autistic, I'd punch him right back!" And the people behind me all agreed with her. She went on to say that the boy was known to have violent tendencies. All I could think about was my book, *Autism ABC*, and that I *didn't* address the issue of violence. *How could that be?* I thought. I know the clerk (named Barbi), and that she can take care of herself. Barbi acts like a marine, and has a haircut and attitude to match. She works long, ten-hour shifts, and doesn't like distractions. Whoa! I think that kid was lucky he left in one piece.

"I lose my temper, but it's all over in
a minute," said the student.
"So is the hydrogen bomb," I replied.
"But think of the damage it produces."
—George Sweeting

When you live with anger, you send it out
with every step and action you take.
—Suzan Hilton

The best remedy for a short temper is a long walk.
—Joseph Joubert

NOW I ASK YOU . . .

Have you ever been in an accident (car, taxi, truck, bus, boat, or plane)? Were you hurt? Was anyone else involved? Was anyone hospitalized? Who was at fault, or was it a mechanical issue? How did this experience make you feel? What were the repercussions?

HIGH FLYIN'

I was upset. After a two-week stay in the hospital, Jay, my six-month-old son, was scheduled to be released that morning. But his temperature had elevated *one* degree, and the doctor decided to keep him an extra day, just to be on the safe side. I couldn't believe that *one* little degree was the cause for such concern, and I was unhappy about it, in the extreme. In fact, I was as mad as a wet hen. I missed Jay.

Nursing heartsick feelings, I was driving home on the freeway at a very fast clip. (This was back in the days when there was plenty of room on the freeways.) The traffic was lighter than usual, and I was traveling a number of car lengths behind a large moving van, with an open back door. I wondered if the company boss knew that a motorboat was being hauled therein. I doubted it. I figured that the workers had already delivered furniture early that morning, and on the QT were moving the privately-owned motorboat, without their boss's knowledge or consent.

I no more than considered that scenario, when the boat took flight out of the moving van, sailing straight for me. I began swerving back and forth across the wide open lanes trying to avoid the boat, while honking my horn wildly, in an effort to alert the drivers behind me. The boat hit the pavement with sparks flying, as it bounced erratically, then skidded over to the middle divider, ricocheted off the cement wall, and then flew in an arc back across three lanes, for a perfect crash landing on the hood of my car. It then bounced over the top of my car, and proceeded on its way in bumper car fashion, back down the freeway, damaging vehicles left, right, and center.

Later, when the California Highway Patrol finally arrived (this was long before cell phones), there was a scraggly line of twelve or so vehicles stretched along the side of the freeway—with various amounts of damage—alongside the freaked out drivers. It took a long time for me to get home. Few people believed me when I said, "A boat fell on top of my car on the freeway."

I was so thankful, and relieved, that my son *hadn't* been released from the hospital that morning. The elevation of a mere one degree temperature may have saved his life. (This happened at a time before seatbelts and children's car seats were mandated, and Jay would most likely have violently landed on the floorboard, and rolled around, from pillar to post).

I have often wondered what happened to the two workers that were driving the van (if anything). Did they lose their jobs? Did they have to pay restitution? Did the insurance cover all of the vehicles? And, I have pondered, as well, about just how much damage was caused, by not taking the time to tie down the boat, or simply close the moving van's backdoor.

All is not necessarily what it seems to be
at first blush,
and that the significance of what occurs,
may only be obvious later on.
—Robert H. Hopcke

Sometimes being in a car accident
happens to remind you of
everything and everyone
we are grateful for.
—Jimmy Hanaie

Accidents happen.
But what is important is our reaction.
—Jimmy Hanaie

In survey after survey, people report that the greatest
danger they face are in this order: terrorist attacks, plane
crashes, and nuclear accidents. This despite the fact that
these three combined have killed fewer people in the
past half-century than car accidents do in a given year.
—Will Self

NOW I ASK YOU . . .

Have you ever broken a rule or a law unwittingly? (Surely, you have jaywalked in your life. It was against the law, up until January 1st, 2023, when the Freedom to Walk Act was passed by California's Governor Garin Newsom). Have you ever broken a rule or law deliberately? Did you give it much thought, or were you worried? (Close to my house, there is a posted traffic sign, saying No Right Turn on Red, which half the neighborhood ignores). If caught, were you given a chance to explain yourself? How did you feel about the situation?

DEAD RATS

As I passed by the playground, the pupil's voices had changed from a low roar to the high-pitched squeal of delighted children running wild. Uh-oh. Something's a foot. I 180ed the grounds like a cop, looking for the telltale signs of a crime in progress: the youngsters could be playing just a simple game of hide and seek, or a more serious one of hit and run, or the dreaded search and destroy.

Hordes of students—of all ages—were running and screaming in mock terror, while a little blond second grader chased them all around the playground. *What in the world?* I thought, as I stood transfixed, watching the noisy demonstration. I couldn't figure out why the little girl was holding her hand in front of her in such an awkward position, as she merrily charged after everyone.

"Dead rats! Dead rats!" the pupils obligingly shouted out to me—on cue—as they gaily galloped by, happily pointing and gesturing behind them. They thundered past in vast circles. Then I spied a long thin tail hanging out of her hand—oh, boy—as I motioned the little girl over.

"What do you have in your hand?" I softly asked, as a curious crowd of onlookers gathered around.

"Just Silky," she said, as she proudly showed me a small live mouse.

"Whatever made you bring Silky *here*?" I further questioned her.

"My class is going on a field trip to the zoo today," she explained, and I wanted to show Silky the animals." Ah, I decided, an act of love, not willful disobedience.

After I explained the field trip rules ("Sorry, no pets allowed!"), I sent her to the kindergarten room that houses a vast supply of critters, to see it they could provide Silky with a safe habitat for the day.

The little unremembered
acts of kindness and love
are the best parts of a person's life.
—William Wordsworth

There are no great acts,
only small acts
done with great love.
—Mother Teresa

We can judge the heart of a man
by his treatment of animals.
—Immanual Kant

See a world where all animals—
large and small, courageous and timid,
wild and domesticated, strong and weak—
are treated as we ourselves
want to be treated.
—The Intenders of the Highest Good

The love for all living creatures
is the most noble attribute of man.
—Charles Darwin

Some people talk to animals.
Not many listen though.
That's the problem.
—A.A. Milne

NOW I ASK YOU . . .

Have you ever had one of those days, when every thing goes haywire? Days where you felt you were in deep doo-doo? Days in which you would like to never, ever, remember?

HO, HO, HO

Well, I had one of those days, on Christmas Eve, no less. Who would have thought that *anything* would go awry? (My husband had died two years earlier, and our adult children live in different states, so his family always invites me to their family functions.) Just as Laureen (his niece) was to drive me to her daughter's party, a long, long ways away, Jack, her little dog that was seemingly on his last legs, was sick. And shit BIG TIME, in my living room, hall, library, the walk through, and the den. He was desperately trying to get to the outside den door, where he always used the back grass to do his business. You wouldn't believe that his little body could hold that much. What a mess! Eek! So there we were, in all our Christmas finery, cleaning up fecal matter all over the carpet throughout the house. Now Laureen was a nurse for 38 years, so this experience didn't bother her in the least, like it did me. I was unaccustomed to such (Dookey! Poo-poo, Ka-ka, Shit!). At length, as we were finally finished and ready to go, I went out onto the patio, before I realized that I had walked right through another trail of crap! So then we had to not only clean the cement patio, but my shoes, as well. (The soles of which had a deep, intricate design, which made it hard to remove the waste matter).

We finally got to the party, and everyone was enjoying the festivities (about 30-some friends, neighbors, and family members). After socializing and eating, we all moved into the large living room, for the gift exchange. So what did I receive? The only gift gag of the evening: a big monthly calendar of dogs *shitting!* (Have you ever heard of such a thing? Who knew there would be buyers for such?) Laureen and I looked across the room at each other, as neither of us could believe it, since we'd spent our earlier hours taking care of #2. Nor had we shared our earlier experience with everyone. It didn't seem to be the time or place to do so. I left the calendar there (I think I was the only person who didn't look at the pictures). The crowd of twenty and early thirty-year-olds though, thought it was hysterical. Ugh! (They all had dogs, so they were accustomed to such, I imagine).

Later, as an aside, to change the subject, I asked Laureen who the older man was, who came late to the party and left early. I noticed that everyone had greeted him with lukewarm hugs, with very few smiles or talking involved, and he spent most of his time playing with the young children (the 1, 2, and 3-year-olds). With a stoic look on her face, Laureen said that he was her ex-husband, and they had been divorced for **29** years! She did not appear to be a happy camper around him. It seems that he would pop up every now and then, at family functions. A third negative experience happened (which will forever remain unsaid), after most had left the party, so I couldn't wait to get home. It was simply a *shitty* day, one that I never want to repeat.

The family partiers went back to the same house on Christmas morning (even though they had hangovers, and had to drive so far away), to exchange their personal gifts. But I stayed at home, with Laureen's cat and dog. And I was happy to do so. Then, the very next day, I bought two new pairs of shoes, just in case.

Now you really have to think about the incredible odds, of having those two experiences happen on the same day. They were a unique, unrepeatable, and a once-in-a-lifetime experience. And it is well-known that the more improbable the synchronistic event, the more significant the meaning. So what was the Universe trying to tell me?

I have been trying to figure out the personal meaning involved in this experience. And I have come to the conclusion that because I was one of the two oldest persons there (both Laureen's mother and I were 83 years old), and I don't drink, which meant that I had a tad more serious bent than all the other party-goers; that the personal message to me was that I need to loosen up, relax, and laugh more; that at this late stage of my life, I need to get past my *prudish* ways (in speech, conduct, and dress) and *squeamishness* (unpleasant images or words, as in blood, poop, gore, etc.). Yikes! A tall order, but I am working on it.

Shit happens
when you're busy
making other plans.
—Unknown

NOW I ASK YOU . . .

Have you ever visited a psychic? Were you curious, perplexed, or indifferent? How did you *feel* about the reading? Did you learn anything?

PSYCHIC

I am somewhat psychic myself. I have been, all my life. As a result, I have always been interested in psychic phenomenon—the whole nine yards. You name it, I was passionate about it (ESP, telepathy, precognition, clairvoyance, psychometry, handwriting analysis, dreams, etc.). I read everything I could about each subject, and about psychic authors, some I believed and some I didn't. And I went to various psychic fairs, and private psychics. Whenever I went to tarot card readers, I could actually read the cards upside down, and would know when someone was new at it, or faking it. Friends would come to me asking for a Palm reading or handwriting analysis. I always told everyone that I was a novice at whatever they asked for. And we'd laugh a lot, during the sessions. Until, that is, the counselor at my school wanted info about her boyfriend. She gave me a letter he had sent to her, asking for a handwriting analysis, and whatever else came to mind. But it was all gloom and doom. I recognized that he knocked her around (she said she fell down the porch steps, but I knew differently). So I stopped practicing on people, although I did have a spoon-bending party one time. That was still fun. And I continued to give lectures on various psychic topics, whenever such groups asked me. I was always happy to share new info with others.

Throughout the years, I have experienced a number of psychic situations. I only shared them with a few close friends; even so, the word got around. For instance, when my son was in high school, he and three other members of the football team, were in my car. I was driving down Los Alamitos Blvd./Seal Beach Blvd., when a squad car pulled out in *front* of me. And, I'm moaning, "Oh, no! Oh, no!" The boys naturally wanted to know what I was upset about. "He is going to give me a ticket!" I explained. They all started laughing, trying to persuade me to not worry about it. Naturally, I didn't want to get a ticket, so when we got to the stop light at Pacific Coast Highway, I went straight across into the town of Seal Beach, instead of turning to the left, in the same direction the police car went. So, to waste time, I drove up along the beach, and finally turned onto Main Street, and drove back to PCH. I thought plenty of time had passed, and we were okay to complete our journey. So we're driving down PCH, past the beach (which used to be called Tin Can Alley when I was a child), and there, sitting on the side of the highway was the same police car. "Oh, no!" I complained, while we passed, as the cruiser pulled back onto the road. So now it was behind us. I drove a little while longer, and then pulled over, and they drove on by, over a tall hump in the road, so we couldn't see them anymore. We all shared a sigh of relief. Then, after waiting awhile, and not wanting to see the police again, I made a U-turn, and we were headed back the way we came. There were no other cars on the road, either going or coming. We were all by our lonesome. A few minutes thereafter, the squad car came back over the hill, and red-lighted me. I received a ticket for making a U-turn. Apparently, one had to drive all the way into the next town—Sunset Beach—before turning around at the 2nd stop light. *Can you believe?*

This experience, of course, only added to my reputation as a psychic. That particular incident ran swiftly through the high school rumor mill, as the four boys told their football teammates, who told their girlfriends, who told *their* girlfriends, and such.

A later psychic incident happened, when my mother died. She came back for a visit, and showed herself to my father, my brother, and myself, all in the same evening. She was an angry sight to behold. And we all lived elsewhere. My brother called me from Oregon, and we both realized that we had the same scary experience. I lived in Signal Hill, and our Dad lived in Long Beach. Now, he had the mind of a scientist, and didn't believe in such nonsense, and freaked out to the point that he didn't sleep at night for several weeks, leaving all the lights on. He wouldn't discuss his experience, because he didn't want to believe it. We all decided that Mother was *angry* that she died so young (she was only 52 when she passed). All three of us were stunned—kind of rooted to the spot—and didn't really remember the bulk of what she was yelling about. At a later date, she blamed it on the drugs the doctors had given her, but that doesn't seem right. *Who knows?* But that became a subject I hadn't followed before: apparitional experiences (ghosts, spectral evidence, teleportation, and hauntings). It is one thing to read about such things, and quite another to actually experience them.

A psychic is a person
who knows without being told;
who learns without being taught;
who sees without being shown.
—Michael Bassey Johnson

NOW I ASK YOU . . .

Have you ever found an interest or a skill that you didn't know you had? Were you surprised, happy, stunned, or shocked?

HYPNOSIS

In my early thirties, I became enamored with the study of hypnosis. And John (around my age) was practicing to become a hypnotist. He was able to put me under, easily. So I would go to his two friends' apartment, and he would practice on me. It got to the point that, during one summer, there would be a few people in the room when he would put me under. I was told that they were his buddies' friends, and didn't give it another thought. But every time I would come out of a trance, there would be more people in the room: 8, 10, 14, or so. I thought it odd, but I was always trying to clear my head afterward (since I had been basically deep asleep), and would rush out, to drive home to my family. Come to find out, the room was soon crowded with people, wall-to-wall, standing room only, because I was giving messages to those in the room. I was a *clairvoyant*, and didn't even know it! Then it all made sense to me, as to why the crowd kept getting larger each evening. Word was getting around. I started getting huge headaches each day, and later found out that one shouldn't be hypnotized that many days in a row. But what did I know? It was all new to me. Then I started getting really uneasy, thinking that at some point, someone would surely recognize me, and I might lose my teaching job. And I *loved* teaching. Then those three guys wanted to start a new *religion* around me. *Say what?* (At that point, I think they were thinking of me as a money-making machine.) They started talking to each other about the possibility, like I wasn't even there. They were *serious!* They had even made a special fancy chair for me to sit in, as I gave readings. I couldn't believe it! I don't know what I had been saying to all those people, but I'm pretty sure that John made the suggestion each night, that I wasn't to remember anything I had said. In any case, I didn't want to be a part of a new religion. I just wanted to teach! So I stopped meeting with those guys immediately.

> *The state of hypnosis is actually an ordinary*
> *human experience. It is like just before*
> *falling asleep, getting lost in thought,*
> *music, or even a movie.*
> —Unknown

NOW I ASK YOU . . .

White lies are known to be harmless or trivial, mostly to avoid hurting one's feelings or to avoid small troubles. In this case, I needed to escape a potentially bad situation. Some people say they have never told a white lie. I don't believe it. Have you ever told any white lies? I bet you have. Have you ever seen an ugly baby, and said, "What a cutie!"?

WHITE LIE

Many years thereafter, I suddenly received a constant flow of mental communications from John (the hypnotist). I would wake up in the morning, and would get the message to connect. This went on throughout the day, for many days, and I finally set out to find him, to stop his nonstop messages, and to hear what was so important. I did not know his last name, nor did he of mine, nor did I remember the names of his two friends. So, I just got in my car, and started driving.

(This is something that I used to do in my 20s and early 30s, and it flat-out scares me senseless, now. I would hear that there was a psychic lecture in some other city, or a specific person was giving a speech somewhere, and I would set out to find the place. I would drive the freeway to other cities, until I thought I had gone too far, and get off the freeway, and wander around, and suddenly, there the site would be.)

So, I stopped on a street that I thought John might live on, and slowly drove until I saw a bunch of apartment buildings. There was a huge square, grassy area, in front of the side of one of the buildings that had a side door. I knocked on the door, and—wonder of wonders!—a woman opened the door. I asked if she knew a man named John, who might live in any of the surrounding apartments. She said that her husband's name was John. "Really?" (You could have knocked me over with a feather.) "Is he interested in hypnosis?" "Yes, he is," she said. "Why do you ask?"

"My name is Sherry, and John used to practice various hypnosis methods of putting me under," I explained. And she got all excited. And said that he had been mentally reaching out to me. "Yes, I received his messages, and wondered what was so important," I replied. She was all excited, knowing that he had actually gotten in touch with me. Then her attitude completely changed, as she took a good look at me. And stared.

"But you're beautiful," she said. "You're *beautiful!*" she echoed. (*Say what?* I wasn't used to anyone saying that to me.) Then, in a flat, grim, *ugly* tone, she repeated herself again, "You're beautiful!" Uh, what does one say to that? (I could imagine what was going on in her head, all those hours John and I spent together, and didn't like the implication, as I began to backtrack.) I didn't want to become embroiled in a family argument. "Please tell John, that I received his messages, but that I have no time to dabble in hypnosis anymore, as I have other fish to fry. Thank you," as I made a hasty retreat. (Which was a big, fat white lie, because I am still interested in hypnosis, but I couldn't think of anything else to say.)

Mama says a little white lie
Never hurt nobody.
—Forrest Gump

If I only had three words of advice,
they would be, Tell the Truth.
If I got three more words,
I'd add, All the Time.
—Randy Pausch

I suppose everyone tells little white lies,
quite often they're necessary to make someone
feel better or prevent feelings
from being hurt.
Whoppers? No, that's dangerous
and they'll boomerang.
—Richard Chamberlain

Sometimes, truth causes pain and suffering.
At such times, silence is preferred.
In fact, there may be times
when a white lie could actually lead
to a good outcome.
—Amish Tripathi

But little white lies
here and there
is human nature.
—Lucy Hale

BIG or small, lies is lies.
—Unknown

NOW I ASK YOU . . .

Have you ever experienced an event in which people saw things differently? Did you focus your attention on what you considered important, and were surprised to find someone focusing on something else entirely? Was the emotional intensity different?

WHITE CORAL BELLS

Francis enrolled as a third grader late in the year. She did the work expected of her, and took part in daily activities in a robot-like way, with no emotion involved, but she wouldn't speak. She had not uttered a word to anyone, not even me. She and her beloved sister had recently been separated, taken away from abusive parents, and placed in separate foster homes. Francis was having a hard time adjusting, to the loss of her total family, as well as a new family, a new home, a new neighborhood, a new school, a new teacher, and new classmates. She followed directions well, making no trouble for anyone, but took part in school activities with all the joy of a wind-up toy. She had definitely been traumatized by her experience. Since we didn't know what would work, we did what we could, feeling our way, by guess and by golly. The class tried new things to interest her every day, hoping to find the combination that would open Francis like a safety-deposit box, to no avail. Her elected mutism remained intact. Finally, after three weeks, she became one with the group—during music, of all things. I was teaching the class to sing a two-part melody, titled, "White Coral Bells." We were doing a good job of harmonizing, when her voice joined ours in song. It was immediately apparent to all. I could see the youngsters bright eyes and matching smiles, as they continued to happily sing. Francis had finally decided to become a full-fledged member of our class family. She later confided, shyly and hesitantly, that her big sister used to sing that song, and it reminded her of the good times they had shared together. We made it a point to sing it often.

We were all thrilled with this turn of events. My principal, however, sent me a message. It simply said that two-part harmony was scheduled for fifth graders only.

Behind every favorite song
there is a story.
—Meggan Roxanne

NOW I ASK YOU . . .

Have you ever known of a neighborhood problem that got out of hand, and carried onto the local school? Were you ever involved in such? This happens frequently in inner city schools (high-poverty, with a host of associated conditions). One can't run and hide, because everyone knows where to find you on a school day. But a fight is usually carried out before the school day begins, or after it ends.

HELP!

As usual, I led my students into the third grade building. We walked along in an orderly, quiet, single-file line. I unlocked the hall door, and entered the classroom, but no one followed me. I dashed back into the hall, as I heard an unfamiliar voice, shouting, "I'm gonna kick yo' candyass, you little fucker!" I was just in time to see Lolo, as he launched, throwing a carefully aimed haymaker—POW!— connecting with the mouth of a fourth grader. *Crunch!* A tooth fell out. Suddenly, blood was gushing everywhere, as the bully emitted an ear-shattering scream.

The class went bonkers, scurrying around, looking for the tooth, while trying to stay out of the blood. Doors flew open up and down the hall, as other children yelled for details, and ran to join the crowd.

"Go inside, and occupy yourselves with a book, or something!" I yelled, as I ordered my students into the classroom, and shouted to a neighborly teacher to hold the fort. Demanding that Lolo follow me, I half-carried the howling victim to the nurse. The boy was quickly spirited away to the hospital, where he received several stitches.

Lolo was not a trouble-maker; not a fighter. He was a popular, easygoing kid. It turned out that the fourth grader had come *looking* for Lolo, to settle a disagreement that had started in the neighborhood the night before. Things were settled all right. And Lolo had the wisdom to stake his rep on that one lucky punch. No one ever bothered him again.

My dad used to always tell me
that if they challenge you to an after-school fight
tell them you won't wait—
you can kick their ass right now!
—Cameron Diaz

NOW I ASK YOU . . .

Can we agree that English is the hardest language to learn? It has plenty of rules, but do you always follow them? If you do follow the rules, do you have a difficult time listening to those who are grammatically challenged (like newscasters and street reporters)? Do you cringe upon hearing dialog that is unnatural, but sounds right and communicates meaning? I always console myself by saying that the errors I'm hearing are the result of family tradition, or learning a second or third language, or are using the latest words coined (from science, technology, business, finance, and pop culture).

SLANG

While supervising a student teacher at Poly High School, three tenth grade boys liked the shoes I was wearing. One excitedly proclaimed, "Them shoes is vicious!" Another boy expressed the same sentiment in a different way: "Her kicks is sick!" The last shouted them to be "Wicked!" I smiled, and thanked them for the compliments, hoping that the student teacher would later discuss grammar issues, as well as the time and place to use slang language (a type of informal language, that is more common in speech than in writing, and is often restricted to a particular context or group of people.)

For last year's words
belong to last year's language,
And next year's words
await another voice.
—T.S. Eliot

Usage is the only test.
I prefer a phrase that is easy
and unaffected
to a phrase that is grammatical.
—Somerset Maugham

"OMG! Did you hear that Jessica ghosted Charlie?"

"Dude! The show last night was killer! You missed out!"

NOW I ASK YOU . . .

Surely you know what cussing is. Do you use it? Sparingly, or every day in every way? There are some people who can't talk without swearing. Whether you call it potty mouths, toilet mouths, or foul mouths, swearing and cursing are modes of speech, existing in all languages. And it is a fact that one hears more swear words in the inner city schools, than on television!

PROFANITY

The story, *Tough Eddie*, by Elizabeth Winthrop, is about a brave little kindergarten boy who also secretly played with his very own dollhouse. The second graders all had the same reaction to the tale, but expressed themselves differently, as they yelled in unison:

"Faggot!"

"Pervert!"

"Nerd!"

"Pussy!"

"Queer!"

"Fruit!"

Later on in the year, the class had the same response to Charlotte Zolotow's *William's Doll*. These children definitely made their gender choice early on, and weren't deviating from it one whit. Of course, now that action figures for boys are all the rage, I'm unsure if the response would be the same.

One Monday, a third grade boy was in trouble for using foul language. He regretted using such words, saying, "I apologize! I apologize! I'm a good boy, I'm not a cusser."

His teacher sweetly said, "I know you aren't," and that was the end of it. On Friday, however, the boy didn't receive a star for a half-hour of work, and loudly expressed his displeasure: "This is *bullshit!*"

"Ms. Meinberg! He called me the 'A' word! The 'A' word!" Francisco shrieked, as he started ripping off his jacket in preparation for battle. "He called me an American! I'm a *Mex-ican!*"

True, profanity is mostly the voice of the ignorant and the verbally challenged. Although some see it as a game, as to how many fuckity fucks they can use in each sentence. In some groups, such as construction workers, for instance, nobody pays attention to each other, unless they swear every other word. But swearing is also what children learn at home; the way in which their families communicate.

Upon hearing the assignment, a third grader exclaimed, "You gotta be fuckin' kiddin' me!" As another helpfully explained his buddy's response: "He don' give a shit."

Ricardo's frustration was even lower than usual. "Jesus Christ!" he shrieked, as he stomped down the aisle to the pencil sharpener.

"Hold it right there!" I yelled from across the room. "Wait just a minute," as I launched into an obligatory discussion about the proper words for seven-year-olds to use in a classroom.

He looked at me with round, disbelieving eyes, and in all seriousness, explained: "Ms. Meinberg, I don't think you understood me. All I said was 'Jesus Christ.'" Indeed.

Under certain circumstances,
urgent circumstances,
desperate circumstances,
profanity provides a relief
denied even to prayer.
—Mark Twain

GRAMMAR
POLICE
To Correct and To Serve
—Tee-Shirt

*Granted, it takes emotional courage to be honest in print. Heartfelt, go-for-broke truth-telling can be risky, scary, difficult, and hard to do. Experts tell us that dialog shouldn't all sound the same. And yet, when I wrote about those inner city children with a Black pop culture vocabulary, or a Southern dialect, or the poor with little learning, I was accused of being racist. You can't please everyone.

NOW ASK YOU . . .

Have you ever had a sub-par teacher that was just going through the motions? One who only did the bare minimum? One who was boring, forgetful, and inattentive? One who never answered questions? One who showed favoritism, while publically humiliating another student? Of course you have, and it puts the best teachers under the same dark cloud, unfortunately.

KINDERGARTEN TEACHER

My third grade classroom's set of windows looked out upon the kindergarten playground, and one of the kindergarten classrooms. That teacher often seemed to be in trouble, for one infraction or another. The principal went down to talk with her, and found all the children asleep on the rug, and she was asleep at her desk. He woke her up, and gestured for her to follow him outside, so the youngsters would not hear what he had to say to her. "This is a safety issue!" he bellowed, and so forth and so on. At length, he finally finished with "You cannot *sleep* on the job! Ever!" In the Teachers' Lounge, she often loudly complained about how her students never remembered anything she taught the day before. This was her constant grievance. Later, on another day, she dropped something on the floor, and yelled, *"God dammit!"* Well, her students all heard her, and when they went home, every single one of them *remembered* what she said, and told their parents, neighbors, and friends. The teacher had to expect some consequence for her actions, but she was not prepared for the scene that awaited her. The next morning, when the teacher opened her classroom door, she was met with an angry mob of adults (picture pitchforks and torches), with some waving signs, that read, SHE'S GOT TO GO!, and such. Some grandmothers took a fire and brimstone approach, yelling at her, saying "You took our Father's name in vain!" and "You're going to Hell!" They were all riled up, and extremely loud. Then the rather large group crowded into the principal's office to lodge their complaints, and then went downtown to the Board of Education, to chat with the Superintendent of Schools. Yikes! Then, if that weren't enough, the next time the principal went into her classroom, she had her bottom desk drawer open, and he saw a bottle of Vodka therein. That was the last straw! She was never seen again, as her husband instantly checked her into a rehabilitation center for a lengthy stay.

A good example is the best sermon.
—Benjamin Franklin

A good example has twice the value
of good advice.
—Albert Schweitzer

Example is not the main thing
in influencing others.
It is the only thing.
—Albert Schweitzer

What you do
has far greater impact
than what you say.
—Stephen Covey

We learn so much
from how teachers behave—
so much more than
what they actually teach
us in the classroom.
—Unknown

Children seldom misquote.
In fact, they usually repeat
word for word
what you shouldn't have said.
—Unknown

If you set a good example,
you need not worry about setting rules.
—Lee Iacocca

NOW I ASK YOU . . .

Do you like your given name? Does it suit you? Or do you wish you had another more expressive name? Have you ever considered changing it? I have known three Barbie's, none of whom match a Barbie doll, in any way, shape, or attitude. None liked their name, feeling that it is a great burden to carry.

NAME CHANGE

A new student from another country was admitted to my inner city third grade classroom. Her name was Bich, which was a common name in that country. You can imagine the class response, when she was introduced to us by the office clerk. Recognizing many future problems for her regarding her name, the counselor spoke to her father, and explained that she needed a different name, in order to save her reputation. She was called Ellen, thereafter.

My friend absolutely hated her given name, and refused to tell anyone what it was. She only whispered it once to me, and I wasn't sure what she said, as she mumbled it so fast (something on the order of Hildegard), but she refused to repeat it. Once was enough. When she was a youngster, and for years thereafter, she idolized a high school girl, by the name of Pat Joseph—who was beautiful, smart, and talented. She wanted to be just like Pat Joseph.

When my friend was in kindergarten, her grandfather always walked her to school. He affectionately called her Pet, but the children misheard him, thinking that he called her Pat, so that's what everyone called her. As such, she was known as Pat to everyone throughout her school years.

After graduating from high school, and moving to California, she became a hairdresser in Long Beach, working for the prestigious Bob Joseph Salon. In time, she married her boss, and she became known as Pat Joseph—who was beautiful, smart, and talented. Talk about obtaining a long-term private goal!

I'm not my name. My name is something I wear,
like a shirt. It gets worn. I outgrow it, and
I change it.
—Jerry Spinelli

Do you have an unassuming, common name, such as Mary Smith, Bob Jones, or just an average Joe? Or might you have a given name that appears to exude status or wealth (think: Thurston Howell the Third in *Gilligan's Island*)? I loved my name, until I later found so many younger girls were also named Sherry. I wanted to be different.

UNUSUAL NAMES

I charged into the office of my new school, to inform the principal that Ali Baba was missing. Mr. Biggs snapped his desk drawer shut with enough force to make a sound like a pistol shot. Clearly, he did not like to be inconvenienced by intrusions. "I don't have time for such foolish nonsense!" he shouted. "Ali Baba, indeed!" he snorted, fanning his hand in the air to motion me out. I had to convince him that I did have an Ali Baba registered in my class, and that, although he had been present earlier in the morning, he had yet to return from recess. I was wounded that Mr. Biggs seemed to have such a low opinion of teachers' dedication to duty, and nursed a bundle of injured feelings all day. I am not, and have never been, a practical joker.

Inner city school populations have given names that are much more unusual than that of most other schools. My student roll sheets often looked like the names on a Burlesque marquee: Lovette, Sparkle, Dazle, Treasure, Velvet, Tiara, Princess, Mahogany, Cocoa, Cinnamon, Caramel, Ambrosia, Destiny, Liberty, Velvet, and so forth. Also, Emerald, Ruby, Diamond, Pearl, Jewel, and Star were thrown into the mix. And I was startled to find that Riley, Murphy, and Emerson were gender neutral names.

Vendetta's mother told me that she had so named her daughter because that was the most beautiful word she had ever heard. I refrained from telling her what it meant.

Cassandra's mother also didn't know what that name implied. Greek: She who ensnares or enflames men. Or, in a mythological sense: Knowing the future, but cursed with the fate of not being believed.

Another mythical name was that of Pandora, whose mother obviously didn't know the story: Out of curiosity, Pandora—who was considered to have a *deceitful, feminine* nature—opened a chest (or a jar, or urn, depending on the version), which released all the evils of mankind, (plagues, famines, diseases, etc.) leaving Hope trapped inside, when she quickly closed the lid.

So, it seems that all of the problems in the ancient world were the cause of women. Hmmmm.

I had been conversing with a group of teachers (and a few of their friends), about the unusual names of our students, when I mentioned that one of my boys was named Chili. It turned out that one of the women in the group was named Chili (her given name, not a nickname). Gulp! We became fast friends thereafter, thank goodness. (Cue: "*The Name Game*," by Shirley Ellis.)

My third grade boy's names were also distinctive: Prince, Beethoven, Chili, Zero, Hallelujah, Yono, Lolo, Tiger, and so on. One third grade Samoan was unhappy to be named Sandy, because in his culture, given names sometimes pertained to the geography of their conception or births. As such, he didn't think his name was "manly" enough. I've wondered if he still thought that his name wasn't bold or powerful, given the strength of Hurricane Sandy (2012) that caused so much damage.

> *Me, I'm still waitin' for Hurricane Ed.*
> *Old Ed wouldn't hurt ya, would he?*
> *Sounds kinda friendly.*
> *"Hell no, we ain't evacuatin."*
> *Ed's comin'!"*
> —George Carlin

> *Names have power like magic spells.*
> —Cinderella, 2015

> *In order to be irreplaceable*
> *one must always be different.*
> —Coco Chanel

> *It's funny how my name has always*
> *been such a big deal.*
> *When I was growing up, my family was always moving.*
> *I had to meet new people all the time. And they'd laugh.*
> —Calista Flockhart

NOW I ASK YOU . . .

Do you have a nickname? If so, do you like your nickname? Do any members of your family or your friends have nicknames? Monikers are usually related to one's interests, personality, or physical appearance. But there are other reasons for nicknames, that substitute for proper names. And they have staying power.

NICKNAMES

During the turmoil of my first day as a third grade teacher, at an inner city school, the hall door noisily flew open, to reveal my first white student. For maybe about fifteen seconds, everybody in the room froze like players in a macabre tableau. I immediately focused on the newcomer's eyes, as the banjo music from the movie *Deliverance* eerily twanged through my mind, growing louder and louder as he moved ever closer to me. He stomped over to where I stood, swung his fist at my nose, and shouted, "I don't like school, and you can't make me!" Then he bolted through the outside door, slamming it for emphasis. He was a good way down the street, and still going full steam, before I made it to the door to yell at him. And, by the time my hollering was through, he was long gone. Needless to say, the noise level in the room rose several decibels.

I couldn't believe that I hadn't even been given a chance to say "Hi!" or "Good Morning," or "Welcome to Room 14." I couldn't believe that I still had a nose on my face. If I had bowed my head just a fraction of an inch . . . Oh well, one can't afford to dwell on the negative. None of the other students looked real happy to be there either, but at least no one else bailed.

The office staff did not seem surprised that I had a missing runaway. And although I did not know his name, they did. Suffice it to say that Randy ran away six times that day! The last time they dragged him back to school, he didn't have his shoes on, so they had to send him home. (He wasn't called RUNAWAY RANDY for nothing.)

Many young inner city students use more swear words than adults. But Rodney, a third grader, had such a tendency to lash out with verbal abuse, that his foul language had almost lost its shock value. His classmates learned early on to tune him out. However, when he clashed with a third grade teacher while on yard duty, she was having none of his nonsense, and asked several men to remove him from the playground. As Rodney was being carted off, kicking and bucking, he finally crossed over the threshold into truly inappropriate behavior, when he screamed at the rather buxom teacher, "Mrs. Hernandez! Mrs. Hernandez! Next time I see you, I'm gonna *rip your tits off!*" That instantly got everyone's attention, and imagination, as well. He was immediately dubbed, RODNEY THE RIPPER, and the nickname stuck like flypaper, much to the teacher's chagrin.

One tall, beautiful third grade girl in my class, was dubbed THE MOUTH, schoolwide, because she knew the most rude swear words, and loudly spewed them whenever riled. She would get in someone's face, and stand in their space, yelling vile words like machine-gun fire, while pointing and gesturing with her finger at the hapless victim. She was a sight to behold. I was always in awe of her loud delivery, as she never used the same words twice. She was very clever. One day, she was furious with her reading teacher, and launched a scathing verbal attack, in no uncertain terms, ending with, "And you is a tight-assed Honky *Bitch!*" My reading class was right across the hall, so we heard it all, and everyone was happy in their hearts that they weren't on the bad side of such treatment. I was shocked that I wasn't shocked by her language! She slammed the classroom door shut, then slammed the hall door shut, ran across the grass, and into the office, and shouted obscenities at the secretaries, then opened the principal's door, calling him names, and finally ran on home. The next day she sent a note with her little brother, to give to the principal. She apologized for her rude behavior, and suspended herself for the day. Now that's what I call taking charge of a situation.

When my husband, Wayne, was a teenager, tricked out cars and car clubs were all the rage in high school. And a friend of his placed all of his old baseball and bowling trophies in the front of his car (a '55 lowered Chevy, with high-gloss black paint and a cherry-red interior). He knelt in front of it, and had a photograph taken of the display. It looked like his car had won numerous awards, and he used this photo to impress the girls. When the guys finally figured it out, they called him THE GREAT PRETENDER thereafter (from the popular song, recorded by the Platters, in 1955). The nickname still stands, all these decades later.

Nicknames stick to people,
and the most ridiculous are the most adhesive.
—Thomas C. Halburton

NOW I ASK YOU . . .

When you think you are totally organized, with all your ducks in a row, think again. Remember, you can't control the weather. Have you ever scheduled an event (a meeting, birthday, graduation, wedding, funeral), and the weather didn't cooperate? Have you ever been on vacation, and the weather wasn't what you expected? You must take Mother Nature in stride. Don't let things that are beyond your control ruin your special days. Laugh and move on to Plan B, C, or D.

BETTER LATE THAN NEVER

The December wedding and reception took place in a beautiful old house at the Fort Vancouver National Historic Site, in the state of Washington. Most of the family and guests were coming from the Portland, Oregon area, and the only way across the Columbia River was the I-5 or the 205. Unfortunately, a massive storm hit midafternoon, and at one point, both freeways were entirely blocked. As a result, the wedding got a late start, as guests staggered in at all hours. In the meantime, the guests entertained themselves, by going through the General Miles (1839-1925) Headquarters Museum, reading about the grounds history, and observing the memorabilia: old photos, swords, pistols, and souvenirs of days gone by. When all the wedding party was finally assembled, the ceremony was performed on a lavishly decorated staircase, which was absolutely gorgeous to see. Afterward, all the guests left early, during a break in the storm, hoping to beat the worst to come. With only three little girls left, as family members were packing up the last of the flowers and decorations, the youngest thought she heard distant jingle bells. She kept saying she could hear Santa, but no one believed her. Until, that is, a thoroughly drenched and bedraggled Santa Claus came stomping through the door, loudly shouting, "Ho, ho, ho!" He carried a huge wet bag of presents for all the little children who had already come and gone. Oh, well. Santa sure made those three little girls, very, very Happy!

There is no such thing as bad weather,
only inappropriate clothing.
—Sir Ranulph Fiennes

NOW I ASK YOU . . .

Have you ever had to take at test? Of course you have, throughout your school years. Or maybe for a job? Do you look forward to taking tests (like my friend)? Another friend said she was a really good guesser, so testing didn't faze her, in the least. I have always freaked when taking tests. Once, in a city college history class, I knew all the answers going in the door, but the minute our tests were given to us, I had a brain freeze, and didn't remember anything. I waited, but the answers never came, until I was walking out the door. That's how stressed I was. So I made it a point to easily practice with my students together, and I gave each third grade student, one of those little red SUN-MAID raisin boxes, telling them that scientists said raisins were good for their brains. I watched the nonreaders who just randomly marked the boxes without reading the questions. So, I would casually ask the questions on the test out at recess, and had some great conversations with them (separately). It was clear that they knew the answers, but just couldn't read yet. So I gave them good grades in history, geography, and health, because they knew the material. The interesting thing was that they *argued* with me about their good grades. In the third grade, they already saw themselves as dummies and losers. That really shocked me. So I made a point to work on confidence building, motivation, and encouragement.

UNIVERSITY FINALS

You can understand the stress I was under, back then, as the last week of the doctoral four-year program was ending with Finals Week, and I had a medical condition, that I didn't understand. I could feel my blood coursing throughout my body, lickity split, and knew that wasn't normal. It was flat-out scary. I was afraid that if doctors were to check me out, that I would end up in the hospital, and miss the test. So each night, I would park by the front doors of the hospital, and try to sleep. If I got worse, I figured that I would just open the car door, and fall out. *Surely someone would find me*, I thought. I didn't tell my husband for a few days, not wanting to worry him, what with him being in California, and me in Utah. And this final test was too important not to take, which probably meant that if I missed taking it, I would have to fly back to Utah, to take the test at a later date (after I had forgotten everything). But the last time I talked to him, I was shaking so bad he could hear the nervous tremor in my voice, and so he kept asking me what was wrong. I was a mess, so I finally started crying, and told him. (He worked in a hospital, and he went nuts upon hearing my condition, as I suspected he would!) So Wayne took the first flight out, and I drove to the airport to find him. I was in such a state, that when I saw him coming through the door, he dropped his carry-on case, and ran to catch me, as I fainted. I was sliding down the wall, as he pinned me against the wall, so I didn't land on the floor. (Remember, I first met him on the restaurant floor.) He drove me to my dorm and then he started packing all four months of my stuff in my car, while I took the final test. Good Grief. Then he drove me 12 hours straight, to our Kaiser hospital in California. When the nurses would put a blood pressure cuff on me, and listen to my heart or breathing, they thought their stethoscopes were defective, and tried two or three times, and then would try again with a new one. After trying yet another one, they all would scream, "Get this woman a bed, she's *hypertense!*" That response happened so often, that I had to steel myself, because the nurses would always shout into my right ear. It turned out that I had *extremely* high blood pressure, and I still do, to this day (over 35 years later), and I take three different blood pressure meds, each morning, noon, and night. (High Blood Pressure has no symptoms, making it known as "the silent killer.") Yikes!

Success is not final,
Failure is not fatal:
It is the courage to continue
that counts.
—Winston Churchill

You don't have to be great
to start,
but you have to start
to be great.
—Zig Ziglar

It's not that I'm so smart
it's just that I stay
with problems longer.
—Albert Einstein

NOW I ASK YOU . . .

Have you ever had an unexpected phone call that you couldn't understand at first? But there was some urgency to the request? Was it about a legal problem? A will perhaps? Or a person in the hospital? Or a birth, a death, a divorce? Or an adoption, or jail? How did it make you feel?

BETTER NEVER LATE

One day, I received an unexpected phone call, from BYU. "Am I speaking to Dr. Sherry Lynn Meinberg?" I answered in the affirmative, wondering what in the world this was all about. She was a young, new assistant, and had found my diploma in the bottom drawer of a desk. "Do you want your diploma?" she asked. *What a silly question,* I thought. "Yes, of course. Please," I answered. Shortly afterward, I received it in the mail. The shocking thing was that I had never even missed it! And no one ever asked to see it. I was so glad that those four grueling years were over, and that I had graduated with a doctorate. My diploma was only **29** years late!!!!!!! And I had a good belly laugh.

> *It all started with*
> *an unexpected phone call*
> *which led*
> *to unexpected changes.*
> —Meemakshi Gupta

*Your cell phone has already replaced
your camera, your calendar,
and alarm clock . . .
Don't let it replace your family.*
—Unknown

*Life is what happens
when you put your phone down.*
—Unknown

NOW I ASK YOU . . .

Was there ever I time when you didn't get a message? Have you ever shown up, when a meeting, a date, or a party was canceled? How did that make you feel? Snubbed? Embarrassed? Were you upset? Worried? Or happy to not be included?

UN-INVITED GUESTS

One example of last-minute cold feet, before a looming wedding date, is that the groom might cheat on the bride, or vice versa. This was the case when a teenage couple got into a terrible row, and broke up, unofficially, even though the invitations had already been sent. Shortly thereafter, the bride cried on the shoulder of the groom's football buddy. Alcohol was involved, and one thing led to another, and they were intimate. Later, she went back to her intended. The couple determined that they were still in love, and committed to each other, and the wedding went on as planned. The ceremony was meant to represent a new chapter in their lives, a fresh start, a brand new beginning, with no reference to what went on before. The buddy was then, understandably, *uninvited* to the wedding. However, not knowing the situation, the buddy's mother and father, who had also been invited—showed up, with him in tow. They didn't get the memo. AWKWARD!

Uninvited guests are often
most welcome when they leave.
—Aesop

265

The place of an uninvited guest
is behind the door.
—Unknown

The art of being a good guest
is knowing when to leave.
—Prince Philip

NOW I ASK YOU . . .

Do you believe that one sex is superior and more valuable than the other? Do you think that gender stereotypes about women and men, and the roles they play, are valid? Or do you think that such sexist assumptions breed prejudice and discrimination?

EARLY SEXISM

My third grade students loved my new car, and excitedly asked about it.

"Did your daddy buy it for you?"

"No."

"Did your boyfriend buy it for you?"

"No."

"Did your husband buy it for you?"

"No."

"Did your uncle by it for you?"

"No."

"Well then, who *did* buy it for you?" they demanded, not grasping the fact that I—being a mere woman—could buy my own car.

I raise my voice—
not so that I can shout,
but so that those without a voice
can be heard.
—Malala Yousafzai

Sexism goes so deep
that at first it is hard to see;
you think it's just reality.
—Alix Kates Shulman

Equality is like gravy,
it is a necessity.
—Joss Whedon

NOW I ASK YOU . . .

Have you ever been bored? Have you ever been idle for any length of time, with nothing to do but twiddle your thumbs? Have you ever indulged in naval gazing? Do you prefer doing something, rather than doing nothing? Have you ever waited for something to happen? *Anything* to happen? I worked in inner city schools for many years. In fact, one school was considered the worst in the district. It was called the "Blood and Guts" school, because something off-beat happened every single day. Fights were routine. There was never a dull moment in that school. I always went home to tell my family the unbelievable events of the day. It was never boring working at that school.

BORED

Feeling under the weather the night before, and still not feeling quite up to par in the morning, I called in sick at work. By the afternoon, however, I was feeling much better. Sitting in the front of the house, staring out the large window, I was bored out of my mind. Nothing was happening, since all the neighbors were at work or at school. All was quiet on the Western Front. I was wishing that I *was* at school, with all the students, where something exciting would be going on. I sported an expression that fairly shouted: I AM EXTREMELY BORED! I was feeling lonely and sad. Poor, poor pitiful me.

Suddenly, a ratty old car turned onto my street, with two teenagers in it. My first thought was, *Why aren't they in school?* The girl was driving, and stopped the car in front of the driveway, cattycornered across from my house. The boy got out and walked up the driveway, so I figured they were looking to score some drugs, and would be sorely disappointed, because no one was home. I expected to see him return forthwith.

Not so. At length, I heard the back door slam with such force, that the windows shook. The phone was at my elbow, so I immediately called 911, and told the operator that I was witnessing a burglary in process. She advised me to stay on the line, and describe everything I was seeing. So I did.

The girl had made the U-turn in the cul-de-sac, and came back to idle in front of the driveway. Soon, the guy came out, laden down with two large speakers, a skateboard, and a bunch of other stuff. When the girl saw all the stolen property, she was trying to decide what to do—as the car made several fast start/stop/start/stop/start/stop movements, and then she took off in a cloud of smoke, leaving the guy with a shocked look on his face. He immediately dropped the skateboard on the ground, and took off on it. The speakers became too unwieldy, so he dropped them on two front lawns, as he sailed on by. I lost track of him, as he rounded the corner onto Stearnlee Street.

A few minutes later, *five* police cars zoomed onto the block, so I went out to talk with the officers. I told them that they had just missed the teenager, and they said, don't worry about it, as he was being taken care of. The officer in charge asked if I had ever been in that house. And I said of course, as I used to babysit there, for two different families. So he asked if I would escort him through the rooms, to see if any other damage had occurred. So the two of us went into the backdoor. I was talking a mile a minute, as I trailed him through the kitchen, and started into the hall, where we abruptly froze. We were met by a huge, low-growling Doberman Pinscher. Uh-oh.

The three of us didn't move, and the only sound was coming from the dog. I have always been afraid of big dogs, and this did not bode well. As the officer gradually got his gun out, he quietly whispered that we were going to slooowly back out, because otherwise, there would be blood and guts all over the place. *Yowsers!* As I began moving backwards, two other Doberman Pinschers came bounding around from the living room, and stood behind me. Not good. Although these two were big, they seemed to be young, and didn't quite know what to do. Unsure of the situation, they kept looking over at their mother for guidance. But her eyes never left the two of us. So we both, in slow motion, finally backed out the door.

As we walked down the driveway, on rubbery legs, thanking our lucky stars that we were in one piece, we saw that more squad cars had arrived on the scene. An undercover officer was also there, who, it turned out, was the father of the girl in question. After she had left her partner in crime, she called her dad, to tell him that she was in big trouble.

In addition, a huge school bus full of students, was also parked on our street. When I asked why it was there, I was told that the skateboarder had tossed a number of items, in at attempt to get away, and had accidently thrown something through one of the open windows of the bus. So the bus became part of the crime scene.

There were so many vehicles parked on our little cul-de-sac street, that the neighbors couldn't get through to their own houses, when they came home from work. So they had to park along Stearnlee Street, and hike in. So the block went from absolutely nothing going on, to a full-out catastrophe. And I certainly got my wish: something exciting going on, with students involved. Oh, boy.

For me, the opposite of happiness
isn't sadness but boredom.
—Sushant Singh Rajput

Perhaps the world's second-worst crime
is boredom; the first is being a bore.
—Cecil Beaton

I've got a great ambition to die of exhaustion
rather than boredom.
—Thomas Carlyle

The Beatles saved the world from boredom.
—George Harrison

Life is intrinsically, well, boring and
dangerous at the same time.
At any given moment, the floor may open up. Of course,
it almost never does; that's what makes it so boring.
—Edward Gorey

The two enemies of human happiness
are pain and boredom.
—Arthur Schopenhaur

NOW I ASK YOU . . .

Have you ever been in a situation, in which something you desperately wanted was coming to you, and at the very last minute, it was whisked away? Through no fault of your own? Did it feel like the rug was jerked out from under you? Did it feel similar to that of a bride being left at the alter?

NO CAN DO

When my third book. *The Bogeyman: Stalking and its Aftermath*, was published (2003), several newspaper articles were written about it. The Los Angeles Times had a half page article (by Jill Stewart), above the fold, with the response being immediate and huge. Former students, from all over the state, were calling the newspaper, asking for my contact information ("How dare someone mess with their third grade teacher!"), as were producers with movie offers. During that period, I was teaching full time, delivering stalking speeches on weekends, and giving interviews, while mentoring victims on a face-to-face basis, as well as having book signings at various bookstores. So I didn't have the time or inclination to deal with all the offers that were pouring in (some with checks upfront). As such, I hired a lawyer, to sift through them, to find the best representation.

She suggested that I sign with the William Morris Agency, which I did. I was under contract for a year, and the scriptwriter and some of the actors were already in place, when everything came to a screeching halt. The O.J. trial began, and everyone in the whole wide world knew who Marcia Clark and Christopher Darden were, due to the daily televised court proceedings, and no one knew me from Adam's Ox. So I was kicked to the curb, and they were both hired. It certainly made sense, from a business point of view. Oh, well. That's showbiz!

*AFTERWORD: Over nine years later (2012), the book raised interest in some producers of the Investigation Discovery channel. One called (I initially hung up on him, thinking he was a telemarketer, and didn't answer his call the second time. He called a third time, after lunch, and I recognized his voice. I proceeded to give him a lecture, before finally realizing that he was legitimate). A film crew arrived from New York, during the summer. Three producers were involved, and later complained about having too much material, for such a short time-slot.

As mentioned earlier, according to the FBI, I am considered to be the longest-stalked person in the nation, at 50 years. So my episode became the Premier of a new TV season of *"Stalked: Someone's Watching,"* on December 12th of 2012 (12/12/12). Strangers still come up to me, saying that they recently watched my show (saying "It was *scary!*" and words to that affect), and I'm always flabbergasted, because it was filmed over 11 years ago.

Books and movies are
like apples and oranges.
They both are fruit,
but taste completely different.
—Stephen King

*What makes a good book
and what makes a good movie,
are totally different things.*
—Seth Grahame Smith

*The book is a film that takes place
in the mind of the reader.
That's why we go to the movies and say,
"Oh, the book is better."*
—Paulo Coelho

*The book's always
better than the movie.*
—Richelle Mead

*Never judge a book
by it's movie.*
—Unknown

NOW I ASK YOU . . .

Have you ever taken a trip that was the worst ever? A trip that was so bad, that you couldn't even laugh about it afterward? A trip that was so terrible, you'd rather not remember it at all? Know that you are not alone in this matter . . .

WINTER WONDERLAND

Our friends were getting married, some 600 miles away, in the mountains of Placerville, California, so Wayne and I caravanned with his brother and sister-in-law. We only planned to stay one night, so we all traveled lightly. We only had the sports clothes we were wearing, and packed our fancy wedding attire. I brought along my pajamas and a toothbrush, and we set out. It was a beautiful sunny day, as we traveled up I-5. We found a nice motel, and hooked up with many friends that had converged from all over for the wedding, toured another friend's property, and returned to the motel, to stay overnight.

The next day, we were dressed in our finest, and attended the beautiful wedding and reception. We then changed back into our traveling clothes, to make the return trip home. The four of us decided to take the scenic road, over 395. Other carloads of friends tagged behind us, so we could all stop at the Tahoe Casino for an early dinner, and gamble for a couple of hours, before we went our separate ways.

By the time we decided to leave, an unexpected weather front had moved in, and it began heavily snowing. Our friends left in a hurry, hoping to beat the storm home going north. We could have left going south in our truck, but Wayne's brother was driving a limited edition Mercedes, which was very low to the ground. And it couldn't handle either the snow or snow chains. Then the PA system announced that 395 was closed. Suddenly, everyone was stuck, as both highways and the airport were also closed. The few limos that finally arrived from Reno had icicles hanging all over them, and the Caesar's workers had to get long extension chords, and use hair dryers to get the doors open, and let the passengers out. No one could leave. Even the working staff couldn't leave, even though their shifts were over, because the late-shift employees couldn't arrive.

Of course, the hotel ran out of rooms. The only reason we got a place to sleep, was because Wayne's brother was a high-roller, so he got a room. As such, we had to double-up in their room, with rollaway beds. So embarrassing! The room was on the 9th floor, and looking down in the parking lot, one could see huge 12-and13-foot snowdrifts. The buses couldn't even be seen! They were completely covered. It was amazing.

Suffice it to say that we were snowed in for *five* days, with no extra clothes, few toiletries, and little cash. Thank God we had our meds. Having lived by the ocean for all of our lives, we had no need for heavy clothes, so I bought several heavy sweatshirts to stay warm. The first few days, our food trays were decorated with beautiful fresh orchids, but soon they ran out. I was concerned that the casino would run out of food. Then, to make matters worse, the hotel lost power. Since we were on the 9th floor, we had to walk down nine sets of stairs, in the dark. The backup generators were running only on the first floor, so all the machines were working, but not the lights or elevators. It was an unbelievable experience!

Finally, we were able to follow the snowplows out, the way we came in. Deep snowdrifts were piled along the road, and road rescues were in force. Many accidents had happened, with cars going off the roads, to be covered in snow, and no one knew they were there. In several instances, I saw brightly colored Christmas packages littering the sideways, indicating the sites where some vehicles had veered off the roads. All in all, we were lucky to have missed all of that.

> *There is no such thing*
> *as bad weather,*
> *only soft people.*
> —Bill Bowerman

> *Life is not about*
> *waiting for the storm to pass . . .*
> *It's about learning to dance in the rain.*
> —Vivian Greene

> *There are some things*
> *you learn best in calm,*
> *and some in storm.*
> —Willa Cather

> *Storms don't last forever.*
> —Unknown

NOW I ASK YOU . . .

Do you have a favorite sea life animal? A major proportion of all life lives in the ocean. It is not known the extent, since many of the species are yet to be discovered.

OCTOPUS

Orange is my favorite color. So you can imagine my surprise to see a brilliant, bright orange octopus moving quickly among the rocks in the Sea of Cortez. Its head was about as big as a baseball. My nephew pointed it out to me, as he quickly jumped from rock to rock, in an attempt to follow the octopus, but soon lost it. We both looked around for it, but its use of camouflage and speed were too much for us to deal with.

Yes, I knew that white is the color of a relaxed octopus, and red tells us that an octopus is excited. And I knew that octopuses can change their color and texture, in order to blend in with their surroundings, but I had never seen photos of a solid orange octopus in any magazine, book, or documentary. So I was stoked.

I have always had a soft spot in my heart for octopuses. One day, Wayne (who loved the ocean and all its inhabitants), had found a teeny tiny octopus in a tide pool, and brought it home. We named him Octavious. He had his own aquarium, since he would more than likely have eaten the fish in our other five aquariums. Another matching aquarium sat next to his, with his food living within. Octavious always knew when he was going to be fed, while he saw Wayne scoop out his dinner, and pour it into his aquarium.

Octopuses are considered to be the most intelligent of all invertebrates, and I was concerned about the boredom he must have felt, all alone, with nothing to do. But I didn't know what to do about it. He must have been depressed, with the lack of stimulation. Octopuses can solve problems, remember solutions, use tools, recognize other people, think strategically, plan and execute escapes, play, do tricks, and even show emotion. Octavious was also super smart. (Oddly, all octopuses learn nothing from their parents. The father dies shortly after mating, and the mother dies as soon as their eggs hatch, at the time of *her* choosing.)

Octopuses are known as great escape artists (Houdini-like), and so was Octavious. He lived for almost a year, but when we came home from work one day, he was no longer in his tank. He had found a way out of his home, traveled across the living room, down the hall, and into our bedroom, and died next to my husband's side of the bed. (Octopuses can only last for 20 to 30 minutes outside their salty seawater.) We were so sad, even though we knew that they have short lifespans to begin with (they are said to live fast and die young), from six months to five years, depending on the species. We knew that only *two* of the 100,000 octopus hatchlings survive to sexual maturity. And that Octavious had a good life, and that on his last day, he died as a great explorer. He was widening his horizons, while facing unknown dangers.

There are around 300 known Octopus species (with even more to identify), ranging in size from a few centimeters, up to 17 feet in length. Octopuses have nine brains, one at the tip of each arm, and the major one, which is wrapped around its throat. They have a dominant eye (like people have a dominant hand). Octopuses can taste with their entire bodies, especially with their suckers.

Surprisingly, they will gently embrace you in a friendly way, with their suckers gently kissing your skin (as a way to get to know you), and when pulled apart, their suckers will make a popping sound. Not only does their skin change colors, but it can taste flavors. And their saliva dissolves fish flesh. They have eight flexible arms, although a recent scientist is now saying that two of the back arms are actually legs (pushing off with those two), which would mean six arms and two legs. (We'll let the scientists battle that out!) Amazingly, an octopus can regrow lost limbs.

Octopuses have a small beak (like that of a parrot), which is the only hard thing on their bodies, making it easy to squeeze its entire body through tiny spaces. (Their bodies are covered in a slimy mucus, which also helps in this regard.) Octopuses have three hearts and blue blood. Each arm is strong and muscular, with around 2,000 suckers on each arm. Even with all those suckers, sharp beaks, and venom (all actually have poison!), the vast majority will not hurt humans, even though they can bite, and do some damage. Unless, of course, they must defend themselves. There are, however, three (to maybe six) Blue-ringed Octopuses that are dangerous to humans. Luckily, they live in an area from the Sea of Japan down to South Australia. They hide in deep trenches of the oceans in the day, and only come out at night. One drop of their saliva can kill you. Yikes!

Octopuses can communicate with others of their own species. They build dens, using shells and whatever else is available. Some are loners, and some live in groups. When threatened, they will squirt black ink, in order to escape, which will interfere with not only the predator's sight, but smell, as well.

Scientists used to say that although dogs, cats, and rats, dreamed, and even fruit flies, fish, and platypuses dreamed, they said that octopuses didn't sleep or dream. Now, however, several recent laboratory studies show that Yes! octopuses don't just sleep. They experience sleep cycles like humans do, leading scientists to speculate that there *are* such things as dreaming octopuses. They have a *quiet* sleep time, in which they keep their eyes tightly shut, and they hardly move. During this time, they are a pale, white-gray. Then they will have an *active* sleep of about a minute, during which time they will flash an array of colors across their bodies, and their skin texture will change, as they twitch their arms, and have rapid eye movement.

Even though all octopuses are born with the same abilities, they have highly individual personalities, as workers in public aquariums and zoos will tell you. They have thoughts, and feelings, and are so curious, they want to know about everything all around them. Some octopuses are very active, some are shy, some are bold, and some are troublemakers. It doesn't take long before they like some people, or dislike others. They behave differently towards those people they trust. And they will often blast painfully cold, salt water, drenching those workers they do not like. And they have long memories. Yet, they will use their funnel to hose off friends, too, as a way of being playful, wanting others to join in the fun.

The aquarium staffs invent new toys or interesting ways to serve their food (inside locked boxes or balls) to keep their complex, clever brains active. No one wants to see a bored octopus, because then they will use their time to plan an escape.

Many people say that octopus DNA proves that they are aliens from a distant galaxy. They have a staggering level of complexity, with 33,000 protein-coding genes (which is more than we humans have). Scientists suggest that the frozen octopus seeds, or eggs, were sent to Earth on icy meteors or comets, crashing into our oceans, some 540 hundred million years ago. *Who knows, for sure?*

I don't care how they got here, or when they got here, I'm just glad they are here. They are the most fascinating creatures! All in all, it was quite exciting to see an orange octopus in the wild!

> *What we consider to be scientifically true*
> *is merely that which science has*
> *been able to observe so far.*
> —Pieter Elsen

NOW I ASK YOU . . .

Do you have a favorite color? Or do you have several favorites? Or do your favorites change with the seasons? In Western culture, blue is traditionally for baby boys, and pink is for baby girls. Although many parents have chosen yellow for their newborns. Experts tell us that popular colors vary by culture, gender, and time.

FAVORITE COLOR

One day, the second graders asked me about my favorite color. I said that I preferred orange, whereas my husband liked red, and therefore, I had an orange V.W., and he had a red V.W. I looked upon a sea of blank faces.

"What's a V.W.?" they wanted to know.

"Oh, it's a Bug!" I explained, thinking that everyone had seen the Walt Disney movie, *Herbie the Love Bug*. Silence again.

"What's a Bug?" they chorused.

"A VeeDub." Nothing.

"A Volkswagen!" Nada. Zip. Zilch.

Not until I took them outside and showed them, did they get the picture. The word *car* would have sufficed.

Sunset is still my favorite color, and rainbow is second.
—Mattie Stepanek

Color is the finishing touch on everything.
—Marc Jacobs

I am a believer that color affects people's moods.
—Lully Pulitzer

Color in a painting is like enthusiasm in life.
—Vincent van Gogh

NOW I ASK YOU . . .

Roses are red, violets are blue, and in between are a million other hues. Do you like the variations of color? Would you want to choose between the over 3,500 paint colors by Benjamin Moore? Mostly we work with the eight basic colors in the Crayola box—red, orange, yellow, blue, green, purple, black and brown, with gray and white thrown into the mix. Were you lucky enough to get the popular 64 colors in the Crayola box? I wasn't, but my friend was, so I liked coloring with her. Do you like to see all the colors? Do you like to see the change of color with the seasons? Does your wardrobe change with the seasons? Do you choose colorful flowers, candles, or pictures to augment your decorations?

COLOR

Color is a part of your everyday life. It is all around you. We see it all the time, but we take it for granted. Color is so important. It would be a bleak and boring world—like the old-time, black and white movies—if we had no color. Some individuals only wear black. How confining. One woman I knew was nicknamed Pinky. Her hair and total wardrobe were pink. I often wondered if she ever tired of it.

It is my observation that many Americans are *afraid* of color: beige clothes, beige furnishings, beige lives. A lawyer friend jokes that everything in his life is beige, or a variation thereof: his turkey dinner with a roll, his file folders, his Post-it notes, his khaki pants, the couch, his cat, and so forth). Don't succumb to the cultural pressure toward sameness. Beige is bland, impersonal, and anonymous. It fairly screams, "Don't look at me!" You are here to be colorful. Do everything with your eyes wide open. Allow yourself to be seen! When I was a professor, I always wore colorful outfits, and I received many positive comments from professors and students in other classes. Once, when I was at a symphony, everyone else was wearing black or gray, and I had a colorful outfit on. Many women came up to me, asking where I bought my clothes.

And when I had applied for a Doctoral degree (that ran four years), 5,000 people around the world had also applied. *Who knew?* The organizers had finally reduced the candidates to 100, and we all met one evening, to mill around and get acquainted. The professors were mingling in the crowd, speaking to everyone. Who knew that they were choosing only 42 of us? Yikes! I think I was chosen because of what I was wearing. The invitation letter said that we were all to wear blue. I knew they meant navy blue (as in business attire), but I chose to wear baby blue. I wore a white blouse, with a baby blue sweater vest, and a matching baby blue jacket and pants, with baby blue earrings, and both baby blue heels and purse. So I definitely stuck out from the crowd. The psychology professor grabbed me first, and hauled me over to the head guy, introducing me as being creative, imaginative, courageous, a thinker outside the box, and so on, and so forth. So I think I was chosen simply because of the color I brought to the meeting.

Be uniquely you. Stand out. Shine.
Be colorful.
—Amy Leigh Mercree

Life is about using the whole box of crayons.
—RuPaul

Colors are the smiles of nature.
—Leigh Hunt

Color is my day-long obsession, joy, and torment.
—Claude Monet

The purest and most thoughtful minds
are those which love colors the most.
—John Ruskin

People need color. It defines their world,
and makes them feel alive.
—Simon Bull

Sometimes all you need
is a little dash of color.
—Unknown

Colors speak all languages.
—Joseph Addison (1672-1719)

Color in a painting is like enthusiasm in life.
—Vincent van Gogh

NOW I ASK YOU . . .

Do you have a lot of gray in your life? Gray clothes? Gray car? Gray hair? Gray is a dull, gloom and doom, moody and sad color. It affects both your mind and your body, causing unsettling feelings, which can lead to depression. The world can seem flat, or dull, or boring, causing disinterest, loneliness, and isolation. If you have a gray attitude, your picture will always be bleak. My mother chose the color gray for the walls in our house, and the wall-to-wall gray carpeting. The couch was also gray. I always felt like we were in prison. However, others say that the color gray encourages authority, strength, and calm, which is the reason many psychologists paint their offices gray. The role of color in your life may be far more extensive, and important, than you are aware.

GRAY DAY

Any teacher can tell you, that there are some children who are in class in body only, as there doesn't seem to be any activity going on in their heads. Terrance was one such child, who always seemed to have a vacuum between his ears. Several months had gone by, in which he seemed to have no connection whatsoever with what was going on in the classroom. I had to resist the impulse to knock on his noggin, and ask, "Yoo-hoo! Are you in there?" Clearly, he had the brains of an ouster.

Whenever he contributed to class discussions, it was always some off-the-wall comment that was not even vaguely connected to the subject at hand. We all had come to expect this kind of behavior from him, and the class largely ignored his attempts to communicate. He was definitely marching to the tune of a different drummer.

One day, however, will live long in my memory. We had taken a field trip to Marineland, and on the bus ride home, he had a heretofore unfamiliar look about him, as he shared a startling discover with me.

"Ms. Meinberg! Ms. Meinberg!" Terrence yelled (as a lightbulb seemingly flashed above his head, like a character in a cartoon strip), as he excitedly pointed out the window. "See how the sky is the same color as the Pacific Ocean!"

I just about died from the shock, as he actually merged two subjects (geography and art), into one understandable sentence. And, furthermore, his observation was correct, as the gray of the day was so pronounced that you couldn't find a line between the waves and the sky. (He had, previous to this moment, called the ocean "the big waters," and only recognized the sky as big, blue, and up high).

I almost cried right there on the spot (but I couldn't tear up in front of my students). The whole trip had been worth all the hassle involved, for just that one sentence alone. It was as if someone had flipped a switch on inside his head, and his synapses, and neurons, were firing, and finally connecting with his dendrites. Hallelujah! Terrence was always on target thereafter, and his subsequent learning was phenomenal. He had successfully broken out of his intellectual coma. You just never know what will turn a child "on." So, after this experience, I was much more open to the color gray.

But no, then I'd remember that during my first marriage,

my last name was Gray. And then I'd be reminded of the horrible things that took place (I was lucky to live through it!), so I was back to NOT liking the word gray again. My life back then had settled down to never-ending shades of abandon-all-hope gray: shifting from dove, to iron, to lead, to zinc, to dull pewter, to battleship gray, in which I identified with Ansel Adam's theory, that the world could be represented in nine zones of gray.

Gray is the queen of colors,
because she makes
everyone else look good.
—Helen Van Wyk

You are the rainbow
that adds color to my gray skies.
—Avijeet Das

Gray has no agenda . . .
Gray has the ability
that no other color has,
to make the invisible visible.
—Roma Tearne

This jail's so neat;
all the colors match!
Gray, gray, gray!
—Jamie Greenberg-

NOW I ASK YOU . . .

Are you a dog lover? I am not. I love cats! I am queasy around large dogs, although many of my friends have them. I try to stay away from them, but big dogs always seem to find me. I am afraid of them, although I don't know why. My niece recently moved in with me, and—Surprise! Surprise!—she came with her small dog, and big cat. I am adjusting . . .

COYOTE

One dark early morning, I was walking down the middle of Stearnlee street (In an effort not to wake the neighborhood dogs, that would start barking and howling and awaken their owners), on my way to the local park. When I was around six feet from the park curb, I saw a coyote loping along, from my left. I stopped dead still. The coyote walked right in front of me, as if he didn't even recognize me as a human, and halted. I seemed to be just a stationary object that it was hiding behind. I couldn't believe how big he was. I bizarrely thought that, if I were to slightly bend over, I could actually pet it. Then I questioned *why* I would want to pet such a big, wild animal, when I was afraid of tame dogs that were smaller. We both stood silently for awhile, without moving a muscle, as he stared down Strearnlee. Then the coyote suddenly took of like a shot from a cannon. I was immediately concerned for the small dogs, cats, squirrels, and rabbits in the surrounding neighborhood. Then I wondered about where the coyote's den was, and if cubs were involved, where would they find enough to eat, and so forth. And I was dumbfounded at my initial reaction, realizing that I knew next to nothing about coyotes. I only had the cartoon Wile E. Coyote as a model, and knew that coyotes are considered to be tricksters in folklore. That was the sum total of my knowledge about them. So I nixed the idea of walking through the park, and zoomed home to safety, and my computer, to research coyotes. I found out that coyotes are not friendly to humans, but will attack if threatened; so it is best to freeze, because you cannot outrun a coyote (at 35 to 43 mph), and they can jump an 8 foot high fence.

Coyote is always out there waiting,
and coyote is always hungry.
—Navajo Proverb

NOW I ASK YOU . . .

Did you ever have secret clubs when you were a child? A club in which you had secret signs, handshakes, and rules? A membership where if you broke the rules, you would be banished forever? Oh, what fun!

COYOTE KIDS

Later, in the dim mists of my long-ago memory, I realized that when I was six or seven years old, we neighborhood children banded together in what we called our Coyote Kids Club. In order to be a member, each individual had to vow, that even if it was pouring down rain outside, and he or she heard our coyote distress call, that each would immediately come outside to help one another—*even if their mothers and fathers wouldn't let them*. Yikes! This was a heavy decision. We pictured ourselves climbing out our bedroom windows, if we couldn't sneak out the door. Oh, the horror of it all! There were consequences to consider. After much discussion and consideration, everyone solemnly promised. It was a very big deal. And we swore that it was a secret, and that we would *never* tell anyone, as we were united as a family of coyotes. If someone didn't show up in the rain, that kid would be kicked out the club. Forever. This was big stuff! Luckily, it never rained, so no one was ever put to the test.

I don't think we did much more than run around, barking, yipping, howling, and growling, while hiding in the bushes from imaginary unwanted predators, and pouncing on our own prey. I imagine that the adults on the block were tired of our noisy antics, and were pleased when we eventually turned to quieter distractions. Come to think of it, maybe this is why I have such a soft place in my heart for coyotes. (Oops! I just realized that I broke my long-ago vow.)

Coyote Power:
Surviving by one's intelligence and wits
when others cannot;
embracing existence in a mad, dancing, laughing,
sympathetic expression of pure joy
at evading the grimmest of fates;
exulting in sheer aliveness;
recognizing our shortcomings with rueful chagrin.
—Dan Flores

Have you ever received unwanted attention from anyone? Did it happen only once, or was it a repeat performance? Did it make you feel uncomfortable? What did you do about the situation?

FOUR HOUSE PAINTERS

I don't know why I have had such a problem with painters. I have had four different painters working at my house, who had become more trouble than they were worth. I keep putting off contacting any more painters, because of my past experiences with them.

(1) The younger painter was very courteous and professional, and went about his work in a timely manner. I was pleased with his personality and work ethic. Then, he didn't show, and he didn't show, and he didn't show. At length, a policeman came to visit. And I found out that early one Sunday morning, the police saw the painter's truck, that had crashed into a traffic light pole, and they figured the driver was drunk. When they looked at him, he was sprawled across his steering wheel. But when they pushed him back against the seat, they saw six bullet holes in his chest. It turned out that he was a member of a small criminal group that dealt with credit card fraud. One of the members was a postman, who found many new credit cards in the mail. With the credit cards or debit cards, the group was able to obtain goods or services or money. Apparently, my painter wanted out of the group, and the crew let him go *permanently.* So I was left with his

ladders, paint brushes, cans of paint, tarps, and such. His family wanted none of it.

(2) The second painter was a much older grouch, who said he had been in the business for years. I told him that he was to remove the furniture, and then paint the room, one room at a time, before moving on to the next room. As such, moving the furniture wouldn't be an inconvenience for the family. On the 4th of July, the day he was to start, he brought along an older worker (a bum he had picked up off the street), to help him move the furniture. Then Wayne and I left for the annual holiday block party. Much later, when I returned home, I found that *all* the furniture in the house (except for our back bedroom) had been moved to the outside patio! I was freaking out about that, and went to find the two old guys. I found them having a *fist fight* in my empty living room and dining room! It seemed that the helper was tired, and wanted to go, and he wanted the promised beer, and money. He also wanted a ride back to his street. It turned out that the two did not even know each other.

That night, after the fireworks displays were all over, Wayne and I were exhausted, and fell into bed. He went right to sleep, but I sensed something was wrong. It was difficult to open my eyes a bit, to look out the drapes. I could see a bright light up high, and thinking it was the moon, I closed my eyes again. And did it the second time, and then a third time. I didn't want to get up, but that bright glow bothered me. I pulled the drape back, and saw to my astonishment, that the garage was on fire! As was all of our furniture, and such, in the patio. And the flames were leaping across to our bedroom roof. I immediately yelled for Wayne to wake up, and we struggled to get through the doors to the front of the house. Of course, our phones were not working.

A Good Samaritan was driving down Bellflower Blvd. in the dead of night, and upon seeing the fire, and not hearing sirens, he drove down three other streets, to find the house in back of us, and rousted those neighbors, telling them to call the Fire Department, and then check out their own backyard. (This was all before cell phones, of course.)

I realized that my car was parked with its front bumper against the metal garage door, and both were on fire. But my car was packed with show-and-tell materials, for a presentation that I was to give the following week, at different schools, and I didn't want the children to miss out! So I jumped in the car, and backed up, just as the whole garage door melted onto the driveway. I zoomed backwards down the driveway, while my husband and next door neighbor used garden hoses to shoot water on my blazing car.

I was in my pajamas, and Wayne was in his undershorts, as we met the firemen. They thought they had a five-alarm fire in the making, in which the whole row of houses on our side of the block would be burned to the ground. But luckily, there was no wind at all, which saved everyone else's houses. People all around the surrounding area came in droves—all in their night garments—to watch the fire being fought. (But none of my block neighbors woke up!) The strangers were either crying, moaning or groaning, while I was patting backs, and hugging them, and telling all that everything was okay, that we were alive and well. (At one point, I thought, *What is wrong with this picture?* as others should have been comforting me, but I carried on). The Fire Captain was yelling for my husband, "Where's the man in his underwear? Where's the man in his underwear?" So we all started looking, to no avail. Wayne had realized that he needed his glasses, and crawled through the house to the back bedroom, to get them. He grabbed a pair of jeans on his way out, so nobody recognized him thereafter. The smoke was so low, it damaged his lungs, and it took several weeks for him to get his voice back.

There were spent bottle rockets on the front lawns of the houses on our side of the street. We all knew that they came from the guys in the next block. Every year, they went down to Mexico, and loaded up their car with illegal fireworks. So their 4th of July party was huge. The Fire Marshall also knew who fired off the bottle rockets (three guys), but couldn't prove which one actually did it. And he apologized profusely. (One of the guys was standing in the crowd, watching our house burn.)

We were safe, but our money wasn't. We had to buy new furniture for every room in the house (except our back bedroom), as well as T.V.s, computers, lights, paint, paintings, plants, sheets, blankets, and all the tools you don't even think of. The next morning, Wayne had to go to the store, to buy a shovel, a broom, and a dustpan, just to start cleaning up.

Insurance men came with cameras, because they couldn't believe all the stuff that was in our garage and patio. They wouldn't pay for a lot of things, like my Mother's trunk, my Father's trunk, my son's trunk (all family history items) because they didn't live there anymore, nor all the Lion's Club stuff (for which Wayne was the President), because none of it actually belonged *to him!* We also had a double shake roof, which was outlawed long after we had it installed, so it was grandfathered (which the insurance wouldn't cover). We replaced it with a mission tile roof, so we wouldn't have a fire again (for which the insurance wouldn't pay). Then an inspector said that the new roof was too heavy, and had to be retrofitted. (Which cost us even more!) To make matters worse, a whole neighborhood had gone up in flames elsewhere, and, as a result, the insurance guys said that they had run out of money, and couldn't give us all that we asked for, at the same time. As I recall, we had a choice of a smaller amount now, or we could wait for years, and *hope* to get the larger settlement later. Something like that. It was one of those take the money and run situations, and we were in a bind. So we decided that less was more, and went for it.

(3) I finally had the front bathroom remodeled. It seemingly took forever, while waiting for shipments to come, during COVID. Finally, at long last, everything was in its place, and a young Hispanic man came to paint the room. I smile at everyone whenever I greet them, and hand out water bottles when they needed a break, and laugh or joke with them, whenever I'm leaving or coming home. Apparently, this young man thought I centered my attention upon him, and him alone, and that I more than "liked" him. He would come in, sit down on my couch, and chat, during his break, and after work. This bothered me, but he had told me that he had recently moved from Texas, and had a girlfriend, and such. So, I thought he didn't have any friends, and listened to his stories. Then, he started coming in after the work shift. That bothered me, but he said that he was just waiting for his girlfriend to get out of the Hair Salon, so he could drive her home (to Los Angeles). He

was staying later. And later. And I was uncomfortable. Then I found out that he had been *fired* several weeks prior, since he was unpredictable, coming in late, or not at all. I was thunderstruck. So I called the foreman, and asked him to come over and escort the young man off my property, and tell him to never come back. I thought he had ulterior motives. He told the foreman that he thought *I* was lonely, and needed a friend. *I am alone, but not lonely.* There is a difference. And I have many friends. He came back a couple of times, and I called the foreman again, and he took care of the situation.

(4) The replacement painter was an older Hispanic man. I sighed in relief, making it a point not to engage him in conversation, other than hello and goodbye, considering my recent experience. He, however, started asking personal questions: "Is that your car?" "Yes," I answered, giving no extra information. (I drive a 370Z classic, which I love.) Next, he asked, "Is this your house?" "Yes," I answered, with no follow up discussion. Later on, he asked, "Where is your husband?" "He died two years ago," I responded. I didn't like the way this was going, and made it a point to stay out of his way.

On the day the painting was completed, I was walking from the hall into the kitchen, as he started howling and crying in the bathroom. "Oh, my mother! My mother!" he sobbed. *I don't believe this*, I thought, as I leaned against the kitchen doorway, with my arms crossed against my chest. I watched as he fell across the hall, onto the wall, and sort of slid down a bit. "My mother! Oh, my mother!" This guy couldn't act at all. He was making crying noises, yet no tears were evident. "What happened to your mother?" I asked. "She died!" he exclaimed, and continued fake crying. "When did she die?" I asked. "Two years ago!" he cried. It was clear that the mental script he was following, would show that I would have empathy with his problem, having lost Wayne two years prior, and that we shared a common tragedy. I wasn't going for it, nor was I going to pat him on the back, saying "There, there, I know just how you feel," as he obviously expected. As I walked out the back door, I found a beer bottle cap on the cement, which meant that he was drinking on the job, to get the courage to act out his plan. *Give me a break!* I said to myself, as I called the foreman, telling him to come pay this guy off, and get him out of my life. It was embarrassing in the extreme, as this guy said that he thought I was lonely, and was coming on to him. Yeah, right! *I am not a cougar!*

Women who chase after
younger men are called "cougars,"
whereas men who chase after younger women
are called, "Men."
—Unknown

COUGAR
IN AREA
Please stay on trails,
Travel in small groups
and do not allow men
under 30 to travel alone.
—Unknown

Animal lover that I am,
a cougar I am not.
—Betty White

NOW I ASK YOU . . .

Have you ever seen someone pick a fight? A bully at your old school perhaps? A best friends fight? Or teenage girls fighting over a boy? (Yikes!) Or a husband verses wife fight? Or a bar fight? None are pretty sights. Especially, if you are involved. Picking a fight is when someone is deliberately provoking a fight.

PICKING A FIGHT

One year, I taught summer school in a building with open classrooms. This meant that each set of four or six classes were housed in one humongous room, with no walls or partitions between them. (What brain came up with that idea? And what brain okayed it? Obviously they were saving money . . .). The students in my building trooped through my door each morning, since it was the closest to the front of the school. As a result, one angry mother kept trying to choose me off, every day when school let out. She constantly challenged me to fight with her, in the middle of the street—with her fists clenched, her face flushed, and her eyes fiery—calling me vile names in the process, in an effort to rile me in fisticuffs. She was belligerent, trying to get the other parents involved. It was truly disconcerting, to have acquired so violent an enemy, without any effort, whatsoever, on my part. I could never convince her that I was NOT her son's teacher. (Indeed. I didn't even know the name of said student.) Since the pupils for all the classes walked through my door each morning, she didn't believe me. Although I constantly asked the principal to do something about the situation, nothing ever took place. Every afternoon, I would go to the office to ask him to walk me to my car, but he was never there. So I ended up taking verbal abuse, in various doses, while trying to sneak unnoticed to my car. Both of which go against the grain of my nature. Each day, I wondered if I could make into the next, worrying that the situation might escalate. Since there are those who are known to hold grudges, I felt that I might easily be maimed or killed by this wacko stranger—who mistakenly had it in for me. (And remember, I have the dubious honor of being the longest-stalked person in the nation, and I didn't think I should have to deal with the same kind of situation at work!) To this day, I don't know what her complaint was all about. I just know that her son was not in my class, and that I received zero support from the administrator. (I later heard that the principal was new, just learning the ropes, and he didn't want another problem to mar his unsteady position).

Do not fight the person.
Fight the problem.
—Abel Starc

He will win who knows when to fight
and when not to fight.
—Sun Tzu

Arguing isn't communication,
it's noise.
—Tony Gaskins

If you want to stop an argument.
close your mouth.
—Charles R. Windoll

Control your "Anger"
because it is
one letter away from "d"anger.
—Unknown

Say what you mean,
but don't say it mean.
—Andrew Wachter

Pick your battles wisely,
because if you fight them all
you'll be too tired to win
the really important ones.
—Unknown

NOW I ASK YOU . . .

Have you ever been robbed? Or have you been in a store that was being robbed? Have your keys, wallet, or purse been stolen? Have your lunch or soft drinks disappeared at work? Has your car ever been vandalized or stolen? Has your house been burgled? Have personal items been lifted, when you were out and about? Has anyone leveled a gun at you? Have you ever been stalked? Have you been in a vehicle accident that was deliberate? Have you or someone you know, been beaten, raped, or kidnaped? Did you ever feel the need for personal protection, at work, or at home, or even while out shopping? What kind of protection did you need? Did you actually get it?

CONCEALED WEAPON

All of the above has happened to me. Even so, it was a hassle when trying to get a weapon! For decades, I'd been putting up with my stalker's sick, twisted behavior, but his lengthy, threatening letters were getting even more erratic. And he had set a specific date for my demise. Unfortunately, the police had not been helpful, since Chuck had to "do something" first. So I needed something to protect myself, just in case his threats became a reality. So I had to go back to the police station to get an application. When I walked in, a group of policemen were surrounding their boss. All talking stopped as I walked up to them. I asked where I could get an application for a concealed weapon. The boss and his men all tried to dissuade me. I kept asking, as they kept shaking their heads back and forth. They told me that it would cost money (as I recall,

I paid around $79 or so, but now the total cost for a CA CCW is anywhere between $200 to $300, adding insult to injury. *Who can afford that?* It's outrageous!). And then they said that after I sent the application and fee in, it would automatically be *denied*. So my money would be wasted. I still wanted an application. Finally, I said that if I didn't get an application, I was going to sue them all, as well as the whole Police Department. The crowd quietly parted like the red sea, and I went to the desk, and picked up the application, and happily went home.

Suffice it to say that I was the *first* private citizen in the City of Long Beach, to be issued a permit to carry a concealed firearm. I took two gun training courses, which included indoor live-fire shooting exercises (a long story), and I bought a 357 magnum hammerless, snub-nosed, Smith and Wesson revolver (another long story), for personal protection. However, it turned out that because I worked at elementary schools, middle schools, high schools, and universities, by California law, I was unable to carry a gun even in the trunk of my car. So, my time, effort, energy, and money, was all for naught. Oh, woe!

A gun in the hand
is better than
a cop on the phone.
—Unknown

Don't like guns?
Stay out of my house
and we'll be just fine,
—Unknown

Why carry a gun?
Because a cop
won't fit in my purse.
—Unknown

Country Girls don't retreat.
They just reload.
—Unknown

It takes 43 muscles to frown
and 17 to smile,
and only 3 for proper trigger squeeze.
—Unknown

I would like to see every woman know
how to handle firearms,
as naturally as they know how
to handle babies.
—Annie Oakley

NOW I ASK YOU . . .

Have you ever made assumptions that were totally off the mark? Guesses that were not even within the same ballpark? I tend to make up stories on the fly, when I don't know what's going on. It's an automatic response. Some of my stories are right on the money, while others are not so much.

TOTALLY WRONG

My friend, Di, and her two young boys, were coming over for a visit. At seemingly the last minute, I decided that I must go buy some milk, just in case it was needed. So I took off in my car, without telling anyone, as I didn't want to waste the time it would take.

As I roared up to the grocery store, I saw a young, good-looking, tall man (mid to late twenties, or so), marching back and forth in front of the store's doors. He seemed agitated, as he kept looking at his watch. I immediately thought that he was meeting his girlfriend there, and that she was late. I also noted that he was wearing a tan trench coat, and thought that he must be from New York, because no one wore them out here, in the California sun. Luckily, a car had just moved out of parking slot, directly across from the grocery store door, and I easily slid in, and parked. The man looked startled, as I ran across the street, and started through the front door. He followed me so closely, it felt like he was right on my heels. I assumed that he was heading for the phones (no cell phones then), to call his girlfriend to ask why she was so late.

I was in such a hurry, that I picked up clues, but didn't

put them all together. As I charged through the door, I could see a ton of people, all grouped together against the far wall, and that they all seemed to be quietly staring at me. I then grabbed a cart, and of course, it had a bad wheel. The music wasn't playing, and the PA wasn't working, and my cart was the only thing making noise, as I rolled through the isles, at a fast clip. I saw no people, and heard no babies crying, or any talking whatsoever. WEIRD! After grabbing the milk, I roared over to where the checkout stands were, and all the same people were still there in the lines, but not one was talking. So I lined up behind a man, and loudly asked, "What's going on? These lines don't seem to be moving!"

He tried to ignore me, so I asked louder. He finally turned around to shush me, whispering, "We're being robbed!"

"*What?*" I asked, dumbfounded.

"Shhhh!" everyone around me said. So I looked up front, and saw *five* guys, all wearing tan trench coats, all holding long guns of some sort, taking money out of all the registers. Jeez! Have a clue!

Then the burglars stashed their weapons *underneath* their long coats, and left. Shortly thereafter, the police came in, and then later, everyone had to wait for money to come from the other chain's grocery stores, in order to make change for that days' customers. By this time, my milk was warm, and time was wasting, so I ditched the milk, and left. All the people told the police that I didn't witness anything, and I didn't know anything, being the last customer to arrive. So I got to leave, whereas everyone else had to be interviewed by the police.

When I got home, I was met by two angry adults (my

husband and my friend), both wanting to know where I had gone for so long, and why. I don't think they believed me.

Assumptions are made, and most
assumptions are wrong.
—Albert Einstein

Assuming things is the equivalent of sleepwalking
blindfolded on a cliff edge
fully expecting a safety net to be there
to break up the fall
should you topple over the precipice.
—Stewart Stafford

Assumptions are terrible things to make,
and like all dangerous things to make
—bombs, for instance, or strawberry shortcake—
if you make even the tiniest mistake
you can find yourself in terrible trouble.
—Lemony Snicket

But you are making assumptions
without all the facts,
and that's not a sign of intelligence.
—C.C. Hunter

NOW I ASK YOU . . .

Have you ever been astounded by an overflowing of love directed at you? An unexpectedly love so warm, that it felt like you had received a group hug? A love expressed by family members? Neighbors? Friends? Or those you work with? Or even strangers? It is said that the greatest happiness of life, is the conviction that we are loved; loved for ourselves, or rather in spite of ourselves.

UNFORESEEN LOVE

It was sometime around 1984, when NASA began looking for a teacher, to be a part of their Teacher in Space Project. The chosen teacher would be a part of the 7-member crew (4 men and 3 women) for the STS-51-L Challenger mission. I thought it would be a fantastic experience, and wanted to take part in the adventure. But I didn't know how to apply. I asked top educators in several counties, newspapers, radio and TV hosts, as well as government officials, but no one had an answer. I knew that NASA had a phone number, but thought it was only for important dealings. I was wrong, as 11,000 other teachers, from all over the country, had applied. At any rate, I had mentioned my problem to a couple of teachers, and a handful of students, and thought that was the end of it. I was unprepared for the follow-up.

The rumor mill was outstanding, as suddenly, everyone around me knew that I was interested in such an experience. Throughout the days, my students, as well as previous students, came to me, to express their sentiments about my plans. Older students in middle school and high school

NOW I ASK YOU...

(that I hadn't seen in years!), came by after school, to express their concerns, as well. Some parents, along with unknown neighbors, came after school to speak to me regarding same. No one wanted me to go. They actually pleaded with me, NOT to pursue the matter any further. It was such an unplanned outpouring of love, that I was filled with wonder. It was pretty amazing. To the point that I felt like I was wearing a warm coat of love, or that I had a cocoon of love surrounding and supporting me. It was breathtaking. With smiles, hugs, and laughter all around, I felt safe, secure, and deeply loved. So I happily chose not to chase after NASA any further.

After Christa McAuliffe was chosen to be the first teacher in space, she said, "If you're offered a seat on a rocket ship, don't ask what seat. Just get on!" She took a year-long leave of absence from teaching her high school classes, in order to train for the shuttle mission. NASA paid her salary, as well as that of her runner-up. Christa was going to conduct experiments, and teach two lessons from the space shuttle, while communicating with students in orbit. The lessons were to be broadcasted to millions of school children via closed-circuit TV, which was to include a tour of the space craft, called *The Ultimate Field Trip*.

All eyes were on the Challenger Space Shuttle, as it began its 10th launch (January 28, 1986), and watched as it broke apart 73 seconds into the flight, at 43,000 feet, killing all of the crew instantly. Which immediately changed NASA's space program forever (trying to do too much, too fast, with too little money). Children all across the nation were crying.

The shocker for me came about *after* the Challenger disaster. Day after day, teachers, students, former students, parents, neighbors, and friends, all came to wish me well. They all talked about the Challenger, and regretted the death of the teacher, Christa McAuliffe, and the crew. And yet, they were so happy that I wasn't a part of that tragedy; that I was still with them, safe and sound. I was simply dumbstruck, to say the least.

AFTERWORD: Thirty-seven years later (4/20/23), with little fanfare, Space X's Starship, the world's biggest and most powerful rocket, blasted off, in an attempt to orbit the world. Elon Musk's company plans to send people and cargo to the moon, and eventually Mars. But, like the Challenger, the Starship failed, just minutes after launching from Texas. It blew a huge hole in its launching pad, flinging concrete chunks up to 6.5 miles away, across 385 acres (damaging equipment and storage tanks, while igniting a 3.5 acre fire in a nearby state park). It carried no people or satellites. Both the booster and the spacecraft were ditched into the ocean. It was a day of mourning and remembering.

> *I cannot join the space program and*
> *restart my life as an astronaut,*
> *but this opportunity to*
> *connect my abilities as an educator*
> *with my interests in history and space,*
> *is a unique opportunity to fulfill*
> *my early fantasies.*
> *I will never give up!*
> —Christa McAuliffe (1985)

NOW I ASK YOU . . .

Do you know anyone who has had a mini stroke? Mini strokes happen when a blockage occurs to a major artery to one's brain, which disrupts the flow of blood and oxygen. It lasts only for a few minutes. It is said that with the right amount of rehabilitation, a person's speech, cognitive, motor, and sensory skills will steadily be recovered. One can live a full life after having a mini stroke. I am a good example.

MINI STROKE

My whole life revolved around books. I buy them, I read them. I share them, I donate them, I edit other's books, and I write my own books (this book is #24). I was considered an expert in Children Literature, and, as a result I taught courses for teachers, and soon-to-be teachers, about books they could use in the classroom, as motivation for subjects, or for use as a culminating experience, or books to use just for FUN. Then I had a mini stroke, and all that activity skidded to a stop. I couldn't hold a pencil or pen, so I couldn't write. I couldn't read, because the words kept jumping around on the pages. And I had trouble speaking, because I wasn't able to remember specific words (so I wasn't able to be a guest speaker, or be interviewed on live radio or TV anymore). And I couldn't walk a straight line, and I fell a lot. And I couldn't drive, of course. I had no strength at all. The easiest things were hard to do, like simply getting dressed in the morning.

One middle of the night, I walked into the kitchen to get a drink of water, and my husband was sitting in the kitchen chair. I didn't recognize him. (We had been together for almost 54 years). I didn't think it odd to find some guy in my house in the middle of the night. I felt comfortable with him, so I leaned back against the sink, and chatted with him. I thought I was speaking to him, but Wayne said that I was just gibbering, not making any sense at all. Wayne recognized that I was having a mini stroke, and came over and hugged me, saying "I think we need to go back to the hospital. What do you say?" "Okay," I answered. He asked another question, and I said, "Okay." He was being as gentle as possible. Since it was the middle of the night, he said, "I'm going to go into my bathroom, and change clothes. Can you go in your bathroom and change clothes?" And I answered, "Okay." After a while, he tapped softly on my bathroom door. "Honey, are you all right?" I paused, and then said, "No." "What's the matter?" he asked, and I answered, "I don't know how to get dressed." So he quietly asked if he could come in and help me, and I said, "Okay." As he came in the door, I held up my bra, and asked, "What's this for?" I was totally flummoxed. He helped me get dressed, and he walked me to the car, and off we went. He knew something was terribly wrong, because I didn't say one word, and I'm usually a chatterbox.

I have a few snapshot memories of my stay in the hospital, but at the time, I couldn't tell anyone about my complaints. I didn't have the words. The worst experience: My wedding ring (that hadn't been off my finger in all those years), and a double-heart ring that Wayne had given me, were pried off my fingers, using tons of lotion. I had gained weight over the years, so it was tough to remove them. I kept saying, "No, no, no!" but two young gals wouldn't listen, and they stole my rings. I couldn't fight them off. I felt drugged, and didn't have the strength. I was home for several weeks before Wayne noticed, and asked me where my rings were. And I started moaning, realizing yet again, that my rings were gone forever.

I was told that I had a year to get better, and how I responded at the end of that year, would determine how I would be for the rest of my life. So I was determined to get better.

The limits of my language
are the limits of my universe.
—Goethe

My brain seems to take the scenic route.
Things come to the forefront of my mind
sooner or later. It just takes time.
—Richelle E. Goodrich

My spelling is wobbly.
It's good spelling, but it wobbles.
And the letters get into the wrong places.
—Winnie the Pooh

Life is not about how many times you fall down.
It's about how many times you get back up.
—Jaime Escalante

NOW I ASK YOU . . .

Have you ever been in a situation where no one knew what to do? Where all the etiquette rules of conduct didn't apply? Where even basic common sense seemed to be out the window? Where all the onlookers were seemingly paralyzed? Where everyone was hoping that someone else would take charge? It is an uncomfortable situation to be in.

OUCH!

It was a backyard wedding, with only family and a few friends in attendance, for a close-knit, cozy effect. Spring had provided the perfect weather—the flowers and trees were in full bloom, and friendly birds chirped in the background. Everyone was beautifully dressed for the happy occasion, and looked forward to taking part in this blessed event. The ceremony was moving along without a hitch, when, just as it came time for the bride to say "I do," she screamed at the top of her lungs, and fled into the house. All were stunned, riveted to their seats, looking around at each other in dismay. "Is the wedding off?" everyone whispered. "What's going on?" No one knew the proper thing to do. "Do we stay?" "Do we go?" Everyone was at a loss for ideas. The mother of the bride finally ran into the house, and didn't come back out. Everyone stayed in their seats, waiting for directions, which never came. It turned out that a wayward bee had flown up the bride's gown, and stung her in the most inappropriate part of her anatomy. After she was attended to, and the barbed stinger was removed, instant redness, itchiness, and swelling occurred. At length, she calmed down somewhat. And ignoring the intense pain, the wedding resumed. But my aunt never got over the experience. For decades thereafter, whenever the word "wedding" was mentioned, she would become hysterical, crying copious amounts of tears. It was one of those situations that no one could ever forget.

The only rule is there are no rules.
—Aristotle Onassis

There are no rules here.
We're trying to accomplish something.
—Thomas A. Edison

NOW I ASK YOU . . .

Have you ever been so dissatisfied with a product or service, that you found it necessary to write a complaint letter? Did you ever get a response? Were you happy with the end result? I have had a positive reaction to all my letters of complaint, except on two occasions. And with those two, I ended up writing to the Better Business Bureau, and local computer sites, to warn future customers. One happily resolved letter of my complaint was eight pages long. The result was that the owner of the boat fired all of the workers (except for the cook, whom I had praised), posted my letter on all the dock marinas where his fishing boats were moored, and sent back eight hundred dollars (which worked out to be worth a hundred dollars a page). So it was definitely worth all the time, effort, and energy to lodge the complaint.

FIGHTING FLEAS

My son and I went to the movies, to see the first Rocky movie, that everyone had been talking about. It was a pretty new theater within the Los Cerritos Mall complex. The place was packed. But we couldn't concentrate on the movie, because *huge* fleas were bombarding us. The whole time Rocky was fighting on the screen, we were fighting in our seats. I finally caught one, and held it between my thumb and pointer finger. I went out into the lobby, to speak to the manager. He looked all of 16 years old, and couldn't empathize with our situation. Nor did he want to see the giant flea that I was holding in my hand. I was not satisfied with his lack of response, so I held the flea all the way home. Then I wrote a scathing letter to the local Health Department site, and scotch-taped the flea to the top of the letter. They called me in response, saying it was a pretty new facility (only three years old), and I said that I knew that, and couldn't believe it either. I told them exactly where we had been sitting, and they checked it out. It must have been really bad, because the theater was closed down for two weeks, while it was being fumigated. Whereupon, my son and I danced a victory dance to the Rocky theme song.

Haste is good only
in catching fleas.
—Alla Yaroshinskaya

NOW I ASK YOU . . .

Have you ever been disgruntled about work rules? Do many of your coworkers complain about the same thing? Had it been bothering you all for a long time? Did you decide to do something about it? Or did you worry about losing your job, and do nothing?

DRESS CODE

The dress rules for teachers were in place for years, without a change. I can remember in my first school of teaching, the principal (a male), ordered the vice principal (a woman), to go home and put on some hose. (It was an extremely HOT day, and the school had no fans or temperature controls, and we all felt for her.) One man at another school in which I worked, was irritated that men had to wear a tie, tight around their necks. So he always hung his tie around his shoulders, until the bell rang for school to begin. Then he would quickly tie his tie. It was his way to object. I overheard a conversation of a supervisor from downtown, asking the principal, *"What's with that guy?"* Like it was a horrible break in the rules. He probably would have been canned at the time, if he wasn't such a fantastic teacher.

When I was in my third elementary school, the women teachers had had enough! Everyone was irritated that we had to wear dresses only (which was difficult to do, when you are sitting on the floor with younger students). So one day, all the teachers got together, and wore fashionable pantsuits to school. We figured that our principal couldn't send all of us home (as there weren't enough substitutes to go around, so who would teach our classes?). Our principal didn't say a word about the uprising, yet she was the only one who wore dresses forever after.

Years later, some student teachers, never heeded the message that they should look *presentable*. Some looked like they had just rolled out of bed, and grabbed the first thing off the floor to wear. When I visited a student teacher for a first grade observation, she was wearing a very short top with loose pants. Every time she raised her arms, her blouse would hike up, and rolls of fat could be seen. It was not a pleasant sight. All the first graders were gathered on the rug, so everything was upfront and personal. The students were undoubtedly used to the view, as they made no comment. Unfortunately, when she dropped an item on the floor, and bent over to pick it up, her shirt hiked up, and her pants pulled down. So there she was with her thong on display, as well as a humongous tattoo of an eagle, that spread from one side of her expansive body, to the other. The students, of course, went bonkers. They didn't know which to focus on, as neither her backside, her underwear, nor her tattoo should be seen in a classroom situation. At length, she pulled herself together, and the class calmed down. Somewhat. If she had been teaching middle school, however, the kids would still be hanging from the ceiling lights.

Use common sense. One student teacher showed up for his first day at a high school, wearing shorts, a Hawaiian shirt, and flip flops. True, this was a Southern California school, but it was a classical one, in which every man wore a suit and tie, and every woman wore professional outfits. This young man stuck out like the proverbial sore thumb.

What you wear is how you present
yourself to the world, especially today,
when human contacts are so quick.
Fashion is instant language.
—Miuccia Prada

Being well dressed hasn't much to do
with good clothes. It's a question of
good balance
and good common sense.
—Oscar de la Renta

Of all the things you wear,
your expression is the most important.
—Janet Lane

If you're going to kick
authority in the teeth,
you might as well
use two feet.
—Keith Richards

NOW I ASK YOU . . .

How do you handle waiting? Is it an enjoyable situation for you? Have you ever had to wait for a long freight train to pass? Have you ever been stuck on a freeway, waiting for an accident to be cleared? (Once, as a child on a family trip in the Dakotas, we had to wait for a herd of bison to move off the highway. It seemed to take forever, as they took their time.) Are you waiting for the right time (to tell someone, or do something, or go somewhere)? Have you ever had to wait for something that was important to you? How did you feel about waiting? Were you just wasting time? What did you do with your time, other than twiddling your thumbs? Have you ever expectantly looked forward to a train, plane, or boat ride? Or a holiday, a vacation, an award, or a special event?

Waiting is hard. It is difficult to remain stationary, while staying in one spot. It is difficult to remain inactive, as time goes by. Any pause or delay can be agonizing (especially if you are waiting for something fun to happen, like birthdays, weddings, or trips). Was your baby's arrival on time? Did an "imminent" death in the family take much longer than predicted? Is time on your side? Waiting is achingly difficult.

WAITING

My husband, Wayne, and I were standing in line before the polls opened, waiting to vote. The election day workers weren't ready, and the people in line were getting anxious. Some were going to be late for work, and others were going to be late for school. People were grumbling left and right, checking their watches, while huffing and puffing and agonizing.

A man and his young son (about ten years old) were quietly standing behind us. The man's hands were laced tightly together, as if imposing external restraint. At length, the boy turned to his father, and asked, "Dad, are you mad at me or something?"

The man slightly smiled, and said, "No, son, I'm trying to exercise patience."

His simple demonstration sure helped all those within earshot, including me.

> *Patience is not simply*
> *the ability to wait—*
> *it's how we behave*
> *while we are waiting.*
> —Joyce Meyer

NOW I ASK YOU . . .

Have you given any thought as to how difficult it is for immigrants to settle as permanent residents in America? Immigrants have to learn a new language, a new culture, and new laws. In addition, children have to learn about new schools, new teachers, new students, and new rules: a tough row to hoe.

CIVIL RIGHTS

I was observing a Lakewood High School student teacher, as he related his personal incident during a lecture on Martin Luther King, Jr. and the civil rights movement, to his 11th grade history students. All were touched by his story.

The student teacher had immigrated to the USA when he was six years old. He was immediately placed in the first grade, late in the school year. He knew no English whatsoever, and his teacher knew only a few Spanish words, so he rarely understood what was going on. Each class was participating in a program for the PTA. Parents were invited to attend the presentation in the auditorium. His teacher, naturally wanting *all* her students to be included in their play, gave him the only *nonspeaking* part. She pinned a star on his chest, as he was to be a policeman, and she modeled his job. All he had to do was walk across the stage, and grab a girl by the arm, and drag her off the stage. As a first grader, he was apprehensive about being on display in front of all those strangers—not only kids, but adults, as well. Not knowing *why* he was told to do what he was to do, was the worst of it, but it seemed an easy enough thing to accomplish. Unfortunately, for him, when he walked across the stage, and grabbed the girl (who was representing *Rosa Parks*), everyone started booing. He thought the audience didn't like him, and he began to cry in the middle of the performance. He didn't know what he had done wrong! It was years before he realized that the audience had been booing the *historical situation*, and not him personally. What a way to be introduced to civil rights! (There was hardly a dry eye in the classroom!)

The roots of education are bitter,
but the fruit is sweet.
—Aristotle

NOW I ASK YOU . . .

Have you ever made a promise? A promise is an assurance that you will do a particular thing, or that a particular thing will happen. No ifs, ands, or buts. It gives a person a reason to expect something. Do you keep your promises? Have you ever broken a promise?

DAWG GONE!

I had written a book called *Bumps in the Night: Fantasy Creatures*, and thought that children would enjoy drawing pictures of their favorite fairy tale characters, so I started an art contest (for all grade levels). There were 58 creatures, and anywhere from 1-to-7 pictures for each. I sent a letter to each winner, and told them that it would take about a year or so for printing, but the timing was out of my hands. So I sent the manuscript, and all the pictures, showing exactly how each page should look (making it easy for them to print) to Dog Ear Publishing. And they took my money and ran!

I didn't realize that anything was wrong, but as the months went by, I became concerned. Then very concerned. None of the delay was my fault, of course. But I had promised the student artists a copy of the book upon publication, and I couldn't do what I had promised, as no one was bothering to answer my correspondence (emails, letters, and phone calls). I was frustrated, worried, and *angry*, because my little artists were growing older. And older, And older. Time was wasting away! It took a long, long time, to find out what was wrong.

The book was under contract to Dog Ear Publishing.

Unfortunately, the company owner/president, Ray Robinson, and his son (the vice president), became embroiled in numerous court actions in various states, by individual authors, as well as various Attorney Generals (under Consumer Protection laws and Deceptive Consumer Sales Acts). When I finally got to talk to the president (he only answered the phone expecting someone else), he blamed all the problems on his son. Much later, the son called me, saying that *he* would use my manuscript and pictures, and print the book under a different publishing company name. But that never happened either, with more time passing.

The Better Business Bureau (BBB) posted an announcement, stating that the Dog Ear Publishers accreditation had been suspended, issuing the most severe level of warning: **WATCHDOG ADVISORY!**

They finally closed their doors at Dog Ear. But did they tell me (or anyone else)? NOOOO! They even failed to show up in court for multiple lawsuits. They were late with royalties, or never paid the authors at all. Come to find out, all the authors were having the same complaints as mine. No one received any money, not even a statement. Now Dog Ear is considered to be "the worst of the worst" publishers. *Who knew?*

Dog Ear Publishing finally filed for bankruptcy in the courts, but any money received would first go first to bank loans, taxes, unpaid employee wages, creditors, and lastly, the authors. So, the cost of litigation would exceed what authors would receive, even if there *was* any leftover money. And since there were few or no assets, a class action would be pointless.

As a result, I never received my manuscript, or the

artwork back, and didn't know what to do about the situation. So I looked around for another company, and finally found one that I thought would work, and wasted another year with them. I gave specific instructions, as to how I wanted it. All they had to do was simply print the pictures the way I had placed them. *How easy could it get?* It should have taken no extra time at all. But it was bounced to someone in the countryside of Canada (slow mail), who changed the layout of every single page (for no good reason), which freaked me out, so I cut ties with them, also.

At the same time, my husband, Wayne, had become extremely ill, and I was his sole caretaker. He was housebound. Then, I almost died, *twice* (for two different reasons: first, I almost drowned, and the next day, my gal bladder exploded. In both cases, two different doctors called Wayne, to tell him that I was not going to make it. But I told everyone that I flat-out *refused* to die, until *Bumps in the Night* was published, and delivered, as promised. Unfortunately, shortly thereafter, I had a mini-stroke (refer back to Mini Stroke), and had to return to the hospital, for the third time. I didn't even know who Wayne was, and we had been married for 54 years!

I had to start retraining my brain. I worked to get my vocabulary back, and then learned how to simply hold a pen in my hand, and how to write and spell. When using a computer keyboard, I would constantly reverse two letters, which was so annoying, and time consuming. My handwriting looked like that of a preschooler. People used to say that my handwriting was beautiful. Not any more. Check out my first attempt:

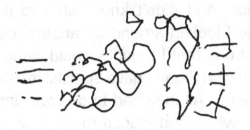

And I lost a good deal of my memory. I still have a hard time remembering the names of people and places that I had known for years. Numbers are even harder to remember. I also had a rough time walking, as my balance was poor, and I was so wobbly, that I often fell. Not fun! So my friends held onto me, until I graduated from a walker to a cane. When I started getting better, my husband got worse, so I became his caretaker again. And at length, after a long, slow decline, Wayne died.

So, after three companies, and *five years*, instead of looking for another publisher, I found a local printer, Eugene Yo, at Innovative Print Solutions (in Long Beach, CA), and he printed 80 copies for me, in a two-week period! Hallelujah! Then I sent copies of the book to all the student artists that were then five years older. A few were even in college by then! Unfortunately, some had moved, and I felt awful when those books were returned. I was able to track down all, but two. Even so, at that late date, wonder of wonders, I have received many Thank You wishes, cards, and letters, in return. Thankfully, at long last, I was able to keep my promise.

> *Broken promises,*
> *like broken glass,*
> *are hard to replace.*
> —Wille Mae Gaskin

It is easy to make promises.
It is hard work to keep them.
—Unknown

A promise means everything.
But once it is broken,
Sorry means nothing.
—Unknown

Never promise more
than you can perform.
—Publius Syrus

People with good intentions make promises.
People with good character keep them.
—Unknown

Promises are only as strong
as the person who gives them.
—Stephen Richards

A graceful refusal is
better than a lengthy promise.
—Ali ibn WAbi Talib

You can't trust a promise
someone makes while drunk,
in love, hungry, or running for office.
—Joe Moore

Never make a promise in haste.
—Mahatma Gandhi

NOW I ASK YOU . . .

Do you like to visit the dentist? Are you careful to schedule appointments each year for checkups? Or do you only go to see your dentist when something goes wrong? Do you fear the dentist, or the bill?

DENTAL PROBLEM

My life appears to move from one extreme to another, leaving me little time to do what I actually want to do. For instance: I took two bites from my sandwich, and heard a crunch. I felt all around inside my mouth, but couldn't find anything wrong. So I took another bite, and heard another crunch. I felt around again, and still couldn't find anything wrong. I finally looked in the mirror, and saw that over half of my **front** tooth was missing! A great big hole in the very front (I must have swallowed the parts of the tooth. Ick!), which wouldn't normally be an emergency, but 10-to-12 people were taking me out for dinner at The Lighthouse, the next night, just to meet me, or thank me, for doing a podcast with them (based on *The Bogeyman: Stalking and its Aftermath*). One man was to fly in from Italy, a woman was flying in from Texas, and the rest were from California. I only knew her. And I didn't want to have to hold my hand over my mouth the whole time we were there. But, since my mini-stroke, I can't remember names, and even though I'd been with my dentist for 40 years, I couldn't remember his name, nor could I find it in either of my two directories. So, in the dead of night, I drove over to his business (I do not like to drive at night, because I have night blindness), just to get his name off the building. Then I drove back home to call his service, and left a message. And my dentist called me right back. Luckily, I got an appointment for 9:30 the next morning. So he fixed me up for the dinner that night. And nobody was the wiser. Whew!

Some tortures are physical
and some are mental,
but the one that is both is dental.
—Ogden Nash

Life is short.
Smile while you
still have teeth.
—Unknown

NOW I ASK YOU . . .

Have you ever had unwanted attention from someone you knew? Or hostile or offensive harassment from a stranger? Did he/she pop up unexpectedly, now and then? Did he/she phone or email too often? How did you manage to get rid of him/her?

TOO MANY CREEPS

I would often complain to Wayne about people that were bothering me (in addition to Chuck or Jerry), and his response was that I always attracted weirdos. His suggestion was that I should never smile, grin, or laugh when I was out and about, because my smiles were *welcoming*, and infectious to everyone around me, and they put everyone in a good mood. But I would respond that my smiles were genuine and automatic; that I couldn't deliberately be poker-faced; that I wouldn't even know how to show a blank expression. As such, I would say something like, "I can't NOT smile. My smiles show that I am happy, friendly, positive, and sometimes even amused or surprised."

"Aha!" he'd say. "Your smiles show that you are *friendly!* That's the thing everyone is seeing in you! And most weirdos don't have many friends. So they latch onto you!"

(1) One older woman was hard to get rid of. She was a fan of *The Bogeyman: Stalking And It's Aftermath*, and showed up at all my bookstore presentations, and lectures. She spun a tale of her having a stalker, and constantly called the police, using my name. I gave her numerous

suggestions, which she never followed through on (since she was actually a stalker, herself). She seemingly popped up wherever I was shopping, so it took me awhile before I recognized her true self.

At long last, I thought that I finally had gotten rid of her, as I hadn't seen her for awhile. Then I was scheduled for a local radio interview. Oddly, the host had previously contacted me, saying that she could have me on her show, for a fee of $2,500. I couldn't believe it, since I had been interviewed on numerous radio and TV shows nationwide, and no one had ever mentioned a fee. Several weeks later, the host contacted me again, saying that the fee had been dropped, because Stalking was such a hot topic then. So we met at a restaurant for lunch, to discuss the upcoming interview. Later, I showed up at her *tiny* office for the interview, chatting with the host again. There were two chairs facing her desk, and she directed me to the one furthest from the door. At one minute to airtime, the door suddenly flew open, and the older woman rushed in, and placed the empty chair in front of the door, and sat, as the host began her live introduction spiel. It was clear that the two knew each other, and there was no way that I could climb over the woman. I was enraged, but I couldn't get out, so I answered the host's stalking questions for the 15 minute interview. It wasn't my best interview, given the situation. The host then offered to take us both out to lunch, but I shouted, "No, thanks!" as I tore out of the room. I was livid, as I roared out of the parking lot. I never heard from either one, again. I figured that my stalker had glommed onto the radio host, thereafter, showing her true colors.

(2) For years, I would stop at my favorite doughnut

shop before going to work. The same crowd of doughnut lovers was there about the same time. We all smiled at each other, or simply nodded our heads at each other, since there was no time for chitchat, much less meaningful conversations. We were all in a hurry. One day, a second grade boy, stopped his bike in front of our house, and called out to Jay, my fifth grade son. The young boy happily said, "You're going to be my older brother!" Taken aback, Jay said, *"What? What did you say?"* And the boy happily explained: "My daddy is going to marry your mother!" Jay replied, "That can't possibly happen, because I already have a dad!" (as Wayne walked out the side door, sealing the message.) Jay said that the young boy lived on the next block, down the far end of the cul-de-sac. I figured that the only place the man could have seen me, was the doughnut shop, so I switched shops, just in case.

(3) Late one night, most people were doing their last-minute Christmas shopping at the Lakewood Mall. As I braved the crowds, I noted a tall, elderly man in a white suit, passing by me in a hurry. He caught my attention because I had never seen a man in a white suit before. Later, as I walked out of the mall, I couldn't see any people at all. They were all inside. It was pitch black, with no lights in the parking lot, and it was scary. Then I could hear footsteps following me. I quickly ran and jumped into my car, shutting and locking the door. When I looked out of my windshield, there was the elderly man in his white suit, ejaculating all over the front of my car. *Eeuuuw!* I was so flustered, that when I started my engine, it stalled, and stalled, and stalled. And he had enough time to move over to the brand new Cadillac luxury car, parked next to me, and ejaculated on the driver's door handle. Oh, gross!

Can you imagine? I was so freaked out, once the engine started, I threw my car into reverse, and then burned up the aisle, drifting sideways and shot over the concrete curb, in my haste to get away from this guy. I drove directly to the Lakewood Sheriff's station, on Clark Street, where the mall is located. I hurried in, to find two Sheriff's—a man and a woman—and no one else. I quickly told my tale, saying, "If you hurry, you can catch him. He is tall, old, and he's very distinctive, in his white suit." Neither were thrilled with my story. Both were furious at my interruption. "But that's *our* territory!" they said several times, like no one would do such a thing, so close to their station. They kept stalling, as I kept saying, "You can easily spot him!" and "You can easily catch him, if you hurry!" But neither were interested, in the least. They just couldn't be bothered, cementing the feelings I had for the inaction of the police, over the decades, when I needed such help when dealing with Chuck.

(4) Jay was in the 8th grade, when he and a buddy had a major disagreement, a falling out of some sort, and Jay refused to talk to him again. As far as Jay was concerned, their friendship was over. The young boy, however, didn't take rejection well, and kept calling the house. Of course, Jay was not at home, but the kid kept calling, and calling, and calling (this was long before cell phones). And I was the only one answering the phone, and it was driving me crazy! Every time, I could hear steady breathing, but it somehow sounded differently, than Chuck's unwanted phone calls. This happened for so long, that I went to the telephone company to complain, but they sent me to the police. I went to the police with my complaint, and they sent me back to the telephone company. We seesawed

for weeks, until finally the phone company decided to do something about it. They traced the calls to Jay's ex-friend. Two men showed up at his house, and spoke to the boy and his parents. They were told that I had a stalker, who called me everyday, and that if the young boy was an adult, he could be arrested for stalking. But because he was young, and if he promised not to make any more calls to my house, then they would leave the phone in their house. But if he made even one more call, then the phone would be removed from their house, and the parents wouldn't be able to make or receive calls. Forever. The parents freaked out, needing their phone for business reasons, so the kid never called again. It was bad enough having one caller . . .

(5) My husband, Wayne, had finally been released from the hospital, after having had major heart surgery. He was still in a delicate state, but he desperately wanted to take me to Harrah's Casino, to celebrate *my* New Year's Day birthday. So six of us traveled in a caravan to Laughlin, Nevada together. We were all dressed in our fancy finery, counting down the seconds—"five, four, three, two, one!"—whereupon a tall, elderly man in a white suit, grabbed me, holding my arms at my sides so I couldn't move, and gave me a long kiss. My mind was reeling, thinking how strong he was for his age. He then let me go, and was immediately lost in the crowd of merry makers, leaving all six of us staring blankly at his departure. No one could react, it had happened so fast! We were all shocked just staring at each other! I told Wayne that the poor guy must wait all year long, just to get a kiss. And that next year, we would definitely go to

Las Vegas for my birthday. All I could think of was, *What's with elderly men in white suits?!*

(6) I was in the local Teacher's Credit Union one day, when I bumped into my old 6th grade teacher. We were both surprised! It was so wonderful seeing him, after some eleven or twelve, years or so. We chatted for quite a while, catching up. While I had moved onto junior high, high school, and college, he had moved up the ladder, having a job in district office. One day, he came to my school, and found my classroom, and asked if I could give him a ride home, as his car was being repaired. So I happily drove him to his home. Then it became evident that he wanted to date. I wasn't interested, having just gone through my divorce from Chuck. By this time, I had moved into my parent's home, while trying to find a new apartment. Now he started calling, and calling, and calling. Mom and Dad were asking what was going on. (They both knew him, and I didn't know what to say. It was so embarrassing!). Then, every time he had business at my school, he bothered me. So I told my teacher friends that whenever they saw him on the grounds, to send me a message (saying: **the ghost walks**), so I would be up front teaching, and couldn't talk to him). One night he called, drunk as a skunk, saying that he couldn't marry me, because his second wife had raised his two children, but that he had rented a year-long lease for me at the Outrigger Inn hotel. *Say, What?* Give me a break! He said I needed to meet him at the bar therein. Yowsers! (And I don't drink!) Needless to say, I didn't show. He was so persistent, that I finally wrote a letter, telling him to leave me alone, and left it under his car window wiper. Uh-oh!

(I had placed it on his wife's car by accident.) He never bothered me again.

> *A creep is someone who claims he's one thing*
> *but he's actually another.*
> —Matthew McConaughey

> *Look around and you will see*
> *this world is full of creeps*
> *like me.*
> —Lyle Lovett

> *Creeps get rewarded for being creepy.*
> —Tom Scharpling

> *There are a lot of creeps on the internet.*
> *There's just a certain amount of risk.*
> —Peter Weddle

> *How to be a creep:*
> *1. Following you on the street*
> *2. Oglling at you*
> *3. Stalking you on social media*
> *4. Calling at unearthly hours*
> *5. Taking 'No' to be 'Yes' and*
> *troubling incessantly*
> —Durga Kannan

> *Beat it*
> *CREEP*
> —Tee-shirt

*We knew that we were
kind of odd and creeps,
and we wanted to do
odd, creepy stuff
for people who
wanted to see that.*
—Penn Jillette

NOW I ASK YOU . . .

Have you ever seen an accident, as it was happening? Did it appear to be happening in slow-motion? Were you rooted to the spot? Were you able to do anything to help? Texas, California, and Florida consistently lead the nation with the most truck accidents (given that trucks are used more in those areas). 27% of truck accidents happen on interstate highways, and 37% of all fatal truck crashes occurred between 6 PM and 6 AM (2022).

TRUCK ACCIDENT

On the way back from a family fishing trip in the High Sierras, in the early morning hours, our three cars were caravanning, to beat the traffic. As we were coming off the last mountain, there seemed to be no one in front of us, for miles. At one point, Wayne suggested that I might want to shut my eyes, so I immediately looked way up ahead. And we could see a large, white truck that had misjudged the turn onto our highway, coming in the opposite direction. And it was overturning, and crashed, and then it slid on its side for a good length of time, before coming to a dead stop, just as we arrived on the scene.

Without discussing the situation, we each decided to do what we could, and we each immediately got busy. Wayne, who worked in a hospital, was checking out the two drivers, who were in bad shape, and he called for an ambulance, and the police. I started picking up the larger glass shards on the road, and items that had fallen off the truck (bumper sections and such), so that any following cars wouldn't get their tires cut. Wayne's sister, Donna, grabbed two blankets from her car, to drape over the drivers, and Jay, started wig-wagging his arms, to stop the oncoming cars, to slow them down while crossing through the debris field.

The white truck had no painted signage on its sides, nor was any information inside the glove box, to give us a clue as to what we were dealing with. One trucker was dead, and the other had a broken back, and was in too much pain to answer questions. This was a safety concern to all four of us, `because the truck was hauling some heavy-duty liquid that was a muddy-colored icky green, that flooded out from the truck, making its own stream across the prairie-like terrain.

We'd been on the scene for almost an hour, when the police finally arrived, and sent us packing. When we got home, Wayne immediately went to bed, as he had done all the driving, and was worn out. Donna and Jay had driven on to their own homes in Idaho and Fresno. I, on the other hand, had not done any driving, so I was wired, and decided to take my car in to have it serviced. So I'm sitting in the Waiting Area, watching the TV news, when all of a sudden, the screen showed a helicopter turning in wide circles, showing the landscape below, that featured a huge stream of icky-green liquid that had stretched far across the field. The next scene showed men in hazmat suits cleaning up the surrounding area. *OMYGOD!* I thought, *we four were all there for around an hour! We might have been exposed to whatever that green stuff was! And if we all perished, since we lived in different cities, no one would have a clue as to what made us sick enough to die.* How weird is that? Happily, we lived to tell the tale.

*It takes 1,000s of bolts
to assemble a truck,
and one nut to scatter it
all over the road.*
—Unknown

*If you know you are driving
so fast to your death,
would you still drive so fast?*
—Unknown

*The ideal man bears the accidents in life
with dignity and grace,
making the best of circumstances.*
—Aristotle

Leave sooner, drive slower, live longer.
—Unknown

*Adversity has a way of strengthening.
If is doesn't kill you,
you learn something.*
—Robert Crais

NOW I ASK YOU . . .

Have you noticed that you are getting older? Do you care? Are you stressing out about it? Or are you happily counting your birthdays? Or might you be steadfastly ignoring them? Take a tip from George Burns, when he said, "You can't help getting older, but you don't have to get old." Are you becoming clearer about what does and doesn't matter?

GETTING OLDER

It was so disconcerting to see my lifespan already in the history books. When observing my student teachers in history classes, I wanted to interject my personal experiences, even through I wasn't supposed to interrupt. It's like the old Henry Youngman joke: "My history teacher is so old, he taught from memory." And so it is. But when the textbook said that the Women's Movement was over, I leaped up to share that it just wasn't *new* anymore, so it didn't get the media coverage as it had beforehand. And I whipped out my membership cards to show that I still belonged to several women's organizations, like NOW. I couldn't let that go unnoticed. The younger girls (7th and 8th graders) should know that women are still fighting for various women's issues.

When observing in a second grade class, I watched the student teacher's face turn from happy to sad:
"You look jus' like somebody on TV!" announced one little boy.

"Really? Who?" responded the young pleased-as-punch student teacher.

"You look like one of them Golden Girls."

"Really? Which one?"

"The Grandma."

And that suddenly got the students off-track.

"She has some wrinkles, that ole lady!"

"Don' mess wit' ole women. They gonna git ya!"

Question: "How old is Dr. Meinberg?"

Answer: "She's pretty old. They say she used to teach Shakespeare."

How old would you be
if you didn't know how old you was?
—Satchel Paige

Old age ain't for sissies.
—Bette Davis

All my life I faced sexism and racism
and then, when I hit 40, ageism.
—Rita Moreno

Wrinkles mean you laughed,
Gray hair means you cared, and Scars mean you lived.
—Unknown

Wrinkles ought to be worn as a badge of honor,
as a mark of survival, if not wisdom.
—Mal Fletcher

NOW I ASK YOU...

Age is strictly a case of mind over matter.
If you don't mind, it doesn't matter.
—Jack Benny

I suppose real old age begins
when one looks backwards rather than forward.
—May Sarton

You know you're getting old
when the candles cost more than the cake.
—Bob Hope

The great thing about getting older is
that you don't lose all the other ages you've been.
—Madeleine L'Engle

Age doesn't matter, unless you are a cheese.
—Billie Burke

If you're not getting older, you're dead.
—Tom Petty

I do maturity exceedingly well.
—Victoria Moran's affirmation

NOW I ASK YOU . . .

Have you ever forgotten what you were just doing? Have you ever walked into a room, and wondered why you went there? Have you ever locked your keys in the car? Have you ever been out driving, and forgot where you were going? Or misplaced your cellphone, or something that you just had in your hand? Have you ever looked for your glasses, and found them on your head? Have you ever put things in a safe place, and then forgot where your safe place was? Have you ever forgotten to water your indoor plants? Have you ever forgotten to buckle your seatbelt, or turn your headlights off or on? Have you ever forgotten to take your meds? Have you ever forgotten to pay your bills on time? Uh-oh.

FORGETFULNESS

Memory slips are aggravating, frustrating, and worrisome, in the extreme. Forgetfulness (aptly called senior moments) is more apparent in our later years. It is said that normal age-related memory loss is generally manageable. And can be the result of stress and anxiety, lack of sleep, depression, dehydration, an underactive thyroid, side effects from various medications, alcohol, an unhealthy diet, or a vitamin B12 or Vitamin D deficiency, as well as overworking, or spending too much time on your computer. Sounds like experts are really not sure. In any case, we each must find a way to deal with it. However, when forgetfulness happens more often than seems reasonable, this may trigger fears of dementia or Alzheimer's disease. A case in point:

My neighbor lived directly across the street from me. I later moved, as did she, and we lost track of each other. At length, she got married, and the happy couple bought an apartment building. They also bought a house to live in. They seemed like such a lovely couple, but both were slowly losing their minds. I only saw her a few times over the following years, and she looked and acted great, as did her husband, so who would know that they were in trouble?

It turned out that she had neglected to place her tenants' checks in the bank. Nor did she pay her own bills. So no money was coming in, and no money was going out. As a result, the water was turned off in the building, which she didn't know about, as she read none of the tenant's angry letters. And then the electricity was turned off. As a result, most of the tenants moved, while all refused to pay their monthly rent, since none of their previous checks had been cashed. Eventually, the couple was in major trouble for not paying state or national taxes. During this hullabaloo, the husband walked to the local cigar store *each* day, to buy wooden boxes of cigars. When he died, there were stacks upon stacks of wooden boxes of expensive cigars piled high in his bedroom. And the daughter whisked her mother off to Minnesota, where she lived, as she had no way to deal with her mother's situation, from afar.

The advantage of a bad memory
is that one enjoys several times
the same good things
for the first time.
—Friedrich Nietzsche

I learn something new each day,
and forget five
of the other things forever.
—Unknown

My brain is like the Bermuda Triangle.
Information goes in
and it is never found again.
—Unknown

I lost my to-do list,
so I made a second to-do list,
but then I found
my first to-do list
which was slightly different
than the second to-do list,
so I made a new to-do list.
—Unknown

I take my forgetfulness
in a positive stride
because I also forget
the problems.
—Hina Khan

NOW I ASK YOU . . .

Have you ever become the center of attention without your doing anything? Were you embarrassed? Or were you able to laugh along with everyone else? (For instance: One party seemed to have lost its punch. I was talking to two couples, about my recent psychic experiences, and suddenly all the other couples moved in closer, and were listening to my tales. A lot of questions and interaction followed. When we were finally calling it a night, the host thanked me profusely for saving his party.)

A HAPPY HOO-HA

Wayne, and I went to Baja Sonora, in Long Beach, California, for an early dinner. It is a small, extremely popular Mexican restaurant, in which the tables are placed close together, in a friendly, casual atmosphere, to accommodate the crowds. We were quietly eating, when Wayne leaned across the table, and whispered, "I love you."

And the woman at the next table went nuts! She stood up as she shouted, "Did you hear that?" as she pointed to Wayne. In a voice to declare the end of the world, she said, "For no reason at all, he just said, 'I love you'—while they were eating!" And she continued on in that vein.

Of course, everyone stopped talking and eating, to stare at us. A few voices tentatively called out, asking if we recently met, or were dating, or if we were newly engaged, or if we were newly weds. The diners appeared focused and interested, so Wayne felt duty-bound to tell everyone, "No, we've been married for 45 years!" Shock and awe. Then, he continued on saying, "And we still hold hands." No one could believe it. "And this is the third marriage for both of us!" which brought down the house. Apparently, we had become an oddity—on many levels.

People keep pushing me
to be the center of attention . . .
I would prefer to be on the sidelines,
because that's where you see more.
—Gong Li

Most people are tormented by
the conflict between their
fear of standing out, and their desire to be
the center of attention.
—Mokokoma Mokhonoana

NOW I ASK YOU . . .

Have you ever had an adventure that you never in a million years thought you'd experience first hand? Something that you'd read about in books and magazines, or newspapers, or had seen on TV, but was *way* too far afield from your everyday life? Were you shocked? Were you prepared?

A HOT MESS

I was excited to have a two and a half week visit with my brother, Terry. He has a house in Cabo, so I was ready to rest and relax, and eager to fit into a slower pace of life, with no worries to bother me, whatsoever. The first days were perfect, without a hitch.

One day, we went to La Paz—a two-hour drive—where Terry's charter business is located. The weather was perfect, the sky was a beautiful shade of blue and the sun was shining brightly, as we strolled around the marina, admiring all of the yachts, and checking out several of his. We then stopped at Captains, his restaurant/bar, and met with many people who work for him (captains, crew members, biologists, cooks, bar-tenders, wait staff, and such), and even some clients. Everyone was smiling, laughing, and genuinely happy. On the way back, Terry took me through the towns that we had bypassed earlier, to give me a most interesting tourist guide.

Suddenly, the next day, things changed, as Hurricane Norma first made landfall in Cabo, wreaking havoc, and leaving tens of thousands without power, water, or the internet (October 22, 2023).

I had seen hurricane clips on the TV over the years, but never expected to be in one. The sky was suddenly pitch black, with flooding and high winds (with a peak gust of 107 mph). Sharp fragments flew through the air like shrapnel. The noise was horrendous, and sounded like a banshee was screeching and wailing, at times. The wind was so strong the house would shake, seemingly ready to fly away. In the back yard, two extremely tall palm trees were broken in half, and a third palm tree was ripped out of the ground, roots and all. The swimming pool and hot tub were suddenly full of dirt and debris. All but one street signs were bent and mangled, and lying flat on the ground.

With no air conditioners, and closed doors and windows, it was hot, hot, hot! We went around with towels hanging around our necks, to soak up the sweat, as it rolled down our faces. Our clothes were uncomfortably damp. There were no lights anywhere, so we used flashlights and lanterns. No water was available to wash hands, take showers, or use the toilet (buckets of water, from the swimming pool, were placed in each bathroom). The microwave and stove, were not working. Neither were Terry's two refrigerators and two freezers, which spoiled all the food (the restaurants had the same problem.) We lived on power bars, bottled water, Coke light (Terry's choice), and Pepsi (my choice). No whole leaves could be seen. They were all ripped and torn into teeny tiny pieces, looking like flying confetti. The toaster was full of twigs, with a jaunty flower sitting on its top. We all went to bed early, because there was nothing left to do (no cell phones, no e-mails, no T.V., no music). All in all, it was like camping indoors.

The beautiful La Paz marina that we had just seen the day before, was a catastrophe. Over one hundred yachts were severely damaged. A 115-foot yacht sank, while tied to the marina fuel tank, causing all kinds of problems. Since some people lived on their yachts, people were checking other downed crafts, hoping for the best. Luckily, all Terry's yachts were saved (two crew members spent two days and nights on his yachts, dealing with bumpers, special sails, and heavy, long double lines tied to posts). However, his restaurant/bar was under a foot of water, which was nothing, compared to others' problems. All he needed to do was drain and dry the site.

Naturally, during the hurricane, we couldn't connect with anyone outside the city, county, or country. All flights coming and going were grounded, leaving all tourists in a quandary. So we all overstayed our welcome, and couldn't wait to return home. Terry had previously lent his generator to someone, who had returned it in poor condition. Naturally, it didn't work during our time of need. So on the day of my flight home, he bought a new generator, just in case.

I survived Hurricane Norma
and all I got was this lousy T-Shirt
and a lot of property damage.
—Unknown

A true Floridian doesn't measure time in years,
but in how many hurricanes they've survived.
—Unknown

A hurricane is just Mother Nature's way of
telling you to clean out your fridge.
—Unknown

NOW I ASK YOU . . .

Are you prepared financially for unexpected expenses? I just had all the fascia boards painted white, and the outside of my house painted yellow, and added a new garage door, and ordered 23 windows (of varying sizes), so I wasn't expecting any new purchases anytime near soon. Oh, woe is me.

SLEEPYTIME BLUES

Several days before leaving for Cabo, inspectors told me that if I was having the weirdest dreams, in which it was difficult to become fully awake. For example, one night I awoke at 2:30 AM, and thought it was time for work (I am retired). So I went into the bathroom, and changed into my professional clothes (which I don't wear anymore). Later, when I saw the clock, I realized that I was way too early for work, and climbed back in bed fully clothed. I was surprised when I awoke, to find that I was dressed for a business day. Strange. Other times, I had to crawl into other rooms, before I could stand and walk. Later, I found out why I was acting so befuddled, and why my dreams were so strange.

When I returned home from Cabo, I was told that if I had stayed one more night in my bed, that I would have *died* in my sleep; that I would have been as dead as a doornail. My whole house was filled with gas, and my back bedroom (formerly the den) had the most gas, and that if someone had lighted a candle or a cigarette, the house would have blown sky high, like a *bomb*. And that the whole neighborhood would have burned down along with me. Egads!

The gas inspectors said that they had never seen a house with so much gas, in all their years of inspections. So they set about to find the gas link. It turned out that there were three leaks: one in the fireplace; one in the wall heater, and one in the dryer (where someone had jerry-rigged the piping years ago).

All my pipes were old, rusty, and falling apart, originals from 1944 (Who knew? They were all behind walls and floors). So I had to replace them all. Then I had to buy new air-conditioner/heaters for various rooms, and combination gas and smoke alarms for all rooms, and pay for new patchwork for the holes in the walls, as well as new indoor paint, not to mention a brand new roof for the house and garage. Ouch!

Beware of little expenses.
A small leak will sink a great ship.
—Benjamin Franklin

NOW I ASK YOU . . .

A caring person is kindhearted and warmhearted; one who gives emotional support to others. Are caring persons in your life? Are you a caring person? Do you show concern and compassion for others? Do you act in a manner in which things, events, and relationships matter?

NOT YET!

Luckily, I have many friends that look out for me. They are affectionate and helpful (I am now 84). Several years ago, I had been in and out of the hospital, so they all kept in touch with me, and watched over me, since I fell a lot. But one week, both my landline telephone and my computer went on the blink at the same time. So my friends were concerned, and later became anxious, since no one had heard from me in a while. So they thought that I was basically down for the count. When one friend came to the house, and I wasn't there, but my car was, she expected the worst. And after everyone was informed of my demise, they decided to meet at my house, to divvy up their favorite things (*unusual* rocks, crystals, art objects, and plants are in each room). One friend called her daughter, with news of my passing, to which she replied, "I'm coming right down! Dibs on the plants!" Later, I think they were all somewhat unnerved to find me alive, well, and upright. It's nice to know that people care, as the background soundtrack of my mind played the Beach Boys singing *Good Vibrations!* Since then, others have begged me to write an I BEQUEATH book, to avoid fistfights upon my demise (L.O.L).

The simple act of caring is heroic.
—Edward Albert

One person caring about another
represents Life's greatest value.
—Jim Rohn

Sometimes the greatest gift
you can give to another person
is to simply include them.
—Unknown

The reports of my death are greatly exaggerated.
—Mark Twain

ENDNOTE

Life is a series of circumstances and encounters, other than plodding through your day-to-day, humdrum routine. Life is all about experiences. Some of them are thrilling and noteworthy events, while others are risky, frightening, or boring. I have literally encountered an endless number of conditions and events in which to evolve. And I am making progress. Explore your very own personal history. Consider your ever-widening horizons. Gradually stretch your sense of self. Question your prejudices. Explore your power to transcend whatever addictions, habits, and obsessions that have held you captive. Know that those moments of peak experiences or important happenings—surprising, motivating, or inspiring—can make a huge difference in your life. Often, the feelings of each event last much, much longer than the event itself. (For instance, Wayne, died in 2020, and I doubt I will ever get over it. One of his favorite songs was "Stayin' Alive", by the BeeGees, and every time I hear that song, I burst into tears, crying out loud in front of anyone and everyone. We saw the BeeGees twice in concert, and Wayne was so happy to see them.) Be alert for those special and unique moments, seize them, and run with them. Every setback teaches you something. Learn from your criticisms and your failures.

Know that you are unstoppable; that you will use your knowledge to keep moving in the direction *you* want to go. Create your own path. Let no one stand in your way. Leap forward. Keep going. Forge ahead. Press on. Thrive past the edges and the margins. Know that you are capable, you are powerful, and you are a survivor!

At any given moment,
you have the power to say:
this is not how the story
is going to end.
—Christine Mason Miller

Learn from yesterday,
Live for today,
Hope for tomorrow.
—Albert Einstein

Life is like a roller coaster.
It has its ups and downs.
But it's your choice
to scream or enjoy it.
—Unknown

Life is like riding a bicycle.
To keep your balance,
you must keep moving.
—Albert Einstein

Life is like a bowl of cherries.
Some cherries are rotten while some are good:
it's your job to throw out the rotten ones
and forget about them,
while you enjoy eating the ones that are good.
—C. Joybell C.

Life is like a camera. Focus on what's important,
Capture the good times, Develop from the Negatives,
and if things don't work out, Take another shot.
—Ziad K. Abdelnour

Life is like a box of chocolates.
You never know what you will get.
—Forrest Gump

Life is like a book.
Some are happy.
Some chapters are sad,
Some are exciting, but
if you never turn the page,
you will never know
what the next chapter
has in store for you.
—Unknown

Life is like a piano.
What you get out of it
depends on how you play it.
—Unknown

Life is like a boxing match.
Defeat is declared
not when you fall,
but when you refuse
to stand again.
—Muhammad Ali

Life is like a mirror.
Smile at it, and
It smiles back at you.
—Peace Pilgrim

Life is like a 10 speed bicycle.
Most of us have gears
we never use.
—Charles M. Schulz

ABOUT THE AUTHOR

"My life is full of stories. I am a lifelong bookworm!" says Dr. Sherry L. Meinberg. "I read books, I write books, I edit books, I donate books. I eat, sleep, and breathe books."

When she retired from teaching in the Long Beach Unified School District (after 34 years), Dr. Meinberg owned several thousand children's books, which is why she had also become a school librarian. Dr. Meinberg later became a core adjunct professor, and supervisor of student teachers, at National University. She retired again (after 16 years), realizing that she had been an educator for **50** years, and figured that her freshness date had long since passed. But her love of teaching was too strong, so she then taught creative writing classes for senior citizens, through the Oasis National Education Organization. Even her car license says READ4ME, and its license plate holder says SO MANY BOOKS, SO LITTLE TIME. On two different occasions, when she returned to her car after shopping, she came upon a small crowd of people, who were looking at her license plate. They had taken bets as to whether she was a teacher, a librarian, a professor, or an author. And she happily said that they were all correct! She has been honored with numerous awards.

Dr. Meinberg is all about raising awareness and opening doors. She is all about getting the word out. This is her 24th book.

I have looked across my years, at
the hoops and the slides,
the ups and the downs,
the ins and the outs,
the good and the bad,
the blahs and the bliss,
the loss and the gains,
the turmoil and the peace,
the agony and the ecstasy,
the sickness and the health,
the cheerful and the gloomy,
the confusion and the clarity,
the bedlam and the balanced,
the denial and the acceptance,
the ignorance and the wisdom,
the cowardice and the courage,
the rejected and the redirected,
the mistakes and the successes,
the heartache and the happiness,
the delighted and the disappointed,
and I am now thoroughly satisfied,
with all of it.

ALSO BY DR. SHERRY L. MEINBERG

The Tree Bridge

The Angry Ants

Bumps in the Night:
Fantasy Creatures

Somewhere Out There:
Aliens and UFOs

EEUUUW: Animal
Gross-Out

An Army of Ants,
A Colony of Bats,

A Pounce of Cats:
Animal Name Groups

Breadcrumbs for
Beginners:
Following the Writing Trail

Diabetes ABC

Imperfect Weddings
are Best

Recess is Over!
No Nonsense
Strategies and
Tips for Student Teachers
and New Teachers

It's All Thought!
The Science,
Psychology, and
Spirituality of Happiness
(Teacher's Guide)

WHOA!

A Squirm of Worms

Alzheimer's ABC

In the Nick of Time:
Coincidences,
Synchronicities,
Dreams, and Symbols

A Cluster of Cancers:
A Simple Coping Guide
for Patients

Seizing the Teachable
Moment

The Cockroach Invasion

Autism ABC

The Bogeyman:
Stalking and its Aftermath
(TV Premier Episode,
Investigation Discovery
12/12/12)

Toxic Attention:
Keeping Safe
from Stalkers,
Abusers, and Intruders

Be the Boss of Your Brain!
Take Control of Your Life

Into the Hornet's Nest:
An Incredible Look at Life
in an Inner City School